FIELDING'S
LONDON
AGENDA

The Freshest, Up-To-The-Minute Guide To London

Nan & Ivan Lyons

Fielding Worldwide, Inc.
308 South Catalina Avenue
Redondo Beach, California 90277 U.S.A.

Fielding's London Agenda

Published by Fielding Worldwide, Inc.

Text Copyright ©1995 Nan & Ivan Lyons

Icons & Illustrations Copyright ©1995 FWI

Photo Copyrights ©1995 to Individual Photographers

FIELDING WORLDWIDE INC.

PUBLISHER AND CEO	**Robert Young Pelton**
PUBLISHING DIRECTOR	**Paul T. Snapp**
ELEC. PUBLISHING DIRECTOR	**Larry E. Hart**
PUBLIC RELATIONS DIRECTOR	**Beverly Riess**
ACCOUNT SERVICES MANAGER	**Christy Harp**

EDITORS

Linda Charlton   **Kathy Knoles**

PRODUCTION

Gini Sardo-Martin   **Chris Snyder**
Craig South   **Janice Whitby**

COVER DESIGNED BY	**Digital Artists, Inc.**
COVER PHOTOGRAPHERS	**Romilly Lockyer/The Image Bank**
INSIDE PHOTOS	**British Tourist Authority, Catherine Gehm, Lorna Pfluke, James F. Rowan, Westlight/Robert Young Pelton**

Inquiries should be addressed to: Fielding Worldwide, Inc., 308 South Catalina Ave., Redondo Beach, California 90277 U.S.A., Telephone (310) 372-4474, Facsimile (310) 376-8064, 8:30 a.m.–5:30 p.m. Pacific Standard Time.

ISBN 1-56952-039-9

Library of Congress Catalog Card Number

94-068333

Printed in the United States of America

Letter from the Publisher

In 1946, Temple Fielding began the first of what would be a remarkable new series of well-written, highly personalized guidebooks for independent travelers. Temple's opinionated, witty, and oft-imitated books have now guided travelers for almost a half-century. More important to some was Fielding's humorous and direct method of steering travelers away from the dull and the insipid. Today, Fielding Travel Guides are still written by experienced travelers for experienced travelers. Our authors carry on Fielding's reputation for creating travel experiences that deliver insight with a sense of discovery and style.

Designed to save travelers time and money, Fielding's *London Agenda* cuts to the chase, telling readers all they need to know to "do" the town. Whether you have a day or a week in London, authors Nan and Ivan Lyons will take you straight to all the right places and off the beaten path.

The concept of independent travel has never been bigger. Our policy of *brutal honesty* and a highly personal point of view has never changed; it just seems the travel world has caught up with us.

RYP

Robert Young Pelton
Publisher and CEO
Fielding Worldwide, Inc.

ACKNOWLEDGEMENTS

For service above and beyond, we want to thank Avraham Inlender, Barbara Settanni, and most especially Janet Rodgers, and Maureen Settanni-Fasulo for being "godmothers" who came through not only with tea and sympathy, but with shoe-leather and love.

Nan and Ivan Lyons

ABOUT THE
AUTHORS

Nan & Ivan Lyons

The Lyons are best known as authors of the best-selling novel turned movie, *Someone is Killing the Great Chefs of Europe,* and for their travel articles in magazines such as *Bon Appetit, Travel & Leisure,* and *Food & Wine.*

Their nonfiction output includes *Imperial Taste, A Century of Elegance at Tokyo's Imperial Hotel,* and several guides to New York City.

A WORD FROM THE AUTHORS

The Agenda Series was designed to put the guide back into travel guides. Unlike other guides that are written by committee, we take full responsibility for the personal, candid and sometimes controversial opinions we have expressed in order to provide our readers with the quintessential London experience.

Today, with travelers having just a few short days to spend on a trip, the only guide that is really useful is one that can distill the hundreds of choices that are available in London into the very essence of the City.

If an old friend were coming to town, everything we would tell them is in this guide. Time is as valuable as money, and you need to know what you can afford to miss and what should be at the top of your agenda. Our goal is to be selective, not provide you with endless details and historical minutiae. The definition of the word "Agenda" is a list of business to be covered and that is our intention as well!

By exploring London locales and listing shopping and restaurant agendas for each, we have made it possible to construct a relaxed agenda for an afternoon or evening without having to leave the area. We also have suggested one- two- and three-day agendas that cover most of what makes London the most exciting, unique city in the world (we told you we were opinionated).

We are looking forward to putting our years of travel writing and globe-trotting at your disposal, so that at the end of your stay in London, you'll leave knowing that you have taken away the very best it has to offer.

The Lyons

Fielding Rating Icons

The Fielding Rating Icons are highly personal and awarded to help the besieged traveler choose from among the dizzying array of activities, attractions, hotels, restaurants and sights. The awarding of an icon denotes unusual or exceptional qualities in the relevant category.

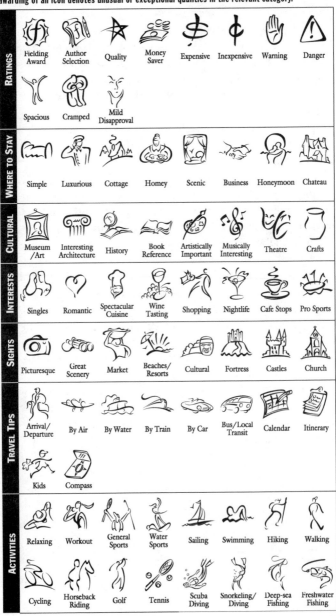

TABLE OF CONTENTS

LIST OF MAPS

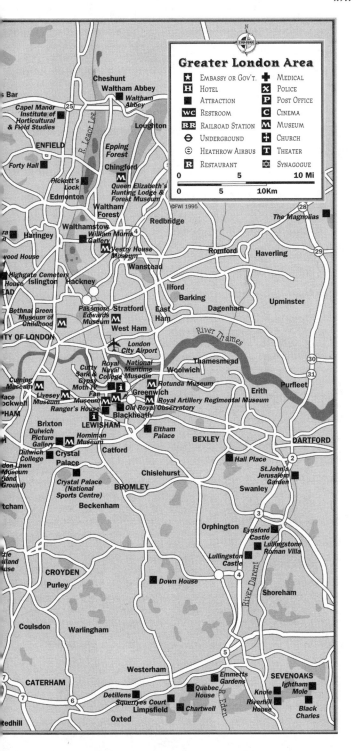

Greater London Area

Symbol	Meaning	Symbol	Meaning
★	EMBASSY OR GOV'T.	✚	MEDICAL
H	HOTEL	✕	POLICE
■	ATTRACTION	P	POST OFFICE
WC	RESTROOM	C	CINEMA
RR	RAILROAD STATION	M	MUSEUM
⊖	UNDERGROUND	✝	CHURCH
☺	HEATHROW AIRBUS	T	THEATER
R	RESTAURANT	☒	SYNAGOGUE

0 — 5 — 10 Mi
0 — 5 — 10Km

©FWI 1995

INTRODUCTION

Parliament Square is filled with interesting statues.

What is London?

Over its long, illustrious past, London has known the best of times and the worst of times. The historical rollercoaster that the British Empire has been on since the city of Londinium was first settled by the Romans in the year A.D. 43, has bestowed on

London not only the imprint of power, but also the heady mystique of royalty. It has made it one of the most exciting, irresistible and compelling of world capitals. London has become, over the centuries, Britain's own best export.

However, despite the glory of the Empire, the chronicle of what Londoners have had to endure in their long-suffering history reads like the plot of a soap opera, played out against the background of Western Civilization. The Great Plague that spread throughout the city in 1665 left more than 100,000 people dead. Just as the epidemic began to die out, the Great Fire of 1666, less than a year later, raged out of control and ultimately burned most of London to the ground. A few centuries later the spread of the Industrial Revolution brought even more misery to the city, as disease-infested slums, filled with the hopeless poor of its factories, were a grim counterpoint to the dazzling growth of the British Empire. Rule Britannia didn't stop the Germans either. London's next and very nearly its most disastrous catastrophe was the Blitz of World War II. Night after night the Germans mercilessly bombed London for over a year until much of the city, including the Houses of Parliament, was destroyed and 30,000 Londoners were dead.

All of these incredible tragedies bring us to the word *indomitable*, which the dictionary defines as: unyielding. This is the key to understanding the psyche of the average Londoner. Through the ages, the people of London have played out whatever hand fate dealt to them with humor, spirit and indomitable optimism. No matter that The Empire has all but disappeared, no matter that the anachronistic "class system" is holding on tighter than a pub-crawler on a Saturday night, and no matter that unemployment is still a constant blight. The people of London go on. The memory of Sir Winston's heroic words are forever in their minds, "we shall fight in the fields, and in the streets; we shall fight in the hills, we shall never surrender," and they never will!

London Bridge may have finally fallen down, but the rest of the city is on an incredible upswing. The recession London went through, much the same as the U.S., is just about over, and the rhythm of the city has accelerated. Things are bigger, older, more historic and definitely more shockingly *public* than ever before. In a city of Victorian sensibilities, bowler hats, pin-striped suits and erudite cab drivers, the queen has just struck oil! However, the whole nation struck oil centuries ago by making "The Firm" (the royal family) its all time, hands down, headline attraction. All the queen's horses, and all the queens men bring over 18 million tourists to London every year.

Even though most Londoners sound like they belong in the second act of *Hamlet*, they don't for a minute mind that your accent is influenced by the American Revolution. No hard feelings, either. The average Londoner is completely accessible to the endless tourists that jam their city. They are always ready with a bawdy joke, a little hot gossip about the "royals," and a good, solid plate of bangers and mash, accompanied (God help us), by a glass of lukewarm ale.

Even though we are fast approaching the 20th century, London is as familiar, or as historic, as you wish it to be. They still have High Tea, they still have bright red double-decker buses, they still drive on the "wrong" side of the road, and they still have fog as thick as pea soup. Most of all, London is still an original: the one city against which all others are measured. In the past it was the capital of the greatest empire the world has ever known. And today, the London that is waiting for your visit, is best described by that very "catchy" tune, "Everything Old is New Again."

The Story of London Is in the Monarchy

From King Arthur to Queen Elizabeth II, London, no matter how much it tries to deny it, is heart, soul and financially tied to its royal traditions. No other city in Europe is as royal as London. Its monuments, its palaces and its "bespoke" tailoring all represent the grip the royal past has on the royal present. As the queen bestows a Royal Warrant to denote a shop chosen by the royal family to trade with, so the city of London has always felt most comfortable with an emotional warrant that is stamped on its very existence.

Playing the Palaces

1. Buckingham
2. St. James
3. Kensington
4. Palace of Westminster
5. The Tower
6. Lambeth Palace

Agenda Priorities

No matter how sophisticated a traveler you may be, it's all too easy to become overwhelmed by the number of "must-see" sights in London. Part of the problem is that the city has so many locales, each with a very distinct personality and pace, that there's never enough time to do everything. Just when you think you've covered all the bases, you realize you've missed the Transport Museum, or that hot new antique market in Islington. After all, you have to sleep sometime.

Make an agenda by selecting your most important priorities and noting their locations. Then read about the areas in which they're found. See if there are other things of interest nearby and estimate how much time you wish to spend at each. The goal is to group priorities by locale in order to avoid zigzagging your way back and forth across the city.

London is a living, breathing, time machine with a choice of the past, the present or the future laid out before you. You can spend the morning at the Tower of London sympathizing with Anne Boleyn, the afternoon in the visitor's gallery at the House of Commons listening to a debate and in the evening, dining in the cheekiest of spots in the Docklands, a 2001 peek at the London to come. Even Scrooge and his ghosts would have had trouble keeping up.

Not to worry, no one ever has enough time in London, not even Queen Victoria, and she hung around for almost a century. If you have only two or three days to tear around town, we'll help you cover enough of the bases, but still have you begging for more on your return trip. The most valuable suggestion we can offer you is to be selective: a.k.a. listening to us.

The Top Three Sights

When the queen is away Buckingham Palace permits visitors.

Buckingham Palace

> *Buckingham Palace Road:* ☎ *0171-799-2331.*
> *Admission to the palace £8 adults, £5.50 seniors, £3+50 children. Call for hours. Mid Aug.-Sept.*
> *Changing of the Guards: 11:30 a.m.–12:05 p.m., Apr.–Aug., daily. Sept.– March every other day.* ☎ *0171-730-3488.*

You can't miss the place. It really stands out because it's guarded by sentries who look like their hats need haircuts. Not anywhere as showy as Versailles, certainly not as romantic as the Alcazar, Buck House (as it's called by people in the "know," although of late, it should be called Pass the Buck House) is a straightforward, no-nonsense structure. It was built by the Duke of Buckingham in 1705 and chosen by Victoria as her new home after she was crowned. There are some 600 rooms, including a few baths, but the Throne Room is at the top of the list for those who care more about their knights than their days. Victoria could also roam through the Green Drawing Room, the Picture Gallery, the Tapestry Room and the State Dining Room. The Royal apartments are up the grand staircase and to the north. Rumor has it that today members of the Royal family live quite simply and have been known to have dinner in front of the "telly."

In truth, what is going on outside the Palace is much more exciting than the tapestries and the ancestral Rogues Gallery within. Do not miss the Changing of the Guards ceremony, which takes place in front of the palace every day from April through August at 11:30 a.m. The rest of the year, it takes place every other day. Even though you have to watch from outside the gate and the crowds are so thick you have to crane to get a good view, it is the best pomp and circumstance of the city.

It is now actually possible to get an inside peek at the Palace. Liz II had to add a few pounds after that disastrous fire at Windsor Castle, so she decided that since she spends the summers away, she would permit the commoners to "play." How could anyone resist? But confidentially, most people think the Dorchester is much more luxurious.

Westminster Abbey's magnificent Gothic ceiling soars 102ft. high.

Westminster Abbey

Admission free, but suggested donation of £1.35—Poets' Corner, Royal Chapels, £3, children, £1.50 seniors.

Mon.-Tues.-Thurs.-Fri., 9 a.m.–4 p.m.; Wed., 9 a.m.–7:45 p.m., Sat., 9 a.m.–2 p.m.; Sun, all day for services only.

Watch your step! You could be treading on the Who's Who of the British Empire. What better place for them to be buried than this magnificent, Gothic cathedral that was begun by Edward the Confessor in 1065. In the chapel that is named for him stands the Coronation Chair, which was carved in 1300. Since then, every British monarch has been crowned on this most fabled piece of furniture. Westminster Abbey has been built, rebuilt and enlarged over the centuries. Christopher Wren added a few last touches in 1745, but, the date of its official completion was 1532. More than 500 tombs, which contain over 15 monarchs, as well as other royals and notables, are under the marble floor and along the sides of the Abbey. Amazingly enough, the atmosphere here is anything but funereal. The beauty of Westminster Abbey is as overwhelming as its size. The ceiling, which is 102 feet high, seems to soar almost out of sight, in the Gothic style of lifting not only the spirit, but the eye to heaven. Over the choir stalls, the banners of the Knights of Bath form a rainbow canopy. It is a heart-stopping experience to actually attend a service as well as visiting the Abbey as a tourist. The Henry VII Chapel (father to Henry VIII, predictably) has the tombs of Elizabeth I and Mary Queen of Scots. At the end of the chapel is the memorial that commemorates the Battle of Britain in 1940, and an honor roll of 1497 Allied airmen who died in it. Everyone is drawn to the Poets' Corner; Chaucer, Handel, Samuel Johnson, Sheridan, Browning, Longfellow, John Gay and Laurence Olivier, are just a few of the ones who rest here. Be sure to leave enough time so that you can wander without feeling pressured. The Abbey is a completely mesmerizing experience with history unfolding before your eyes in the most dramatic of settings.

INSIDE AGENDA

Do a rubbing of one of the ornate tombstones! Don't be shy, it really is the most fun.

The Tower of London

Tower of London, Tower Hill, ☎ 0171-709-0765.
Admission £6.70 adults, £4.40 children, £5.10 seniors. Nov.–Feb., Mon.–Sat., 9:30 a.m.–5 p.m.; Mar.–Oct., Mon.–Sat., 9:30 a.m.–6:30 p.m.; Sun., 2–6 p.m.

More blood was shed here than in any Freddie Kruger movie. First a royal palace, then the Royal Mint, the Royal Observatory, Crown Jewels repository and most notoriously, a prison for the British rich and famous. The Tower has had more personalities than Roseanne, and is really made up of a series of medieval stone structures that overlook the Thames. The most infamous is the Garden Tower, more luridly known as the Bloody Tower, where the two "little princes" disappeared. Centuries later, their tiny skeletons were found buried under the stairs. Where is Jessica Fletcher when you need her?

Yeomen Wardens, aka Beefeaters, conduct Tower of London tours.

Other famous guests of the Towers included Sir Walter Raleigh, the Earl of Essex, a couple of Henry VIII's wives who wouldn't sign "post nuptials," and poor Lady Jane Grey, who really was queen for a day. The oddest prisoner was Rudolph Hess, in 1942, who obviously had a terrible travel agent.

Traitor's Gate, right across from the Middle Tower, is where the prisoners landed after their trip up the Thames. There was little point in any of them getting their hair cut before entering the Tower. After sentencing, which was not an event fraught with suspense, they lost their heads, in the truest sense, on Tower Green. We dare you not to shudder as you walk through the dank cells (some with last messages carved into the stone) and the narrow staircases leading to the dungeons.

Now, after all that misery, anyone would welcome the glitz and glamour of England's dressiest doodads, the Crown Jewels. The Royals who actually managed to keep their heads got to decorate them with some real show-stoppers. They're kept polished and ready for inspection in the Jewel Tower, which has recently been brought into the 21st century with fiber optic lighting to make these knockout jewels sparkle even better. They've even added a moving walkway, which glides you past for a close-up view. Zsa Zsa, eat your heart out.

Those colorful blokes you've grown to know and love on your gin bottles really do exist. They are the resplendent Yeoman Wardens, known as Beefeaters, who number 42 and conduct the tours at the Tower. Aside from having the cheekiest outfits, one of them, the Ravenmaster, is responsible for seeing that all eight (at last count) of the shiny little guys are well fed. Legend has it that if the ravens desert the Tower, the Kingdom will fall. We would be the last ones to point a finger, but perhaps the Ravenmaster should add Princess Di to his list.

The 20 Next Best

An irreverent, but alphabetical list of the runners-up.

Bank of England

Threadneedle Street, The City
Bank of England Museum, ☎ *0171-601-5545. Admission free. Mon.–Fri., 10 a.m.–5 p.m.*
When is an old lady not an old lady? When she's the Bank of England. Britain's most famous "Piggy" was given the nickname "The Old Lady of Threadneedle Street," by an M.P. over 200 years ago, and today, people still delight in using it. Contrary to the gentle allusion to a fragile, tottering old soul, the building looks as formidable as a prison. Gray, windowless at street level, with the most boring of neoclassical architecture, it stands as the best illustration of that famous adage: "Solid as the Bank of England." True to its reputation, it issues bank-notes, fixes interest rates, manages the national debt and generally keeps the British Sterling polished to an impressive shine.

There is a museum, which is the only part of the bank open to the public. You can see the original artwork for the countries' banknotes on display, if you are into royal profiles. Goldbugs will appreciate the bullion and coins on display. How can you resist the most famous bank in the world? Even more impressive, they made it to the top without cash machines.

The British Museum

Great Russell Street
Mon.–Sat., 10 a.m.–5 p.m.; Sun., 2:30–6 p.m. Contribution suggested.
☎ *0171-636-1555*
Two-and-a-half miles of treasure, including the Rosetta Stone (no relation to Sharon), it is the king of museums. It has more than 6-million artifacts. Don't listen to Fred Astaire the British Museum has definitely *not* lost its charm!

Looking more like a great, gray Roman temple, the museum dates back to the middle 1800s, and draws huge crowds due to the ongoing fascination with history the British have, for both their own and everyone else's. They've had a long love affair with the antiquities of Egypt (after all, they deserve a little sweat equity for unearthing Tut). The

Egyptian collection here is superb. M is for the many mummies who reside here. There are also two of the only four existing copies of the Magna Carta, (they didn't have xerox machines in 1215) and of course the Elgin Marbles, which somehow found their way into Lord Elgin's luggage after he took a long walk around the Parthenon in 1816. Talk about having "sticky fingers." To this day the Greeks will tell you to beware of Brits bearing large suitcases. Last but not least, the magnificent Library Reading Room, with its 30,000 reference works that have been thoroughly thumbed by Carlyle, Shaw, Carl Marx, Lenin and Ghandi.

Don't leave without a turn around the museum shop and a snack at the cafe.

Cabinet War Rooms

King Charles Street
☎ *0171-930-6961. Admission £3.90, children, £1.90. 10 a.m.–6 p.m.*
Looking like the background for a 40s film about WWII, the scene is movingly set for a trip back to England's "finest hour." You can almost smell the confidence that seems to linger in the air, even after all these years. The 21 rooms were built 17 feet below ground to ensure the safety of the prime minister and his cabinet during the endless air-raids. The rooms themselves are small and claustrophobic, but the government was able to plan the strategy that kept Hitler hopping. The rooms have been kept just as they were, but the real "tingle-up-the-spine" comes from Sir Winston's, which has his bed made up for a quick nap, and the desk where he made the broadcasts that gave the people of London the strength to withstand the punishment of the Blitz.

Covent Garden

Originally the Convent Garden for Westminster Abbey, the cockneys who worked in the area turned Convent into Covent just in time for Professor Higgins to meet Eliza. The official stock exchange for fruits and vegetables until 1974, Covent Garden's splendid glass-roofed structure now is home to dozens of trendy to-the-max shops and restaurants. Although far more "nouveau mall" than the street markets of Bermondsey, or Portobello road, there is the same kind of boundless energy. It has its own theatricality because of the theaters of the Strand nearby and of course the Opera House, which took root in Covent Garden in 1946. It houses the Royal Ballet and Opera. On the weekends, there is almost always some form of entertainment: mimes, street singers or puppet shows. The very first Punch and Judy show was performed in the square in 1662. Today, it's more likely you'll hear one of the resident waifs crooning "Over the Rainbow" for spare change. (See "Locales.")

Harrods

Knightsbridge
☎ *0171-730-1234. Mon., Tues., Sat., 10 a.m.–6 p.m.; Wed., Fri., 10 a.m.–7 p.m.*
Not since *Camille* has conspicuous consumption reached such dramatic heights. Harrods may have started out as just a department store, but today, it is almost as important an institution in the fabric of London life as the Palace. There is no comparison to it anywhere—

not even Bloomingdale's, Galeries Lafayette, Gums or Takashimaya has the grandeur and dimension of Harrods. If we had but one life to give for our country, let us give it standing at the smoked salmon counter at Harrods, watching the surgical precision of the slicer. (See "Dept. Stores", page 147.)

Parliament's Neo-Gothic splendor houses the Commons, Lords and Royal Gallery.

Big Ben is rarely more than a fraction of a second off.

Big Ben

Westminster, SW1. ☎ *0171-219-4272*
St. Stephen's Entrance, St. Margaret Street. ☎ *0171-219-3000. Commons, Mon.–Thurs., 2:30–10 p.m.; Fri., 9:30 a.m.–3 p.m.*

Neo-Gothic splendor with over 1000 rooms (bigger than Aaron Spelling's house), it pits the Commons against the Lords, which is often more exciting than anything in the NBA. The ministers have been making policy here since the year 1066. But not in the same Palace. The original Palace of Westminster (then the residence of the reigning monarchs) was destroyed by fire in 1834. There was almost nothing left of the original style of architecture. It was decided to rebuild in the Gothic style, but it took more than 20 years before the House of Commons, the House of Lords, the Royal Gallery and the other eight acres of buildings were completed. Put all of this together with Big Ben, the most elegant Tic-Toc in the world, and you have "The Mother of Parliaments," the very heart of British democracy. The Big B stands next to Parliament in all its regal splendor with its four huge faces telling the world that time is marching on. The bell in the tower is used by the BBC on the hour, to start its T.V. shows and radio broadcasts. It's rarely more than a fraction of a second off. Can you say the same about your Swatch?

There are visitor's galleries in both Houses of Parliament, but the lines are long and the sessions difficult to predict. Still, *you* have a much better chance of getting in than the queen, since no reigning monarch has been allowed inside the House of Commons since Charles I raided the place to arrest some hapless M.P.s in 1642. Talk about carrying a grudge.

Hyde Park's 360 acres are a tranquil setting.

Hyde Park

W2, Hyde Park Corner, Knightsbridge
☎ *0171-298-2100. Open 5 a.m.–Midnight.*

Central Park and the Tuileries all rolled up into 360 lush green acres of both gentility and tranquility. It's pram heaven for the nanny brigade, but it's also a haven for pinstripes who need a break from the Knightsbridge scene. All of this pristine beauty belongs to the crown. Henry VIII stole it out from under the Westminster Monasteries and used it as his royal hunting grounds, the only hobby he had aside from his wives. The hunting path he used is today called Rotten Row, no insult intended to Henry, just the anglicizing of the words "Route du Roi." Today, Rotten Row is where all the easy riders in London horse around. The huge man-made lake right in the middle of the park called the Serpentine, is beloved by all the "Wendy's and John's" who have sailed their boats on it for decades. On Sunday, Speaker's Corner has orators that make Ross Perot sound like Mary Poppins.

AGENDA TIP

If you happen to be in the park at about 10:30 a.m., you can catch the exceptionally colorful parade of the Household Cavalry using Rotten Row to get them to the palace in time for the changing of the guards. It's a mini-pageant, not to be missed.

A cruise along the Thames offers dramatic London views.

London, from the Thames

Westminster Pier
☎ 0171-930-4097. April–September.

To understand the beauty of the city, you need to see it from the river. Nothing gives you the views of historic London as dramatically as a Thames cruise. The Houses of Parliament, Big Ben, the Tower of London, all look more regal from the Thames, and London is revealed the way it was when water travel was the best way to get from Westminster to the Tower, without worrying about carriage gridlock. You can go upriver all the way to Hampton Court, which takes the whole day, or downriver, with superb views of the skyline, to Greenwich. The boats leave frequently from Westminster Pier so you may not need a reservation, but if you're a type A personality, you can call ahead.

London Zoo

Regents Park
☎ 0171-722-3333. Daily 10–5:30 p.m. Admission, £6.95, children, £4.95.

Opened by Sir Stamford Raffles (much better known for his Bars than his Zoos) in 1829, London Zoo, of late has had major problems with credibility in the eyes of many an animal-lover in the city. So to soothe the savage beast and their critics as well, they raised over £20 million and flung wide the doors of the cages to update their old-fashioned approach to animal displays. Today, they have transformed themselves into a very P.C. instruction centre for conservationists. The beautiful Snowden Aviary was designed by Princess Margaret's ex.

You can watch the snakes being fed (if you are into horror shows) or the elephants having their teeth brushed, to protect them from pachyderm plaque.

Madame Tussaud's Waxworks and Planetarium attract two million visitors a year.

Madame Tussaud's Waxworks

Marylebone Road, ☎ *0171-935-6861. Daily 10 a.m.–5:30 p.m. Admission, £8.25, children £5.25.*

London has its share of dummies, too. This is *the* kitsch attraction to be seen in the city. The story of London's most famous Madame started in Paris in 1770, where a very young girl got a job as an assistant in a wax museum. As time went by, there was no one who could hold a candle to her in molding and tinting figures. Two of her biggest hits were Voltaire and Benjamin Franklin. The French Revolution came along and Madame T was called upon to mold the death masks of the victims of the Guillotine. Not many people could have found a way to add that to their resume. When things calmed down, Tussaud decided to take her show on the road and she settled in London. Since 1835, people have been "waxing ecstatic" over the exhibition and over two-million people visit the museum every year. Today, it's divided into themed areas such as: 200 years, Legends, Superstars, Chamber of Horrors and the spirit of London that takes you through the Great Fire of 1666 and face to face with Shakespeare. Since all this comes at a pretty high price (£8.25), the only thing the owners have to worry about is waxy buildup.

The Monument

Monument Street
☎ *0171-626-2717. Apr.–Sept., Mon.–Fri., 9 a.m.–6 p.m.; Sat.-Sun., 2–6 p.m.; Oct.–March, Mon.–Sat., 9 a.m.–4 p.m. Admission, £1, children 25p.*

Sir Christopher Wren does it again, or more accurately, did it again in 1677. Unfortunately, The Monument does not celebrate a glowing heroic deed, or the spirituality of the soul; instead it commemorates the catastrophic Great Fire of 1666 that leveled 80 percent of London. The fire started in a bakery on Pudding Lane and burned steadily for four days and nights. Since it destroyed almost all of central London, it is a real miracle that only 12 people died. However, if you are one to look on the bright side, the fire finally and with no help from the Pied Piper, drove all the rats away that had been plaguing London for centuries. The Monument is 202 feet tall and was erected exactly 202 feet from the "pyromaniacal" bakery. There are steps circling around the pillar up to the top where there is a gorgeous view of the city. Unfortunately, they have caged in the platform to discourage those who would prefer to reach the bottom without using the stairs.

National Gallery

Trafalgar Square
☎ *0171-839-3321. Mon.–Sat., 10 a.m.–6 p.m.; Sun., 2–6 p.m. Admission free.*

Their original collection numbered just 38 paintings in 1824, in a townhouse on Pall Mall. From there it was moved to a one-room building at the north side of Trafalgar Square. No one ever dreamed it would grow up to be the venerable National Gallery. Today, it houses one of the world's most important collections of art, from the Renaissance, right up to the 20th century. The building itself kept growing along with the collection. A dome was added, more exhibition rooms and finally the Sainsnbury Wing, a magnificent space to dramatically display the Renaissance masters. Picture this: the Gallery has now spread out into a whole corner of Trafalgar Square and houses over 2000 paintings, including those of Botticelli, Hogarth, Rembrandt, Velasquez and Caravaggio. (See "Museums.")

Piccadilly Circus

SW1, London
The London picture-postcard view we've all grown up with. Even better than 42nd Street (because it's older, snootier and cleaner), it has wall to wall neon, and is overseen by the famous statue of Eros. Don't be afraid of the blue, green and pink spiked-haired kids. They fit right in with the neon. (See "Locales.")

Portobello Road

Notting Hill.
Even if you hate antiques, even if you hate shopping, even if you hate roads, Portobello is so much more than a market. It is part carnival and part happening. Starting from the top of Notting Hill, the 200 or so stores and stalls spill out into the street, which is jammed with the throngs who come to "browse" or to look for a Rembrandt that no one has noticed because he forgot to sign it. The Saturday quest for treasure and trivia is well worth being a part of.

Originally, it was dedicated to fruits and vegetables, but one day the dealers found out there was more lettuce in antiques than lettuce. The dealers are masters of half-truths so if you're not an expert, beware the shills who covet your shillings. Don't bother with Portobello during the week since most of the stores are closed, but on Saturday from 6 a.m. to about 5 p.m., the Hill comes alive with the sound of bargains.

The view of the city from St. Paul's dome is breathtaking.

St. Paul's Cathedral

St. Paul's Churchyard.
☎ *0171-236-0752. Mon.–Sat., 8:30 a.m.–4 p.m. Galleries open 10 a.m.–4:30 p.m. Admission £3, children £2. Galleries, £2.50, children £1.50*
Sir Christopher Wren's biggest hit. Its magnificent dome makes the London skyline that much more elegant. It took 35 years and a miraculous change of design in 1710, when Sir Christopher decided a dome was a lot trendier than the obligatory steeple he had penciled in at the beginning. Whew! We can't imagine the skyline without the gentle curve that seems to melt right into the sky. Amazingly, it came

through the Blitz untouched, as everything went up in flames around it. Inside, all is gold, mosaics, and beneath the dome, right in the center is Wren's memorial carved into the floor and composed by his son, which says: "Reader, if you seek his monument, look around you."

Everyone should stop at the American Memorial Chapel which is dedicated to the 28,000 American soldiers stationed in London, who died in the War. Surrounded by the beauty of the church, it is particularly moving. The views from the dome of the city are breathtaking and the Whispering Gallery is the delight of young and old alike. Because of an acoustical oddity, if you whisper on one side of the gallery, it can be heard with absolute clarity on the other side. It would make Deep Throat green with envy.

Soho

Today, what makes Soho dear to every Londoner's heart is that one of the best Chinatowns in the world is found there. But in the yesterday of Henry VIII, it was a royal hunting ground and So-Ho! was what you yelled when you spotted some poor hapless creature munching on the grass. **Chinatown** is only a part of the colorful restaurant scene in Soho. It has always been *the* place for pre- and post-theater dinners, and today, some of the best new chefs open here first, since the rents are cheaper than Mayfair. The flavor of the area used to be bohemian cum porn flick and sex shop. Now, gentrification has arrived and trendy little boutiques are edging out the "brash and the beautiful". Will Soho keep its raffish image? Tune in after 2001. (See "Locales.")

Tate Gallery

Millbank, Pimlico
☎ *0171-887-8000. Mon.–Sat., 10 a.m.–5:30 p.m.; Sun., 2–5:30 p.m. Admission free.*

From Hogarth and Gainsborough right up to David Hockney, the Tate houses both a major collection of British Masters and also a fine representation of international artists. Best known for its sophisticated and somewhat controversial presentation of its works, the Tate is always making a display of itself. It fearlessly presents artists who otherwise would wind up in the "are-you-kidding" section of the *London Times*. And so, the Tate has won the hearts of the art world by being graciously accepting of the struggling unacceptable.

The "Very Victorian" outside of the Tate belies the relaxed, airy, modern galleries within. Both its funding and its name came from Henry Tate, the sugar king, who was able to sweeten the pot enough for the opening in 1897. Some of the not-to-be-missed works you'll find at the Gallery are: *The Kiss* by Rodin, *The Snail* by Matisse, *The Annunciation* by Dante, and *The Sick Child* by Munch. Of course the Gainsboroughs and Reynolds are a sight for all eyes.

Another art form the Tate celebrates is the art of cuisine. Their restaurant is one of the best in London. Even people who are prone to "art attacks" adore the restaurant, not only for its fine food, but because it has one of the most extensive and fairly priced wine lists in town.

Ten Downing Street's most beloved resident was Sir Winston Churchill the famous prime minister.

Ten Downing Street

One of the most famous addresses in the world, Downing Street, although any Englishman worth his kippers will deny it, is the country's White House. And like the White House, it is made inaccessible by iron gates that close off both sides of the street. Even so, just a glimpse puts you in touch with the historic decisions that have been made here since 1732. Its most beloved resident was Winston Churchill, it's most irritating, Margaret Thatcher.

Trafalgar Square is where Londoners gather for celebrations.

Trafalgar Square

Charing Cross.

Long before M.G.M. was being represented by Leo, the lion quartet in Trafalgar Square became the trademark of an entire city. They sit, like impressive bronze sentries, surrounding the column of Lord Nelson in London's most heroic square. These fabulous felines have been ridden, kissed, climbed on and adored by masses of locals, visitors and pigeons alike. To make the square even more impressive, there are two wonderful fountains that glisten on a sunny day (yes, Virginia, they do have sunny days). There is always a feeling of celebration about the square, and Londoners gather there on New Years Eve as we do on Times Square, to wait for midnight. It is also the sight of the town's most impressive Christmas tree. And at its most moving, it was *the* place to congregate when V.E. day was declared.

Most Absurd Agenda

After he had won the war, Hitler intended to move Nelson's columns to Berlin as a celebration of dominance.

Victoria and Albert Museum

Cromwell Road, Knightsbridge.
☎ *0171-938-8500. Admission suggested £4.50, children £1. Mon., 12–5:30 p.m.; Tues.–Sun., 10 a.m.–5:30 p.m.*

The V&A is best described as London's "walk-in-closet." Anyone who suffers from collectoritis or atticomania will fall in love with this most eclectic of collections that honor the decorative arts. While the British Museum celebrates the history of the world, the V&A celebrates the history of the spirit. The look of the place is in stark contrast to the idiosyncratic, fascinating treasures inside. Every inch of its red brick facade brings to mind the queen who dedicated it in 1899. It has the stoic, massive, institutional look that seemed to give Victoria some comfort as she endured her lengthy widowhood. In an uncharacteristic burst of romanticism, she requested that it be named the Victoria and Albert Museum. Statues of them both stand guard on either side of the entrance. As usual, Vicky does not look amused. A statue of Fame is at the tippy top of the museum's central tower, making its own tongue-in-cheek comment on its attainment.

There are over 150 rooms filled with an irresistible hodgepodge of everything from fashions to Frank Lloyd Wright and Josiah Wedgwood. The newest addition is the Glass Gallery. It has been designed with glass walls and a glass staircase to house 7000 pieces of sparkling, shimmering objects from the 2nd millennium B.C. up to the present. The whole gallery is definitely a "glass" act. Stone throwers need not apply.

HOTELS

The First Entry in Your London Agenda

There is only one word for the hotel scene in London today. SHOCKING! No matter what category you choose from, the cost of a hotel room in London will be a shock. The lowly (but perfectly adequate) bed and breakfasts are now almost all over $100. The mind boggles at being asked to pay three figures for the privilege of staying in someone's spare room. These are the sad facts of hotel life in London today. There is simply no way to sugarcoat your hotel costs. If you are accustomed to a luxury experience, it may translate into four figures before you are ready to check out. Even if you lower your standards to first class status, you will still find that most of your travel budget will be gobbled up by 24 carat sterling.

The good news is that there's a whole new hotel scene in London—they're thinking small, smaller, smallest. The big "Grand Dames" of Mayfair have given way to the three *S's*—smashing, sumptuous and sophisticated. The choice is up to you.

We are not, and never have been, members of the "who cares where you stay—how much time do you spend in your room anyway?" club. If some of you, like us, are official collectors of hotels as treasured travel memorabilia, that's one of the reasons we have avoided including the most obvious members of the chain gangs—despite the security blankets with which they make their beds—a truly British hotel is at least as quintessential a city experience as fish and chips.

Each of the hotels in this section has been stayed in, or at least visited and rooms inspected. We decided not to include a number of hotels for a variety of maddeningly idiosyncratic reasons ranging from too damn inconsistent (the otherwise brilliant Ritz Hotel has some lilliputian lemons), too groupish (the London Hilton), too hard to book (The Fenja, it only has 14 rooms, for heaven's sake), and on and on. Simply, there are too many great hotels in London to start out by making compromises.

How to Select a Hotel

Our choices are based upon three golden rules:

1. When it's time to rest our weary bones, we think our weary bones deserve the best our money can buy.

2. Location, location, location. Since the easiest way to get around the city is on foot, stop and think about the pleasures of being able to walk back to your hotel after a business meeting. It's a lot simpler than dealing with traffic. Try not to stay in Mayfair if you plan to visit Harrods on a daily basis. But no matter where you are, check out transport services, if any, offered by the hotel. (There are often complimentary limos to get you to that first appointment on time.)

3. The least expensive room in the best hotel is usually better than the most expensive room in a moderate hotel. A good hotel buys you a good "Hall Porter," sophisticated business systems, and many extra services and facilities that may even wind up saving you money.

AGENDA TIP

Assuming you've made the perfect choice, you should still take a peek at some other hotels when you're in town. We usually hotel hop for drinks or breakfast. Who knows, the next time you plan a trip, your first choice may be booked solid.

How to Make a Reservation

First, unless your travel agent can do better than the listed or "rack" rate, get yourself another travel agent. Or call up yourself and ask about special deals and weekend or airline-sponsored packages. It's often possible to get a corporate rate just by asking for it. Many hotels cut rates by half on the weekend to fill rooms vacated by captains of London industry. If you're attending a conference, there may be a discount even if you make your own reservation. And sometimes, you can get a special rate just by a little discrete bargaining.

If you arrive, God help you, without a reservation, the London Tourist Board can help. Call them at ☎ *0171-824-8844,* 9:30 a.m.–5:30 p.m. weekdays.

AGENDA TIP

Do not use the hotel's 800 number. Call direct. The last thing you want to do is reach some telemarketing nerd in London who wouldn't know his arm from his armoire.

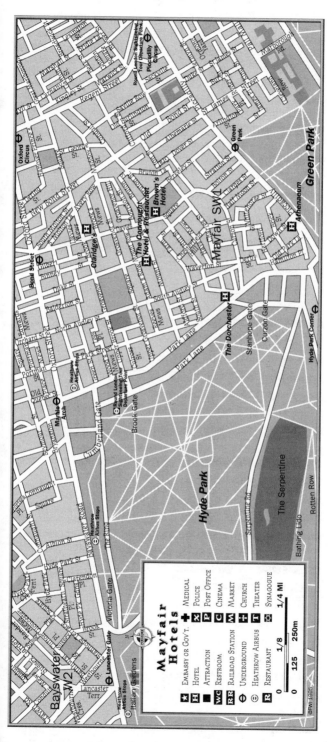

Mayfair Hotels

⭐	EMBASSY OR GOV'T.	✚ MEDICAL
🏨	HOTEL	✖ POLICE
■	ATTRACTION	P POST OFFICE
WC	RESTROOM	C CINEMA
R͞R	RAILROAD STATION	M MARKET
Ⓞ	UNDERGROUND	✚ CHURCH
⊖	HEATHROW AIRBUS	T THEATER
R	RESTAURANT	✡ SYNAGOGUE

0	1/8	1/4 MI
0	125 250m	

©PW 1995

If you have preferences about type of bed, high floor vs. low floor, front views (noisy) or back (quiet), specific views, not wanting to be near elevators or service areas, whatever—let them know when making your reservation.

Be sure you're guaranteed your time of arrival. No hotel is obliged to hold a reservation past the appointed hour. Therefore, you'll have to book with a credit card or a deposit. That's the only way you can rest assured.

That is, if you can forget your hotel's whopping VAT tax and service charges, which sometimes are included, but often are not.

Always inquire as to whether the rate includes breakfast (a wonderful perk that was usually offered at British hotels without charge, but today is fast disappearing.)

HIDDEN AGENDA

It is possible to get a refund on the VAT if your hotel bills exceed a certain amount. Ask for the form!

The Grand Hotel Experience

Claridges/ £250– £500, VAT additional

Connaught/ £235– £750, VAT additional

Dorchester/ £195–£375, VAT additional

Four Seasons/ £210–£335, VAT additional

Lanesborough/ £170–£375, VAT additional

Regent/ £185– £300, VAT additional

Savoy Hotel/ £200–£615, VAT included

Baby Grands

Athenaeum/ £225–£275, VAT additional

The Berkeley/ £200–£400, VAT additional

Brown's/ £185–£255, VAT additional

Halkin/ £190–£375, VAT included

Hyatt Carlton Tower/ £225–£375, VAT additional

Boutique Babies

Blakes/ £125–£235, VAT included

Capital/ £200– £300, VAT additional

Dukes/ £125–£250, VAT additional

Egerton House/ £110– £240, VAT additional

Franklin/ £110 - £210, VAT additional

Halcyon/ £165, VAT included

Lowndes/ £185– £275, VAT additional

Portobello Hotel/ £75– £195, VAT additional

Sterling British

Basil Street Hotel/ £120–£250, VAT included

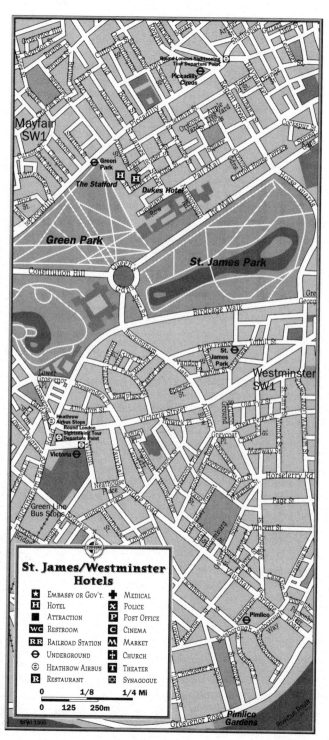

The Cadogan/ £125–£275, VAT included

Diplomat Hotel/ £65–£130, VAT additional

The Goring Hotel/ £125– £220, VAT additional

Milestone/ £190–£275, VAT included

The Stafford/ £170–£306

The Top Agenda Hotel Choices

The Athenaeum

116 Piccadilly, London W1V OBJ
☎ *0171-499-3464, FAX: 0171-493-1860*

Not a very British lobby, not even a very pretty lobby but there is a definite hum in the air. People passing through on their way to the Whiskey Bar or the Windsor Lounge all seem to know something. What they know is that the Athenaeum is "hot" now. The left coast has discovered it and the countryside folk who come up to the big L for shopping have rediscovered it. Right on Piccadilly, overlooking Green Park, the Athenaeum is a hotel for grownups who need a discreet and laid-back atmosphere right in the middle of the madding crowd.

The rooms are geared for warmth and comfort. There are chintz canopies over the beds and bright plaid blankets tucked under the spreads. In the larger rooms there are separate areas for relaxing. Best of all, separate dressing rooms so that you can rattle your Chanel chains without disturbing your "significant" other. And the most caring touch of all, coffee and tea-making equipment and supplies. You may never want to catch that bus to Harrods!

The guiding light behind all this T.L.C. is the Athenaeum's fairy godmother and executive manager, Sally Bulloch. She's as much of an institution here as you-know-who at the Palace. The only difference is that under Sally's watchful eye, things go a lot more smoothly. They even named the dining room after her. Is that like the Academy Award of Hotels or what?

Basil Street Hotel

Knightsbridge, London, SW3 1AH
☎ *0171-581-3311, FAX: 0171-581-3693*

The Basil stands pat in the early 1900s and we hope it doesn't ever give an inch. It is completely committed to the past for all the right reasons. As soon as you walk through the door you've lost 50 or 60 years of architectural development and contemporary furniture.

The rooms can only be described as "yesteryear eclectic." Some are completely wood-paneled in the style of a ship's cabin, some are chintzed to the nines with window-paned closet doors (so that you can watch your clothes in repose), but all have stadium-sized bathrooms. One of the more charming facts about the Basil is that they have tiny single rooms without baths right out of a British boarding school. You can be in the poshest part of London, right opposite Harrods yet, for about 65£ a night.

The Berkeley

Wilton Place, Knightsbridge, London SW1X 7RL

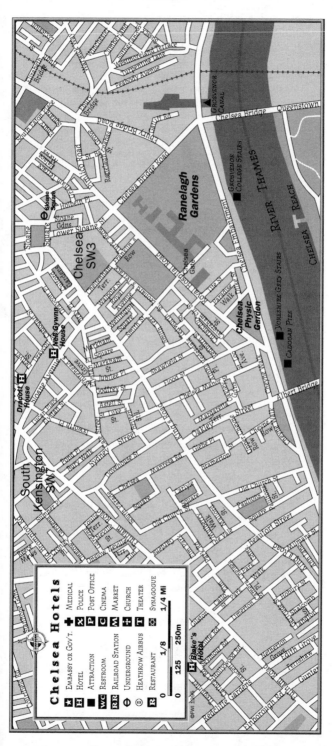

☎ *0171-235-6000, FAX: 0171-235-4330*

Discretion is the *only* part of valor here. Even though the Berkeley is smack bang in the middle of Knightsbridge, its most appealing quality is that you hardly know it's there. The old Berkeley, which dated back to the turn of the century was located right on Piccadilly, and considered to be a venerable establishment. When it was rebuilt in Knightsbridge, its focus changed from establishment to elegantly exclusive. The fact that it's tucked into Wilton Place opposite St. Paul's Church only adds to its spiritual calm.

The rooms match the understated decor of the lobby, although some of the top-priced ones tend to be English-countryside genteel. The Berkeley is not a sumptuous goodie to be used for affairs or second honeymoons. Its strength is top notch service, anonymity and the glamour of Knightsbridge. For very good measure there is a top health spa, and a tiny movie theater right next door, that belongs to the hotel, in case you suffer from "cinema withdrawal."

Blakes Hotel

333 Roland Gardens, London SW7 3PF
☎ *0171-370-6701, FAX: 0171-873-0442*

In the 80s we had restaurants as theater. In the 90s we have The Hotel as theater. And the most theatrical hotel in London is Blake's. Perhaps the reason for that is its compulsively dramatic owner, Anouska Hempel, once an actress now, both a fashion designer and a hotelier. Martha Stewart has finally met her match! Hempel has coupled elegance with extraordinary flair to come up with a hotel that is totally unique. To stay at Blakes is not just to have a room at a beautiful hotel, it's closer to having a part in a Noel Coward play.

The hotel was created by joining several Victorian mansions, so the corridors have twists and turns that lead to random bowls of potpourri and antiques where you least expect them. The lobby is a combination of British campaign furniture, antique suitcases, bamboo furniture, black lacquered walls and a parakeet. There is no mistaking Blakes for your average Holiday Inn. Once across the threshold, there's no doubt you're not in Kansas anymore.

The sumptuous guest rooms continue the mood of elegance, mixed with a little intrigue. Each one acts out a different Hempel fantasy. Ours was Biedermeier cum M.G.M., with black walls and voluminous black and gold silk drapes caught with tapestry swags. The drapes echoed the magnificent silk canopy over the bed and the wood floors were stenciled with a black diamond design. Hidden away in a 19th-century armoire were the crass realities of today (V.C.R, T.V, FAX) but why would you need any of these things if you were in a Noel Coward play?

Brown's Hotel

Albemarle Street & Dover Street, London W1A 4SW
☎ *0171-493-6020, FAX: 0171-493-9381*

Brown's was born back in the 1800s because of a dream. That dream belonged to Lord Byron's valet, James Brown, who thought if he could make Lord Byron comfortable (no small task), then he could do as well for the rest of London. To this day his presence is felt in this clubby "establishment" hotel that is famous for its excellent service

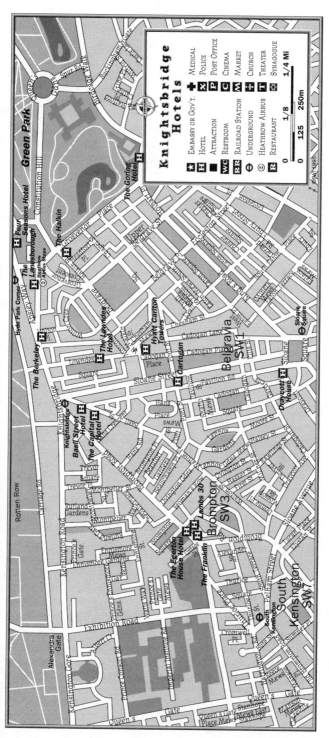

and its atmosphere of calm. Tucked right off Piccadilly (which is not noted for its relaxed pace) Brown's could just as well be in the country. It's used as much by Brits from the burbs who have come to London, as it is by tourists who prefer grace to glitz. It certainly was a favorite with the Roosevelts; Teddy was married at Brown's and Franklin and Eleanor honeymooned there. Alexander Graham Bell made the first phone call in Britain from Brown's. We'll bet they made him pay a service charge anyway.

The hotel has undergone a complete rehab and the Victorian stodginess has been banished while the Victorian charm has been enhanced. Rooms are generous in size and comfort. Colors are vibrant and bathrooms are particularly plush, down to wood-paneled soaking tubs.

If you do stop at Brown's, ask to see Rudyard Kipling's desk. Even *he* felt at home here.

The Cadogan

Stoane Street, London SW1X 95G
☎ *0171-235-7141, FAX: 0171-245-0994*

The Cadogan is yet another hotel in London that echoes the past so loudly you can almost hear Lily Langtry reciting Oscar Wilde's new poem to her "friend" (that's what they called them in those days) King Edward VII. The actress lived next door and finally the hotel incorporated her townhouse and turned part of it into the Langtry drawing room. The whole place reeks of Victorian intrigue and below-stairs bawdiness, even though on the surface it is the soul of discretion and civility. That was what made the Victorian era so much fun; you never really knew what was going on. What was going on at the Cadogan was the arrest of Wilde from his very room and his imprisonment at Reading Gaol. Today you can request that very same room (if you have a Stephen King complex or feel a poem coming on).

Historical kitsch aside, the Cadogan is a gem for anyone who's already bored with the 90s. It's located on the very chic Sloane Street, in the heart of Knightsbridge. Upstairs the rooms are bright and deep-down comfortable. They've been redone in the ever-popular British Mannerhouse style with baths not quite up to Claridge's but generous and workmanlike. The sweetest touch of all is that instead of a chocolate on the pillow, you're left a tiny tin with two squares of shortbread.

The Capital

Basil Street, Knightsbridge, London 5W3 1AT
☎ *0171-589-5171, FAX: 0171-2225-0011*

"Small but luxurious" is the Capital's motto. It translates into a hotel that was made for people who feel their hotel room is an extension of their approach to life. These are the people who make the Capital one of the hottest tickets in town.

Just a crumpet's toss from Harrods, it sits peacefully around the corner on Basil Street with a simple exterior that does nothing to prepare you for the elegance and style inside. The Levins, who own the Capital, spend at least 25 hours a day making sure it's run with an almost military dedication to excellence. They've certainly won the war when it comes to stunning decor, helped in part by high profile designer Nina Campbell, and just a dash of Ralph Lauren. The rooms, although not as large as some of the other Townhouse hotels, are filled with country furnishings, soft colors and superfab baths. The attention to detail is so specific that the Levins had the mattresses made by hand. Is this the place for "The Princess and the Pea" test or what?

The Connaught

Carlos Place, Mayfair, London W1Y 6AL
☎ *0171-499-7070, FAX: 0171-495-3262*

The Connaught must have invented the word "exclusive" because when all is said and done, when the last trendy "boutique beauty" has come and gone, the Connaught will still be sailing on the crest of the Britannia waves. As one of its general managers said, "We don't try to boost the hotel through advertisements or promotions, we don't pretend to be a glamorous hotel and we don't ascribe to artificiality or current fashions." Put that in your kipper and smoke it!

The hotel is right off Grosvenor Square, in the most important part of the British Empire—Mayfair. There are more Rolls Royces, chauffeurs and welch corgis per inch here than the rest of the British Isles, all told, and they all seem to be parked in front of the Connaught. Inside, amid the antiques and crystal of the lobby, there is a hush as the venerable staff discretely greet the Earls, the Lords and the Sirs that have been stopping here for generations. There is no "downstairs" at the Connaught, just wall to wall privilege.

The rooms themselves are as staunch as the staff. Heavy, comfortable, English furniture with fireplaces that are lit to take the chill from the air. The ratio of guest to staff is one to three, so you'll never have to pour your own tea.

If you decide the Connaught makes your lion-heart beat faster, you had better book well in advance. And it wouldn't hurt to include an autographed picture of Winston Churchill.

Claridge's

Brook Street, Mayfair, W1A 2JQ
☎ *0171-629-8860, FAX: 0171-499-2210*

Lavish, without a doubt legendary, but most of all, Claridge's is often described as an annex to Buckingham Palace. The management, way back in 1898, tried to reassure its guests that "the spirit of modernism would not in the least interfere with comfort and privacy." Nothing has changed. Even through umpteen updates and refurbishments, the spirit of Claridge's remains the same right down to the liveried footmen who serve guests in The Foyer.

Royalty, through the years, has had an ongoing love affair with Claridge's. There's always some member of some royal family stopping here, on or off the record. One of the stories the staff loves to tell is that a call came in from a member of the government asking to be put through to the king. The reply was "Which king?"

The accommodations upstairs carry out the majesty and extravagance of the public rooms. Their size can be truly astonishing. One of the standard suites we saw was almost as big as Rumania, with transportation needed to bring you from the bedroom to the sitting room. All the rooms have entrance halls, antiques, buttons to summon the

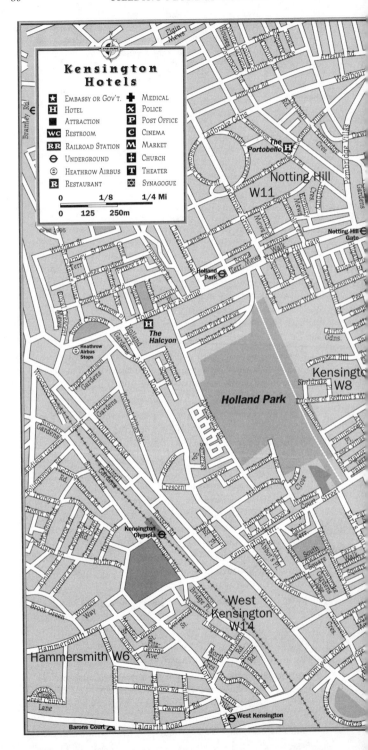

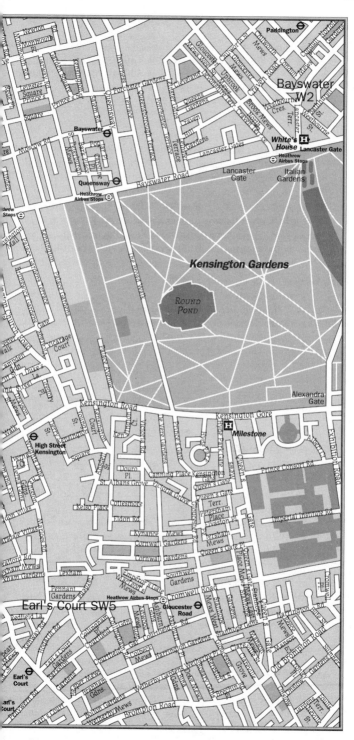

maid, waiter or valet (the buttons are also found right over the tub, so if you miss when you reach for the soap, you're in for an encounter of the closest kind), and most have working fireplaces. With all of this grandeur the staff never makes you feel as if you are part of a museum. A case in point was Spencer Tracy, the ultimate "Everyman": He's quoted as saying"...when I die I don't want to go to Heaven, I want to go to Claridges."

Diplomat

2 Chesham Street, SW1X 8DT
☎ *0171-235-1544, FAX: 0171-259-6153*

Think small, think charm, think wonderful location, but most of all think cheap. Maybe not rock bottom Howard Johnson cheap, but in London today and particularly in as "glam" a neighborhood as Knightsbridge, anything at a rate just above $100 is a reason to cheer. The Diplomat is snowy white on the outside and still retains its 1880s charm in its rooms. After a hard day's shopping on Brompton Road, it's just a short walk back to the comfort of the Diplomat. This is really a Pence-Pinchers delight.

Dukes Hotel

St. James Place, London SW1A 1NY
☎ *0171-491-4840, FAX: 0171-493-1264*

The area of London that is in the shadow of St. James Palace is one of the most prestigious in the world. It's just a few steps from Bond Street, Buckingham Palace, Piccadilly, Jermyn Street and Hyde Park. In the midst of all this luxury stands Dukes Hotel, one of the most luxurious small hotels in London. Since 1908 it's been home for the away-from-home aristocrats. Today, if anything, it's even more luxurious, more exclusive and more personal than it ever was. Even though it's tiny enough to be considered a mansion, it's got hot and cold running butlers and a roster of regulars who come back year after year for Duke's famous T.L.C.

The walls of the rooms are wallpapered or fabric-covered, the furnishings run from airy wicker to lavishly canopied beds, to writing alcoves with antique desks. The plush bathrooms carry out the hotel's dedication to comfort and elegance. All in all, it's hard to leave your room for the harsh realities of the world outside. Not to worry, there's always a bright gaslit lamp outside to welcome you back.

The Dorchester

Park Lane, London W1A 2HJ
☎ *0171-629-8888, FAX: 0171-409-0114*

The Dorchester reeks glamour with a capital G. It stands like a huge art deco ocean liner ready to set sail down Park Lane. Closed for almost two years while its owner, the Sultan of Bruni, gave its aging decor a revitalizing injection of mega-money, it is once again the jewel in his hotel crown.

As soon as you enter the lobby you can feel the energy coming from the special events and parties that never seem to stop here. The Dorchester is club-heaven for the left coast. Maybe Elizabeth Taylor will be having tea (the big D is her favorite), or maybe there's a semi-royal wedding reception in progress. Prince Philip had his stag party here. You can almost hear the flashbulbs popping away back in the 30s when the Dorchester was built.

Upstairs, the rooms are sprawling and done to a turn in Georgian country house style with a nod to the Sultan's oriental rug dealer. Most of the silks have been woven in India and used liberally to give the rooms a rustle of magnificence. Casual is not a word that is even whispered here. The bathrooms are Carrara marble from top to bottom and all have big windows that let the light stream in. The tubs are big enough to do laps.

Just by chance, if you win the lottery, try to book into one of the Oliver Messel Suites. The fab (*My Fair Lady*, etc) theater designer designed two of them; they're really show-stoppers.

The Egerton House Hotel

Egerton Terrace, Knightsbridge, London SW3 2BX
☎ *0171-589-2412, FAX: 0171-584-6540*

The street on which Egerton House is located is so quiet you can hear a souffle fall. In the back of the hotel, beautiful gardens make its setting even more bucolic. But if you click your heels three times, you're right back in Harrods, the Victoria and Albert museum, Beauchamp place and all those other "cool" places. And after you've spent your pounds down to the last ounce, you get to come home to this idyllic townhouse address.

The rooms are splendid, with antiques, porcelain and luxurious furniture. The staff would make Anthony Hopkins sit up and take notice. Downstairs in the drawing room, you can pour your own drinks and curl up in front of the fire. This is a real charmer. As one guest put it, "It's become my London home."

The Four Seasons

Hamilton Place, Park Lane, London W1A 1A2
☎ *0171-499-0888, FAX: 0171-493-6629*

It used to be called the Inn on the Park—well, it's still on the park and it's still technically an Inn but the psyche of the Four Seasons seems light years ahead of its slightly depressing former self. As soon as you walk through the door, someone, even if they are in the midst of a problem, looks up and smiles. That's what makes a hotel "grand."

Outside the facade is rather grim, almost severe, but inside is a 24-carat British welcome. The rooms are very large and well appointed but they are not the most beautiful or the plushest in town. What they are is triple comfortable with baths that are joys to sink down into. They may need a bit of a "re-furb" to bring them up to 90s speed, but they're all solid and substantial like their Mayfair address. Most of them overlook Green Park so the views can be verdantly spectacular. As is the case with most of the Four Season hotels, they are dedicated to fine cuisine. This one has a one-star Michelin dining room (See "Hotel Dining Rooms" page 176).

The staff is everything you would expect from a Four Seasons, excellence on all sides. Best of all, the frustrations of travel just melt away. That's the beauty of the Four Seasons mentality. All *you* have to do is show up.

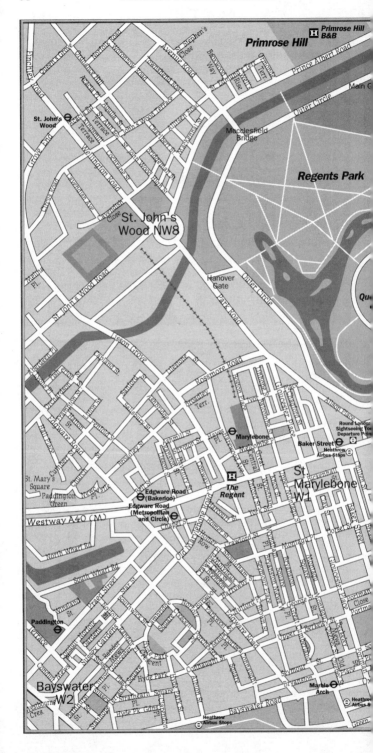

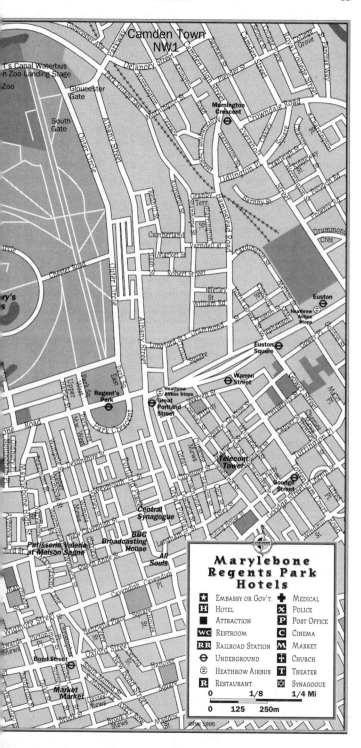

Marylebone Regents Park Hotels

★	EMBASSY OR GOV'T.	✚	MEDICAL
H	HOTEL	✖	POLICE
■	ATTRACTION	P	POST OFFICE
WC	RESTROOM	C	CINEMA
RR	RAILROAD STATION	M	MARKET
⊖	UNDERGROUND	✚	CHURCH
⊜	HEATHROW AIRBUS	T	THEATER
R	RESTAURANT	✧	SYNAGOGUE

0		1/8		1/4 Mi
0	125		250m	

©FWI 1995

The Franklin

28 Egerton Gardens, Knightsbridge, London SW3 2DB
☎ *0171-584-5533, FAX: 0171-584-5449*

From the same folks who brought you the elegant Egerton House comes another Townhouse Tootsie with much the same flair and intimacy. It's like having instant family (the rich branch) as soon as you check in. You'll be handed a glass of champagne while your luggage is spirited up to your room and that's just the first installment of the pampering that lies ahead. Lush to the max, the rooms have four-posters, gorgeous fabrics, oil paintings and beautiful views of the formal gardens the Franklin overlooks.

Downstairs, the bar is small enough to seem as if a cocktail party you've been invited to is always in progress. Shopping bags, the most sought after trophies in London, are strewn around the fireplace while guests exchange harrowing tales about Harrods. The Franklin translates into a warm, friendly and deluxe experience.

The Goring Hotel

Beeton Place, Grosvenor Gardens, London SW1W OJW
☎ *0171-396-9000, FAX: 0171-834-4393*

If you're prone to celebrating world- shaking events, then you should definitely be aware that in 1900, The Goring was the first hotel to have private bathrooms. A sigh of relief was heard round the globe. But as time went on The Goring had to find other ways to keep their edge. They've certainly succeeded. Today, The Goring, which sits regally behind Buckingham Palace is one of the most English of hotel experiences. It has much more to offer than just the grace of a bygone era, or that it is almost close enough to Westminster Abbey and the Houses of Parliament to hear Big Ben chiming, it has the Goring family, whose love for their hotel has kept its incredibly high standards in place for over 80 years.

The lobby is elegant and welcoming with marble floors and leather chesterfield sofas. The tip-off that charm is taken seriously here is the pair of faux sheep that lie in front of the fireplace, warming their hooves. There's no way not to love this place.

The rooms are British traditional, which means they are solid and substantial, with large helpings of warmth and charm. George Goring has claimed to have personally slept in every bedroom in the hotel as an under-the-covers agent, for quality control. If you want a truly British experience as well as a hands-on approach to excellence, this is the place to unpack.

The Halcyon

81 Holland Park, London W11 3R2
☎ *0171-727-7288, FAX: 0171-229-8516*

Luxury, extravagance, discretion and one of the best dining rooms in London are tied up in a gilt-edged package at the Halcyon. Its location in Holland Park is a bit removed from the hustle of Knightsbridge and the bustle of Mayfair, but the Halcyon is the answer to any oil baron's prayers.

As exclusive as 65th Street and Madison in New York, the Holland Park area of London is filled with million £ townhouses, chic little restaurants and gourmet food markets.

The hotel was built from two adjoining mansions in the elegant Belle Époque style which has been carried out upstairs to create some of the most luxurious rooms in town. No two are the same and for sheer drama the Desert Suite, with its tented ceiling, is an "Arabian Nights" knockout. But the Halcyon is more than just a pretty face; the service is superb and the dining room is absolutely wonderful (see "Hotel Dining Rooms", page 177). There's also a Vodka Bar that serves caviar and other sybaritic snacks.

The Halkin

5 Halkin Street, Belgravia, London, SW1X 7D5
☎ *0171-333-1000, FAX: 0171-333-1100*

Perhaps the area is uppity, stuffy Belgravia, and perhaps it's British traditional on the outside, but inside, the Halkin is most definitely a hotel for the 90s. It reeks of Italian sleek right down to the Armani-outfitted staff. No wonder! All its designer's names end in "i." Even its general manager, Nicholas Rittie's name almost ends in "i." In terms of the Halkin's exciting design the "i's" have it.

The lobby is crisp and lean, not a hint of a chesterfield in sight. The floor is terrazzo and mosaic with light streaming in from the atriumed ceiling. The windows are draped in stark white fabric. Minimal is definitely more here.

The hallways upstairs are completely distinctive as they curve around in a ridged design. The rooms themselves are also constructed with curved walls and rosewood paneling that forms an arch with the ceiling. The Halkin is making a statement no one else in London is echoing at the moment. This is a hotel for the pampered individualist.

Hyatt Carlton Tower

Cadogan Place, London SW1X 9PY
☎ *0171-235-1234, FAX: 0171-245-6570*

Big, bright, airy and overflowing with flowers, the lobby of the Carlton Tower is an instant meeting and greeting place for anyone who crosses its threshold. The feeling that you are in very good hands seems to be the reason to choose one of their modish accommodations in the heart of Knightsbridge. Some of these very same hands made the "Chinoiserie," the cheerfully oriental lobby that serves an elegant tea, one of the most festive rooms around. Other hands are busy tending the "Peak," a 21st century health club. This place goes beyond "state-of-the-art" all the way to irresistible resistance equipment. There are also huge conservatory windows, so that London is spread before you as you hone your personal best.

The rooms are oversized, luxurious and furnished in a smart, contemporary style with lots of earth tones and Southwest touches. The baths go on forever, from just your average run of the mill floor to ceiling marble, to luxury in-room spas with whirlpools and steam showers. There are city and garden views from the sweeping windows for a calm, uncluttered and soothing atmosphere to sink down into after seeing the royal sights.

The Lowndes

Lowndes Street, London SW1X 9ES
☎ *0171-823-1234, FAX: 0171-235-1154*

When is a Hyatt not a Hyatt? When it's disguised as a small, intimate hotel that serves as a wonderful alternative to its big beautiful brother, the Hyatt Carlton Tower.

The Lowndes is a country inn right on the doorstep of the snazzy Knightsbridge scene. The rooms are airy, filled with prints and chintz, as well as canopied beds and mega charm. The staff is all spit and polish and very caring. If you're a repeat guest, they'll even monogram a terry robe for you. Another perk is fresh ice in the bucket every night and a refilled nut dish. These people spare no expense to keep you comfy. But the best perk of all is being able to use the state-of-the-art health club at the Carlton Tower, which is just a sneaker's throw from the Lowndes.

The Lanesborough

1 Lanesborough Pl, London SW1X 7TA
☎ *0171-259-5599, FAX: 0171-259-5606*

When the Lanesborough talks about guest amenities, they don't mean bath gel or shampoo and conditioner; they mean "big time" amenities, like a 24-hour butler who will press all your clothes when you arrive, exercise equipment brought right to your room, fresh fruit supplied daily, and when a car is available, they'll make local runs for you. This all adds up to major pampering. The Lanesborough isn't just a great hotel, it's a *really great* hotel!

Located almost on the grounds of the Palace (yes—that Palace), right on Hyde Park Corner, the Lanesborough was originally St. George's hospital from 1733 to 1980 when you had to be very sick to book a room there. Today, all you have to be is very rich. The building itself is one of the most impressive examples of Regency architecture in the city. Add to that 300 million dollars to bring this landmarked building into the 21st century. At night there are two flaming torches over the entrance to add to the drama of the structure.

The rooms upstairs are as opulent as the public rooms. They echo the magnificence of the entrance hall, aglitter with crystal antiques, mahogany paneling and a Gilbert and Sullivan pastiche called The Conservatory, which is, at press time, their dining room.

The upstairs decor is sumptuously achieved with silk upholstered walls, leather couches, brocades that cascade to the floor and every other conceivable luxury. The bathrooms could house a small family. The most surprising thing about this bastion of British Bonhomie, is that it's all being brought to you by Texans. Rosewood, the same down-home folks that own the Bel-Air in LA and The Mansion at Turtle Creek in Dallas, have crossed the Atlantic to score yet another of their hotel success stories. Y'all come back now!

The Milestone

1-2 Kensington Court, London W8 5DL
☎ *0171-917-1000, FAX: 0171-9917-1010*

The Milestone is just a tiara's toss from Kensington Palace, the current residence (but perhaps not for too much longer) of Lady Di. If you stopped at the Milestone, you and she might be standing in the same line at the Cinema or McDonald's. Even if you don't get to share a Big Mac with "Her Chicness" you will probably have a fine view of Kensington Gardens and the royal parklands.

The Milestone is really fascinating. It is a vision of Victorian splendor, Gothic arches and turrets. Inside, most of the detail is paneled in oak with carved ceilings and leaded glass. The rooms themselves are very romantic with antique four-poster beds; some have two levels with stairs leading to a cozy seating area. Every possible care is taken to preserve the very Gothic atmosphere of this charmer. You'll hear a buzz of French and Italian at the front desk; the Milestone seems to attract a continental crowd. If you collect unique hotels, this might be next on your list.

The Portobello Hotel

2 Stanley Gardens, London W11 2NG
☎ *0171-737-2777, FAX: 0171-792-9641*
The Portobello could just be the most idiosyncratic hotel in all of London. It was created to be a 24-room luxury-plus pit stop for rock stars and fashion's playthings. The man who created it, and who also runs one of the most romantic restaurants (Julie's) in town, definitely tapdances to a different drummer. The area is Nottinghill, home to the antique dealers who keep Portobello Road on the right track. Today the gentrification of this quiet section of London is transforming it into one of its "hottest."

The flair and imagination of the Portobello is apparent as soon as you enter. Every detail is lush, theatrical and creative. All of the rooms are different and filled with whimsical touches—a round bed, a painted ceiling and a cabin that makes you want to sail away. The most sensational antique the hotel owns is a bathing machine, half-Rube Goldberg, half-Cecil B. DeMille, which sits in the middle of one of the rooms. A bit off the beaten path but definitely the place for an offbeat hotel experience.

The Regent

222 Marylebone Road, London NW1 6SQ
☎ *0171-631-8000, FAX: 0171-631-8080*
Originally it was the headquarters of British Rail with all the turn of the century grandeur that implies. Today, Regent hotels has given it a £ 75 million new identity as one of the most luxurious of its international hotel group. They've enclosed the whole structure under one huge atrium to make the outside of the building the inside. Add to that a lavish lobby that the inside rooms overlook, and if you're still not on sensory overload, you can feast your eyes upon the palm trees that soar up into the atrium. This must be a whole new school of "cross-pollination" architecture.

Marylebone Road, which is where the Regent is located, is a fascinating section of London to walk. Just a Sherlock's throw away from Baker Street, there's a Holmes Museum that's elementary to anyone, even if they're not Watson. Another resident of the "nabe," Madam Trussaud, waxes ecstatic over everybody from Jack the Ripper to Elvis. Best of all, Regent's park (is this just a coincidence?) with its wonderful zoo, is a short stroll away.

The Regent has some of the most splendid rooms in the city, crammed with the comforts and amenities this group is famous for. Even though the hotel is not in the usual Mayfair, Knightsbridge loop, it is just too extraordinary to ignore.

The Savoy Hotel

1 Savoy Hill, The Strand, London WC2R OBP
☎ *0171-836-4343, FAX: 0171-836-9736*

Of all the hotels in London, the Savoy has perhaps the most romantic of pasts. Back in the late 1800s, a major wheeler-dealer named Richard D'Oyle Carte, built a theater called The Savoy to house the comic operas of Gilbert and Sullivan. D'Oyle Carte, ever the promoter, felt if there was a hotel next to the theater, people could see the show and then have a place to eat and rest. Voilà! The package deal was invented. Next came a hotel manager, who was brought in to get the Savoy on its feet. His name was Cesare Ritz, who persuaded an innovative new "hot" chef named Auguste Escoffier to join him. And so, in this most glittering of environments, the Savoy was born.

Today, the glitter has softened to a burnished art deco glow, but it still has the old magic—squint and you can see Fred and Ginger dancing through the lobby. Since the Savoy is located on the Embankment as well as the Strand, a glint of the river can be seen as you stroll through. There are also pockets of historic elegance in the American Bar and Grill. The "99 percent dry martini" was invented here and the Grill has Winston Churchill's usual table to point out.

The rooms upstairs are all the last word in deluxe, and would still make Cesare Ritz proud. If you plan to be stompin at the Savoy, the definitive experience is a room with a view of the Thames. The bathrooms are all amazing with vast marble tubs and huge shower heads that produce a spray worthy of Old Faithful.

The Savoy is a state of mind, not just a place to spend the night. Its ghosts are the most fabulous in the world.

The Stafford

16-18 St. James Place, London SW1 A1N
☎ *0171-493-0111, FAX: 0171-493-7121*

St. James is known for its monied residents, its exclusive shops on Jermyn Street and its pastoral views of Green Park. In the midst of all this upscale splendor is St. James's Place, into which is tucked the Stafford, a throwback to the London of private clubs and staying in town for a night of theater and fine food. That's the kind of place it is. You can't help being taken aback when the other guests don't all have British accents. It seems so personally devoted to the Empire. This makes it a delightful experience for all the Anglophiles who feel at home here. The only concession The Stafford has made to the passing of time is The Carriage House, a luxurious transformation of 18th-century stables that are in back of the hotel. They've been made into sensational suites that have their own front doors.

The rooms upstairs at The Stafford are all comfortably clubby and cheerful while downstairs everyone is usually drawn to the American Bar, which is an institution in itself. (See "Bars" page 198).

The Stafford is one of the best ways to go native in London.

White's Hotel

Lancaster Gate, London W2 3NR
☎ *0171-262-2711, FAX: 0171-262-2147*

Looking like a grand Victorian confection on the outside, White's hotel is really a small luxury hotel with great charm. A handsome glass canopy, reminiscent of a turn-of-the-century exhibition hall, leads you into the elegant lobby with its welcoming fire in the carved fireplace.

The rooms are quite lavish and some are accented by oriental antiques. If the East doesn't influence the decor then the countryside does, with chintz and quilted spreads over the four-posters. Many of the rooms overlook the very pastoral Kensington Gardens. Being located opposite the park lends an atmosphere of peace and calm. Its the perfect choice for a bit of country added to a London city experience.

Bed and Breakfasts

The B&B scene in London has changed considerably now that prices have escalated to the point of no return. There are still wonderful B&B's all over the city but your chance of finding a first-rate location at a first-rate price has become a bit tricky.

Therefore, why not put yourselves in the hands of a B&B agency which cuts right to the London chase. A couple of the best are:

Central London Accommodations
83 Addison Gardens, W140DT
☎ *0171-602-9668, FAX: 0171-602-5609*
They'll suggest the perfect place for you in whatever price range you find comfortable and they have preinspected all their listings. True to their name, they are most accommodating.

Primrose Hill B&B
14 Edis Street, NW18 LG
☎ *0171-722-6869*
Run by an American woman, this agency is more dedicated to keeping the pounds down than Weight Watchers.

Youth Hostels
8 St. Stephen's Hill, St. Albans, Herts., AL1 2DY
☎ *0727-855-215*
This is an umbrella group for seven different youth hostels in London. They are all well located so give them lots of lead time to make a booking for you.

Apartments

There is yet another choice in accommodations for London that is becoming more and more popular; the apartment option. Since our *London Agenda* is geared to shorter stays, it would probably not be of value unless you had a week or more to spend. An apartment offers you the chance to live like a Londoner. You can spread out, settle in and even make a simple meal. If you are traveling with children, this is most definitely the way to go.

It's relatively easy to accomplish short-term rentals since London is bursting with really good apartment values. You're bound to save money and feel more at home, not to mention have a fridge to store your clotted cream.

Dracott House

10 Dracott Avenue, Chelsea, SW3AA
☎ *0171-584-4659, FAX: 0171-225-3694; £700 - £1800 per week.*

Aston's Budget Studios

39 Rosary Gardens, South Kensington, SW7 4NQ
☎ *0171-589-1105, FAX: 071-589-9433; £190–£1,010.*

Nell Gwynn Apartments

Nell Gwynn House, Sloane Avenue, 3W3 3AX
☎ *0171-589-1105, FAX: 0171-589-9433; £210–£800.*

Lambs

21 Egerton Gdns, Knightsbridge, SW3 2DF
☎ *0171-589-6297, FAX: 0171-584-3302; £650–£850.*

SECRET AGENDA

Shh, just between us, there are two small apartments at Hampton Court that are available for short stays. You can live like a king if you call ☎ *0181-781-9500 (The Landmark Trust).*

AGENDA TRAVEL ADVISORY

The top deck of a doubledecker bus affords a great view of London.

Travel to London from the States is almost as easy to accomplish as travel around the U.S. itself. The choice of airline includes most of the leading carriers, such as American, Delta, United, TWA, Continental and of course, if you'd like to travel with a British accent, British Airways. We decided on Virgin Atlantic because we had heard it was so innovative in its approach to air travel. We were not disappointed. It's a very young, very "on target" operation that is rapidly becoming the airline of choice for the British business community.

Whatever airline you decide on, there are numerous flights leaving daily to bring you to London in time to start your agenda on the schedule you've decided upon.

Continental, ☎ *(800) 231-0856.*
Delta, ☎ *(800) 241-4141.*
TWA, ☎ *(800) 892-4141.*
United, ☎ *(800) 241-6522.*
American, ☎ *(800) 433-7300.*
British Airways, ☎ *(800) 247-9297.*

Virgin Atlantic, ☎ *(800) 862-8621.*

AGENDA FUSS-BUDGET

Some airlines have day-of-departure or day-prior-to-departure reduced fares for Johnny-come-latelys. If you're flexible, you can save enough for more "hot" times in London.

Getting to London

The 15-minute trip from Heathrow to Central London can be a nightmare of traffic delays, which will almost double the normal amount of time it would take to get to your hotel. Armed with that information, you may decide that public transportation is the only way to go. However, if you're able to avoid the horrendous rush hour tie-ups, it should take about 45 minutes to an hour. Keep in mind, people have traveled to London since the Romans arrived by chariot in the second century A.D. *Everybody gets there eventually!*

AGENDA TIP

Try to pay for all purchases with your credit cards. The rate of exchange for the card company could be much better than the rate you receive for your travelers check, since most of the cards are connected to banks. Aside from that, there is a permanent record of transactions for customs and VAT.

Taxi

If this is your very first exposure to these big, comfortable Black Beauties, you're in for a treat. The London cab, as well as the London cabbie, is perhaps the last vestige of polite civilization left! However, they come at a very steep price. A trip into London from Heathrow is likely to cost, during "normal" traffic (we have yet to experience "normal" traffic from Heathrow) £30 to £35. If, God help you, it's rush hour, it might be cheaper to buy the cab from the driver. The tip should be about 15 percent. BE SURE YOU HAVE A LICENSED BLACK CAB!

Airbus/A1, A2

☎ *0171-222-1234*
Departs from Heathrow every 20 minutes. The cost is £5 –£8, with an open return. A1 goes to Victoria Station, A2's destination is Marble Arch, Russell Square. The trip should take about one hour and give you a glimpse of the terrain.

Greenline Bus, No. 767

☎ *0171-222-1234*
This bus will take you directly to Victoria Station. If your hotel is near Victoria, this is a closer alternative than the Airbus. It's £8 and takes about one hour.

Underground/Piccadilly Line

☎ *0171-222-1234*

This is the cheapest and fastest way to get into Central London from Heathrow. The trains leave during peak hours on a five minute schedule, and the cost is £3.10. The only problem is having too much luggage, since the Underground depends on stairs and escalators. If you've only hand-luggage to deal with, this is the way to go. The trip should take about 50 minutes.

From Gatwick Airport

Gatwick is much farther out of London than Heathrow (29 miles), but the upside is that the traffic may not be as insane.

Taxi

Taking a taxi from Gatwick to London is an expensive proposition. A conservative estimate is about £45. If you do opt for a cab, you must make a deal with the driver before starting the trip. Because Gatwick is outside the Metropolitan Police District, meters do not apply, so a price must be negotiated with the driver.

Flightline Bus, No. 777

This is an express bus that leaves every hour from 8 a.m.–11 p.m., for Victoria. The cost is £7.

Gatwick Express Train

This is the most convenient and fastest route to Central London. The train leaves every 15 minutes for Victoria Station and the cost is £8.52. The trip takes a fast 15 minutes.

Stansted Airport

This airport handles flights from other European countries and is 30 miles outside of London.

Cambridge Coach Service

The buses on this line travel to Central London five times a day, Monday-Saturday. On Sunday, service is reduced to three times daily. The service costs £6 and takes approximately one hour and 30 minutes.

Stansted Express Train

Daily service departing every 30 minutes for the Liverpool Street Station. First class tickets, £13.50, second class, £9. The trip takes 45 minutes.

Arrival by Train

If you're arriving by train from another European destination, you might enter at Victoria Station, Liverpool Street Station or King's Cross Station. Each one connects with a Tube stop or has taxis at the entrances. It's a simple matter to reach your hotel from any of them.

Arrival by Car

If you are driving into London from the continent (if you've driven from the States, you must be very wet!), be careful. Remember, the Brits use the opposite side of the road. You must keep left or the balance of your trip will take place in one of London's very fine hospitals.

The Chunnel

Yes folks! The twenty-first century has arrived, albeit a little early thanks to the opening of the "Chunnel". You can now board Eurostar, the high-speed train that catapults you from Paris to London in three hours. No airport traffic, no seatbelts, no airline food. The price of a ticket is, as we go to press, First Class, $312, Second Class, $248, 14-day advance purchase (nonrefundable), $152. For information in the U.S., call Rail Europe, ☎ *(800) 942-4866*, in London, ☎ *0171-834-234.*

A Word About Car Rental

DON'T!

Getting Around London

London traffic can be daunting; exploring on foot is recommended.

There is no getting around the fact that getting around London can be a hectic, debilitating and demoralizing task. It can also be exciting, energizing and enervating, all at the same time. There are districts, squares, places, mews, embankments and lanes! Sounds daunting, doesn't it? But that's what London is all about. Unlike New York, or Chicago, it has been growing for centuries, getting more complex and convoluted with every passing year. It deserves to be a place to be reckoned with, a place that would take a decade or two to really understand.

However, the happy traveler does not live by admiration for world capitals alone, and in truth, the London he or she will want to explore is probably no bigger than a five-square mile area, in which most of the hotels, restaurants and major sights are located. Best of all, London has a brilliant bus and underground network, which will make getting from place to place fun, instead of guerilla warfare. The other part of the sightseeing equation is, of course, walking. Part of the joy of discovering London, with all of its enchanted time zones, is doing it on foot. How could you ever walk in Dickens' footsteps unless you used your own to explore the winding streets of his London. We've always found that walking around London had an almost narcotic effect; just one more street; just around the next corner; down that tiny lane, searching for famous names on "Blue Plaques." Whatever means you use to get around London, you will need:

1. A plan
2. A map
3. Comfortable shoes
4. A well made, preferably windproof, umbrella.

London Traffic Golden Rules

Business hours are the standard, 9 a.m.–5 or 6 p.m. Traffic in the morning and evening rush hours is more like Ringling Brothers than Piccadilly Circus.

There is also an added lunchtime crush, which takes care of most of the afternoon. Not to mention the pre- and post-theatre chaos.

Taking a cab during these hours (read: most of the time), will make your travelers checks disappear faster than a sale at Harrods.

Use Public Transportation!

The plan is an easy one to make. All you have to do is group your activities by area (Chelsea, Knightsbridge, etc.) so that you can walk from A to B to C. Try to explore the shopping and dining opportunities all in the same area. That will cut down on backtracking. If you keep checking your map for landmarks and find the distance is too vast to cover on foot, there are "millions" of bus stops every block or so, and a handy Tube station to take you the couple of stops to your next destination. The street names and numbers may be a bit confusing, but the buses and the Tube have been laid out with the efficiency of an ever-watchful nanny, determined to make sure none of her little charges is ever lost.

How to Take the Tube

If you come from any major city in the U.S., the London Underground system will be a delightful revelation. It's relatively clean and safe, graffiti free and childishly simple to use. It may not be as scenic as those red double-deckers above ground, but the stations are clearly marked at each Tube stop, and the maps are remarkable for their clarity. The trains themselves are comfortable, even luxurious by some standards (excluding Moscow), with plush and leather upholstered seats that the Clockwork Orange Boys have left intact. Londoners who were around during World War II feel particularly fond of the Underground since it was here that everyone flocked to escape the lethal effects of the Blitz. Thousands of people were saved because they sought shelter in the depths of the Underground. The measure of how deep they are is seen in the stupefying height of some of the escalators that look like they could double for amusement park rides.

The London Transport will issue Travelcards that can be used on the Underground, buses and British Rail. Unlimited travel for one day starting from 9:30 a.m. costs about £2.70, which is a substantial saving over single ticket purchases, since the fares are determined by zones. If you are going to stay seven days or longer, and have a small photo, you can buy an unlimited pass for seven days, starting from 9:30 a.m. for £8.50. There are other variations as well. For information, ☎ *0171-222-1234*. It is also possible to purchase Travel Cards in the U.S. before you leave. Just call British Rail Travel International, ☎ *(212) 382-3737*, or the nearest branch of the British Tourist Authority.

DON'T DISCARD YOUR TICKET AFTER BOARDING THE TRAIN. YOU NEED TO RETURN IT WHEN YOU LEAVE.

How to Take the Bus

Everyone knows the method of transportation that is the most fun in London is the beloved bright red conveyance that is synonymous with the City. Children of all ages fight their way to the top deck, no matter how perilous the trip or how impossible the descent at the appropriate stop. There is simply nothing that makes you know you're really in London like a ride in a double-decker bus. The bus stops are clearly marked (white with a red circle) and the front of the bus tells its destination. Since they have so many different routes that overlap, the wait for a bus is relatively short. There are bus stops that say "Request." This means they will only stop if you hail them. Most of the buses run all night, but the late night routes are slightly different, and a late-night bus stop will either have a tiny crescent moon, or an N. Bus etiquette requires that you "queue," which means form an orderly line. Once on the bus, if it's an old model, there will be a driver and a conductor to sell you a ticket. Today, there are more and more "one man" buses, which is too radical a change for us to endure happily. The fare structure on the buses is the same as the Tube, with fare being determined by zone. Travel cards are available in the same manner as for the Tube. Be sure to get a bus map. It will make life so much simpler.

How to Take a Taxi

London taxis are hands-down, no contest, the best in the world. They are also comfortable, clean and tall enough for Wilt Chamberlin to sit back and relax. The London cab driver is the antithesis of, say, the New York cabbie, who usually can't find 42nd Street, and blames you or his unlucky karma. These knowledgeable knights of the road are polite, usually dressed in a handsome, wooly sweater, and most always ready with a smile and inside info on the city. Can you tell that we're in love? Their only drawback is the meter and the traffic. A short trip during rush hour can set you back the first installment on a Bentley. If you do use one, tip about 15 percent and hail the ones with the yellow light, lit-up. They are hardest to find pre-theatre, but if you can make it to the front of a hotel, you may have better luck.

HIDDEN AGENDA

If you're near the Dorchester Hotel, there is a small street in back (Hill Street). Right off that very street is the Diesel Garage that almost all the cab drivers in London use. It's foolproof for snaring one of these comfy darlings during rush hour or before theatre.

LONDON BY LOCALE

Hyde Park sprawls over 363 well-groomed acres.

London has kept its very distinctive identity through the centuries by having many identities, each of which corresponds to an area of the city very much set apart by its own flavor: The glitz and glamour of Knightsbridge; the history of the Empire played out in Westminster the whimsy of Covent Garden, where "upstairs" meets "downstairs" in the most theatrical of settings Chelsea, the birthplace of "Mod" London, where the younger population brought edge and wit to the city of striped suits and pastel feathered hats. Even more to the point, the one-square mile in the center of town known as The City, where, in fact, London began in A.D. 43, is probably the most fascinating locale of all because it summons up more tangibles than any of the others.

In all there are 32 boroughs (local areas of government) excluding The City, that make up the 610 square miles that make up Greater London.

Each year thousands of tourists crowd this dazzling mecca, each responding to a different part of the unique patchwork of the city's locales. History buffs spend all their time in The City, antique collectors haunt Portobello and Islington, theater aficionados find their own nirvana in The Strand and Covent Gardens. No matter how you decide to spend your time in the Jewel of the United Kingdom's Crown, you'll never get enough of it. "So much to do and so little time to do it in," is the rallying cry that will bring you back to London again and again.

Mayfair

Think astronomical, then double it and you have the monetary climate of Mayfair. The streets and the bankbooks of the residents are indeed, paved with gold. It's the Beverly Hills of London with Park Avenue and the Rue St. Honoré thrown in for good measure. The perfect row houses that line the perfect squares of Mayfair are now owned by ministers, rock stars, assorted royals, and billionaires. It got its wholesome name from a not-so-wholesome fair that was held in the area every May in the 1700s. The event resembled a Shriner's convention at its worst. In fact, it was so unsavory it was referred to as "that most pestilent nursery of impiety and vice." Finally, the locals called a halt to the dreaded May fair and the "swells" started to buy up the real estate faster than **Donald Trump**. The most compulsive of the shoppers was the **Grosvenor** family, headed by the **Duke of Westminster**. Today, most of Mayfair is still owned by the Duke, who is considered the richest man in all of Britain. **Rockefeller Center** brings in but a few paltry pence next to the land values of **Oxford Street**, **Regent Street**, **Bond Street** and other savvy investments such as Grosvenor and **Berkeley Square**.

AGENDA GOSSIP

That sly fox, the Duke of Westminster, offered to swap the deed to the American Embassy in Grosvenor Square in return for 12,000 acres of land in Florida (including Cape Kennedy) which the family had lost during that unfortunate "dust-up," the American Revolution. Talk about the art of the deal.

Most of the fine shopping in London can be found in Mayfair. Aside from the huge department stores on **Oxford Street**, the signature of Mayfair is quality. The best tradesmen and craftsmen were drawn to the money and high style of the gentry who moved into the area and hurried to open exquisite shops around **Bond Street** and **Savile Row**.

Mayfair is bordered by **Park Lane**, **Regent Street**, **Oxford Street** and **Piccadilly**. As famous as the area is for shopping, so it is for the luxury hotels that line **Park Lane**. The **Dorchester** is here, as well as **Grosvenor House**, **The Hilton**, **The Four Seasons** and the **Intercontinental**. **Grosvenor Square** is where the **American Embassy**, with its heroic eagle spreading its wings over the stark design of **Eero Saarinen**, is located. The Embassy itself is a boxy horror, but the square is filled with *Upstairs, Downstairs* type Georgian row houses that have always appealed to Americans, way back to **John**

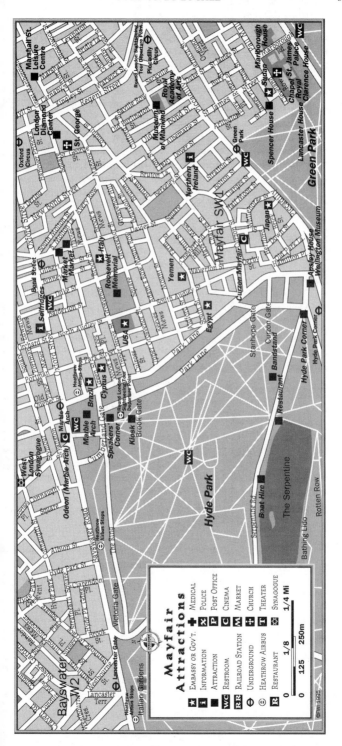

Adams, who lived in one when he was our Ambassador to London. **Berkeley Square** (pronounced as if it were *Barkley*) was the turn-of-the-century address for many of the high rollers in town, among them **Waldorf Astor**, **Gordon Selfridge** and **Clive of India**. Today, the square has mixed usage, with fine townhouses contaminated by grim looking office buildings and ceaseless traffic. The best escape is up **Mount Street** where the very impressive **Connaught Hotel** can be found along with smart shops and cafes.

Shepherd Market is found by turning off at **Curzon Street**, which opens up to a micro-village that dates back to 1735. Tiny streets and alleys have the flavor of 18th century London. This was the very site that the infamous May Fair was held. The market has kept some of the same bawdy atmosphere that the fair generated, with its strolling "ladies of the evening." But, aside from that, it attracts writers and artists in the evening for a bit of La Vie de Boheme. When the weather is balmy, dining spills out onto the street.

The largest of Mayfairs' shopping arenas are **Regent** and **Oxford Streets**. They are both wide boulevards lined with some of London's most prestigious department stores and specialty shops. Off the avenues, you will find **Bond Street**, boutique heaven, and the legendary "bespoke" tailoring community of **Savile Row**, some of whose most devoted customers were the **Duke of Windsor**, and the **Beatles** (yes, all of them). Curzon Street is home to the elegant **Trumper**. the world's most beautiful barbershop.

Regent Street was laid out in 1816, in honor of the **Prince Regent**, who later became **George IV**. It was designed to be a magnificent boulevard and that's the way it looks today, even with the Prince long gone. Royalty is still very much in evidence here, since the queen's own jeweler (a full time job), **Garrard,** has its shop here. Aside from **Hamlay's**, London's answer to F.A.O. Schwartz (actually, several F.A.O. Schwartz's) our favorite on Regent Street is **Liberty's**, in all its pseudo-Tudor glory (see "Agenda Shopping," page 148). World famous for its Liberty Prints, it is also a veritable treasure trove of goods from around the globe. Here's to life, **Liberty**, and the pursuit of shopping. The rest of **Regent Street** has names that are household words, even in the "colonies"—**Wedgewood**, **Aquascutum**, **Austen Reed** and **Burbury's**.

Oxford Street, on the other hand, teems with middle-of-the-road commercialism and sometimes downright "schlock." It's a younger, more restless street with "going out of business" sales and budget chains that have branches all over town. **Selfridge's** (see Agenda Shopping), which ironically was brought to London by **George Selfridge**, an American, stands like a huge Edwardian monument to consumerism. If you need a change of pace to a more down-sized shopping experience, try **South Molton Street**, a very chic little pedestrian mall off **Oxford Street**. At the end of the mall you'll find **Gray's Antique Market**, an upscale collection of vintage jewelry and other bric-a-brac.

JUST AROUND THE CORNER
AGENDA ADVENTURES/MAYFAIR

If the season permits (Oct.–May), one of the most exciting shopping experiences one can have in London is at an auction house. It's immediate gratification and Las Vegas, all rolled into one. The most venerable of the houses is Sotheby's, which has been around since the 18th century. Don't let those accents inhibit you. Be brave, and most importantly, don't rub your nose at the wrong time!

Agenda Shopping/Mayfair

Hamley's

188 Regent Street, ☎ ☎ *0171-734-3161.*
It's been on Regent Street since 1881 and sprawls over an amazing six floors of toys, games, enough stuffed huggables to fill any respectable jungle and the latest in Morphin modes.

Mulberry

11-12 Gee's Court, ☎ ☎ *0171-493-2546.*
Elegantly crafted country clothes and leathers that are really delectable. We dare you to leave without a wallet or a card case or maybe the briefcase of your dreams.

Les Senteurs

227 Ebury Street, ☎ *0171-730-2322.*
Just spending some time in this opulent shop is aromatherapy. They have more than 150 different scents to savor. Don't go if you have a cold.

Heraldry of Mayfair

White House Street, ☎ *0171-499-8335.*
If coats of arms give you a warm feeling, this fascinating shop can trace yours if you have one, or you can choose one that they've already embroidered on cushions and banners.

Nicole Fahri

158 New Bond Street, ☎ *0171-499-8368.*
She's all over town, but this is her most chi-chi boutique, stocked with her latest designs. Her clothes are classic with simple tailoring and great style.

George Trumper

9 Curzon Street, ☎ *0171-499-1850.*
Unguents and wonderful smelling colognes for both sexes, as well as the Royal Family's favorite barbershop. Rumor has it that John Major had all his trims here.

Aquascutum

100 Regent Street, ☎ *0171-734-6090.*

The raincoat that would even impress Gene Kelly! Over the years they've added other sport clothes, with the very British khaki and red Aquascutum color combinations, but since 1851, it's the raincoat that's brought everyone in out of the storm.

Maggs Brothers
50 Berkeley Square, ☎ *0171-493-7160.*
Antiquarian book specialists overlook the Square in great style, with a collection to match. They've been here forever and sell rare autographs as well.

Gieves & Hawkes
1 Savile Row, ☎ *0171-434-2001.*
A stitch in time here means going back to 1785, when the oldest and most famous "bespoke" (made-to-measure) tailor in Savile Row first opened shop. Their clients include British as well as Hollywood royalty. In the past, they've nipped and tucked Lord Nelson, Stanley and Livingston, and Captain Bligh, who had a very different idea of what "off the rack" meant.

Henry Poole & Co.
15 Savile Row, ☎ *0171-734-5985.*
Not quite as old as Gieves & Hawkes, but still a favorite of the Baron de Rothschild.

Thomas Goode
19 South Audley Street, ☎ *0171-499-2823.*
The last word in tabletop fashions. The shop is a series of rooms, each displaying exquisite accessories for the best-dressed table in town. Antiques, silver, china. All in all, there are 14 rooms of temptations to find space for in your carry-on. Even Goode's catalogue is impressive enough to be hard-bound.

Asprey Bond St. Ltd
165-169 New Bond Street, ☎ *0171-493-6767.*
London's 24-carat gift shop, where breathing the rarified air could wind up costing you a pound of pounds. The finest in leather, crystal, jewelry and other distinctive baubles for the aristocracy.

Charbonell et Walker
28 Old Bond Street, ☎ *0171-491-0939.*
A very French name, but in truth, these elegant chocolates come from Kent. They are silky on the tongue and beautiful to behold. Wrappings are done extravagantly, so a box of chocolates becomes a work of art.

Butler and Wilson
20 South Molton Street, ☎ *0171-409-2955.*
The store is almost as dramatic as its fabulously fake jewels. Everything seems to be black except the sparklers that are irresistible. Even Liz Taylor would be impressed.

Molton Brown
58 South Molton Street, ☎ *0171-499-6474.*
Very pure, very natural creams and skin products to keep you glowing. Their line of cosmetics is carried in New York at Barneys, but it's much cheaper here.

Tradition
33 Curzon Street, ☎ *0171-493-7452.*

Tiny tin soldiers make up the entire stock of this shop. They're hand-cast in metal and then painted, or you can buy kits to do it yourself. A joy for any "Tin Horn" who collects.

Halcyon Days

24 Brook Street, ☎ *0171-629-8811.*
Even if you don't have a headache, you won't be able to resist Halcyon's beautiful enamel pill boxes. They can be custom-made for special events or holidays, and the workmanship is superb. With each box, you get a certificate of authenticity.

The Egyptian House

77 Wigmore Street, ☎ *0171-935-9839.*
If you're shopping for your mummy, this is the store for you. A mini Egyptian bazaar, with everything from design-your-own papyrus kits, to high price handmade carpets (not the flying kind). It's a wonderful place to take a break from all that serious stuff on Bond Street.

Brown's

23-27 South Molton Street, ☎ *0171-491-7833.*
Brown's is dedicated to British designers like Jean Quit and Mill Slander. There is a jumble of rooms and lots of great fashions to look through. Best of all, you never know who you'll bump into. Elton John is a regular.

Waterford Wedgewood

158 Regent Street, ☎ *0171-734-7262.*
The two Ws that everyone thinks of when they look for the finest in British tabletop ware. Best of all, they ship!

Reject China Shop

134 Regent Street, ☎ *0171-434-2502.*
Thirty-five years of fun breakables, bargains and clutter. Still fun although the bargains are not aging well.

Filofax Centre

21 Conduit Street, ☎ *0171-499-0457.*
This is the nearest thing to an out-of-body experience for Filofax addicts. A complete line of everything to fill the binders of your dreams, as well as yummy new models to make your heart beat faster. Finally, to be able to say proudly, "our notebook overfloweth."

Agenda Best Bites/Mayfair

Cafe Royal

68 Regent Street, ☎ *0171-437-9090. Credit cards. Expensive.*
Another of Oscar Wilde's haunts, and with him, Aubrey Beardsley and James McNeill Whistler. It was always filled with artists and writers when it opened in 1865. Today, it still has some vestige of its ornate past, but the menu is overpriced and underachieved. Drop in for tea and a drink to soak up the gilded atmosphere.

L'Artiste Muscle

1 Shepherds Market, ☎ *0171-439-6150. Credit cards. Moderate.*

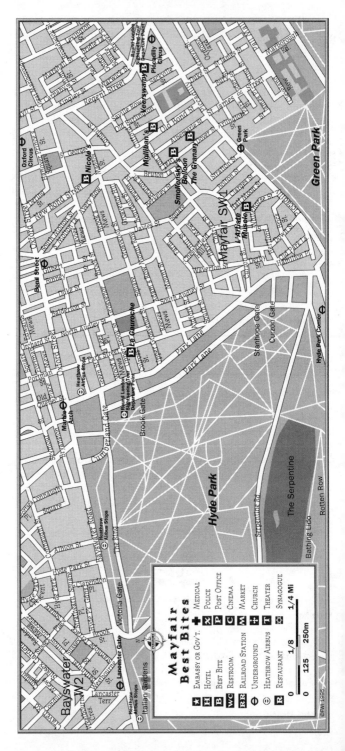

A small bistro in the middle of this ancient little market square, just right for a drink or a soothing Beef Bourguignonne. The rustic atmosphere is perfect after the hustle and bustle of Piccadilly.

Mulligan's

13-14 Cork Street, ☎ 0171-409-1370. Credit cards. Moderate.
If you are not going on to Dublin, stop in for a great plate of Irish Stew in this cozy Pub-Restaurant. Straightforward food, with a little Blarney on the side, and everything is washed down with a giant-sized Guiness.

Nicole's

Nicole Fahri, 158 New Bond Street, ☎ 0171-499-8408. Credit cards. Moderate.
Her classy fashion savvy extends down to the neat, calm restaurant in the basement of the store. Serrano Ham is well dressed with figs and prosciutto, pink duck wears a coat of perfectly spiced bean puree. Her menu is as well dressed as her customers. She also serves a great breakfast and tea.

Goode's

Thomas Goode, 19 South Aubry Street, ☎ 0171-409-7242. Credit cards. Expensive.
Now you can not only enjoy looking at the gorgeous tables here, you can eat off them as well. Goode serves breakfast, lunch and tea on some of the snazziest china in London. Caviar and smoked salmon never looked so good.

Smollensky's Balloon

Dover Street, ☎ 0171-491-1199. Credit cards. Inexpensive.
You just have to love a place that serves fish sticks and Kids Koktails. That should give you a clue as to the age group Smollensky's might appeal to. There are also burgers and fries, served with clowns and magicians.

Veeraswamy

99-101 Regent Street, ☎ 0171-734-1401. Credit cards. Inexpensive.
This was the very first Indian restaurant in all of Europe. It opened in 1927, and ever since, has attracted the crowds on Regent Street. This may not be the best Indian cuisine in the city, but the food is well prepared and the breads, all baked on the premises, are splendid. At lunch, the buffet is the big draw.

Soho

Local color is Soho's biggest asset. Like New York, Soho is a melting pot that bubbles with the many ethnic groups that have come to seek their fortunes in London. The most obvious and probably the largest single block traveled from Hong Kong to set up the exciting **Chinatown** that rivals both New York's and San Francisco's. The other groups were a polyglot of Greeks, Russians, Italians, Indians, and of late, Thai and Vietnamese. Mix well and you get some of the best food in London, with a large helping of crime on the side.

For years, Soho was London's red light district and its narrow-streets were jammed with sex clubs, strip shows and porno movies. Definitely not the place for The Grandmothers of American convention. But even with its very sordid profile, it had some of the best, cheapest and most exotic restaurants in town. Today, Soho is undergoing an attack of the Boutiques. The only known cure is to take two Guccis and call in the morning. Little by little, trendiness is replacing tackiness, and gastronomes are flocking to Soho in even larger numbers.

Gerrard Street is the hub of Chinatown.

The streets that are synonymous with Soho are **Old Compton Street**, filled with some of the area's best restaurants, and **Gerrard Street**, the hub of Chinatown, where dim sum seems to be a national obsession, Wardour, Frith and Greek Streets are all crammed with bistros and brasseries that are haunts of the film and music execs who have recently relocated to this hottest part of town. **Chinatown** opens onto **Leicester Square**, where neon and kids are the order of the day. Teens come here to see the latest flicks at the movie palaces that line the square, and eat in the tawdry fast-food outlets.

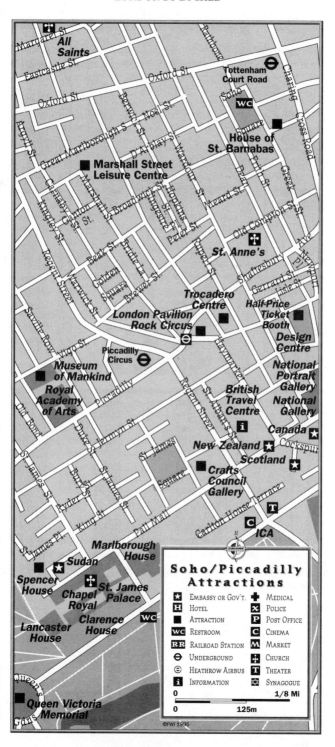

Soho/Piccadilly Attractions

For a bit of culture, there are statues of Shakespeare, Hogarth, Reynolds and London's beloved Charlie Chaplin.

In the very center of Leicester square is the discount theater kiosk, which works much the same way as the TKTS booth on Broadway, in New York (see "Theater," page 185). **Shaftesbury Avenue** is considered the most extensive theater section in London. The gem-like Edwardian houses are one right after the other, The Apollo, The Lyric, The Queens, and at the top of the avenue, the most impressive of all, the **Palace**. Most of them were built at the turn of the century. Every legend of the British stage has trod the boards at one of them and in the 30s, Noel and Gertie and the Lunts twinkled across their footlights. Going from the sublime to the ridiculous, on the other side of Soho you can actually visit the place where the Mods and the Rockers were born, **Carnaby Street**. You'd have to look hard to find Twiggy browsing the racks, but the spirit of the kids who made bellbottoms and the Fab Four household words, is still here (today, it's green hair and nose rings). If you can spare the time, stroll through Dean Street, where Mozart gave a concert at No. 21, when he was seven. If you're in the mood for some fresh fruit, stop into the tiny Berwick Street Market. The fruit monger's calls are music to the ears.

Agenda Shopping/Soho

Shaolin

10 Little Newport Street, ☎ *0171-734-1970.*
Martial arts enthusiasts love this place and always stop in for a few belts or a random brick or two.

Algerian Coffee Store

52 Old Compton Street, ☎ *0171-437-2480.*
They started selling coffees and all manner of equipment to make the perfect blend over 100 years ago. They're not necessarily Algerian but they always have something brewing.

Just Games

71 Brewer Street, ☎ *0171-734-6124.*
Board games, card games and fun and games for the family. Great chess sets at great prices and do-dads for executives who like to play around.

Junior Gaultier

18 Faubert Pl (Newburgh St), ☎ *0171-287-3761.*
For the younger Gaultier collector, Jean Paul has a very tiny boutique, filled with the theatrical fashions he's known for. For the very rich, young-at-heart.

Jess James

3 Newburgh Street, ☎ *0171-437-0199.*
Her collection of contemporary jewelry is one of the best in London. And she displays her treasures with great flair.

Contemporary Ceramics

Blake House, 7 Marshal Street, ☎ *0171-437-7605.*

This is the primary outlet for the Craft Potter's Association, and so they sell the very best designs in London.

Pam Hogg

5 Newburgh Street, ☎ *0171-2187-2185.*
After she left Scotland, she took the high road to design her avant-garde fashions that London's braver souls dote on. Anything that doesn't hug and cling is slit way up the sides.

Agenda Best Bites/Soho

Maison Bertaux

28 Greek Street, ☎ *0171-437-6007. No credit cards. Inexpensive.*
Coffee, tea, and French pastry since 1871. Their croissants have enough butter to be considered lethal weapons. A real institution in this part of town.

L'Escargo's

48 Greek Street, ☎ *0171-437-6828. Credit cards. Expensive.*
The old saying, "too many cooks" certainly doesn't apply here. They have two chefs, which in recent years has made them twice as good. Downstairs is an informal brasserie with straightforward bistro food; upstairs things get "tres" serious and "tres" expensive.

Mildred's

58 Greek Street, ☎ *0171-494-1634. Credit cards. Moderate.*
Mostly veggies on the menu, with a few fish thrown in for tasty measure. Her stir-fries are terrific and she certainly knows her way around a zucchini.

The Gay Hussar

2 Greek Street, ☎ *0171-437-0973.*
Not a reference to life-style, but a venerable old Soho haunt that was always considered to be top drawer. Nouvelle cuisine is definitely not welcome here. But at the top of the Hungarian charts is a rich winey, cherry soup and Transylvania stuffed cabbage. You'll just go bats over that one.

Au Jardin Des Gourmets

5 Greek Street, ☎ *0171-437-1816. Credit cards. Moderate.*
Classic French food with fine wines to match. It's been in Soho for years, living up to the promise of its name. If you drop in for lunch, there is a set menu in the first floor brasserie, so you can splurge a bit on their excellent wine list.

Coach & Horses

29 Greek Street, ☎ *0171-437-5920. Credit cards. Inexpensive.*
This is the closest London comes to the Algonquin Round Table, in New York. The staff of the scathingly satiric magazine *Private Eye* meets here for lunch to trade the latest royal family jokes over a "pint." It's worth having an ale and a pork pie just to see the rude cartoons on the walls and soak up local color from the "inkstained wretches."

The Red Fort

77 Dean Street, ☎ *0171-437-2525. Credit cards. Expensive.*
Some say that The Red Fort has the very best Indian food in London.
Quite a statement for a city that counts its Indian restaurants in the
hundreds. The exotic bar has Indian musicians and women gliding
around in saris. The air is perfumed with the spices of the tandoori
ovens. Easy to see why the days of the Raj were so delicious.

Jin

16 Batemin Street, ☎ *0171-734-0908. Credit cards. Inexpensive.*
Jin is considered hot in Soho in more ways than one. The food of
Korea is as fiery as 10-alarm chili and then some. Even the kim chee,
a pickled vegetable side dish, is breathtakingly hot and that's just the
appetizer! However, when they're not chewing on their chilies, the
Koreans are masters of barbecuing and at Jin, it's done right at the
table.

Cranks

8 Marshall Street, ☎ *0171-437-9431*
There are more Cranks in London than at an AT&T convention.
They all have healthy menus and focus on wholesome veggie specialties. The one in Soho is very popular and more importantly, very reasonable.

Melati

21 Great Windmill Street, ☎ *0171-437-2745. Credit cards. Inexpensive.*
You may have to wait to get in but the food is so unusual it's worth
hanging in. They serve Malaysian and Indonesian specialties that are
both authentic and fascinating. Maybe that's why there are always
lines. Grills come with a rich coconut cream and the satays with a
spicy peanut sauce.

French House

49 Dean Street, Rest. 0171-437-2477. Credit cards. Moderate.
The French House has had a very illustrious past. It was headquarters
to the Free French during WWII. You can't get much more intrigu-
ing than that unless you've met "Victor Lazlow" in person. The pub
on the first floor is rough and tumble grimy, but it is a Soho landmark. The restaurant floor upstairs is quite a different story. Fine food
served by a married couple who chef together.

Patisserie Valerie

44 Old Compton Street, ☎ *0171-437-3466. Credit cards. Moderate.*
Cases and more cases filled with delectables that make a tea break an
occasion. They serve sandwiches, but we advise cutting to the high
caloric chase and ordering the tarte tatin.

The Dog House

187 Wardour Street, ☎ *0171-434-2116. Credit cards. Moderate.*
Depending on how you feel about man's best friend, you might not
mind being sent to the Dog House. This friendly basement boite has
grills, well prepared pasta and very crispy cheese beignets. All this at a
very reasonable price. Arf Arf!

Chuen Cheng-Ku

17 Wardour Street, ☎ *0171-437-5065. Credit cards. Moderate.*
Since the choices in Soho's Chinatown are endless, but not always satisfying, we have to tell you, this is the place we're fondest of. There is

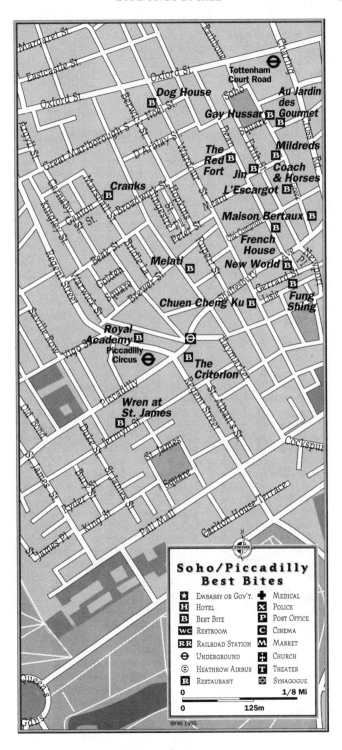

Dog House

Gay Hussar

Au Jardin des Gourmet

Mildreds

The Red Fort

Coach & Horses

Jin

L'Escargot

Cranks

Maison Bertaux

French House

Melati

New World

Chuen Cheng Ku

Fung Shing

Royal Academy

Piccadilly Circus

The Criterion

Wren at St. James

Tottenham Court Road

Soho/Piccadilly Best Bites

★	EMBASSY OR GOV'T.	✚	MEDICAL
H	HOTEL	✘	POLICE
B	BEST BITE	P	POST OFFICE
WC	RESTROOM	C	CINEMA
RR	RAILROAD STATION	M	MARKET
⊖	UNDERGROUND	✚	CHURCH
⊜	HEATHROW AIRBUS	T	THEATER
R	RESTAURANT	✡	SYNAGOGUE

0   1/8 Mi

0   125m

©FWI 1995

a no-nonsense approach to order taking and (heaven forbid) explanation, but on the up side, a comfortable homeyness about Chuen Cheng-Ku. It's always as stuffed as an egg roll with Brits who have been coming here for years as well as enough Chinese to add an important stamp of approval. The Dim Sum lunch is brilliant and best of all you just have to point. The regular menu goes on for miles and most of the choices are wonderfully recognizable.

Fung Shing

15 Lisle Street, ☎ *0171-437-1539. Credit cards. Moderate.*
This small place is a bit more upscale than the rest of the Chinatown regulars, and the menu is much more ambitious. Don't order your old Cantonese favorites; try instead, the salt-baked chicken, shellfish in hot oil or the steamed spare ribs with plum sauce.

New World

1 Gerrard Place, ☎ *0171-734-0677. Credit cards. Inexpensive.*
This just may be the largest restaurant in Chinatown, or at least the largest dim sum palace. They serve them all day, so this is a terrific choice for pretheater nibbles.

dell' Ugo

56 Frith Street, ☎ *0171-734-8300. Credit cards. Moderate.*
Three floors of earthy Mediterranean cooking that makes it seem the sun is shining right down on the menu. Hearty Tuscan soups and dense breads add to the comfort of the one-dish meals that are a specialty here. The hot sausage and white bean casserole or Lamb, and potatoes mashed with olive oil, are a couple of winners.

Piccadilly

Criterion restaurant, Piccadilly, has been popular since 1874.

The part of London known as **The City** may historically be the center of town, but **Piccadilly Circus** is, for most Londoners, its emotional core. They have gathered here to celebrate the end of wars, to support each other through the many disasters they have had to endure, and sometimes they come just to see the marvelous expanse of neon and have some fun. When the troops sailed off for the The Great War singing "Goodbye to Piccadilly," they were only expressing their belief that Piccadilly meant **home**.

The Circus that goes on in Piccadilly has nothing to do with acrobats or clowns; it has to do with traffic. Five different roads all converge in this roundabout, making it both a traffic nightmare and London's most famous postcard. We've always thought that Piccadilly was named after a favorite English relish, but the fact is the name came from a house owned by someone who sold Picadils, a stiff collar, worn in the 1600s. In a playful mood, his customers called the house Piccadilly Hall. But the real symbol of the Circus is its statue of **Eros**. Contrary to what most visitors think, the statue is not a celebration of the citizens' exotic fantasy lives—its guise here is as a very benign **Angel of Christian Charity** (so much for those party animals on Mount Olympus). **Eros** had his wings clipped temporarily when he was given a sprucing. The metal that was originally used to fashion the statue was aluminum, which needed a great deal of restoration to foil the ravages of time.

Piccadilly is a broad, rambling thoroughfare, stretching all the way from **Hyde Park Corner** down to the riotous confusion of the Circus, and separates the area of **St. James** from **Mayfair**. It runs the gamut from elegant luxury hotels to shops that cater to the queen, to famous book stores, to **St. James Church** and at its tackiest, **The Trocadero Centre**, a mini-mall, made up of video arcades, fast food outlets and the Guiness World of records. As if that weren't bad enough, next door, there is an even tackier mall called the **Rock Circus**, which has a Madame Tussaud annex dripping with Britain's favorite Rock stars.

Starting at the statue, take a stroll up Piccadilly. The first landmark you'll come to is **St. James Church**, which was, of all the churches he built, Christopher Wren's very favorite. **St. James** was a victim of the Blitz, but they restored it, and today there is a sweet little cafe called **The Wren at St. James** that's part of the church, serving veggie specialties and trendy desserts.

On the same side of the street is the store to make bibliophiles' hearts beat faster. **Hatchard's** has been around since the 18th century, when books were not electronically generated and you didn't get five for a dollar from Book-of-the-Month. There are three floors of comfortable browsing and a particularly strong children's section. The very civilized sales staff will go to the ends of the Empire to help you search for that volume of Browning you have been looking for.

If you want to know where the queen gets her takeout treats and cumestibles for the royal larder, then you have to stop at **Fortnum and Mason**, probably the most elegant grocery cum department store in the world. A century before Mr. Lord met Mr. Taylor, Fortnum and Mason were a dynamic duo. In 1707, Fortnum, who was a footman in the palace, thought who better would know the food fetishes of the rich and famous. He joined up with Mason, the king of delivery wagons, to start the poshest deli in the world. Today, you can buy cornflakes under crystal chandeliers and have your purchases double bagged by a great grandson of "Jeeves." Upstairs, there is a ready-to-wear department store of limited interest. Try to get to Fortnums near to the hour so that you can watch Mr. Fortnum nod to Mr. Mason from the mechanical clock over the entrance.

INSIDE AGENDA

*Fortnum's sent a hamper of haut cuisine goodies to **Stanley** just to keep his strength up while he was searching for **Dr. Livingston**. (Tea and Crumpets, we presume).*

Right opposite Fortnum's is the **Royal Academy of Arts**, housed in the Palladian-style mansion of the **Earl of Berlington**. It's one of those 1720 beauties that comes up every block or so on Piccadilly. A new facade was added in 1872, but you can still get a taste of the original 18th-century grandeur by visiting the saloon on the first floor. Upstairs, the brilliantly designed **Sackler Galleries**, by Sir Norman Foster, were opened in 1991 to show off the Academy's treasure, "Michelangelo's Madonna and Child." There is an ongoing display of the Academy's permanent collection, but its summer exhibition, featuring over a thousand works, is its most talked-about event. There is a terrific shop and a calm, quiet restaurant for resting tired museum feet. You can't miss the Academy as you pass it because there are always bright colored banners dancing in the breeze.

By now you're sure to be ready for some serious shopping in London's most ravishing "mall" **The Burlington Arcade**. Talk about upscale! The delicate glass roof that covers the Regency style arcade suggests more of a conservatory than a marketplace. You are magically whisked back to a time when the "customer was *always* right." Each of the 35 shops exude luxury and privilege as well as fine craftsmanship (see "Piccadilly Shopping"). There are still beadles (not insects, private patrolmen) in top hats, just as there were in the 1800s to keep a beadle eye out for thieves and beggars. Today they are more concerned with bicycles and in-line skaters.

To understand the derivation of the word "ritzy," one has only to look at the grandeur of **The Ritz Hotel**. You can almost hear champagne corks popping as you pass by. It dates back to 1906, and was named after Cesar Ritz, who made the Savoy a legend. The "Ritz" is spelled out in lightbulbs above its colonnade as if it were an S.R.O. production, and so it has been since it opened its doors. Today it's best known for the very formal tea it serves to the hordes who stand in line to drink it. There is tea dancing as well, to take you back to the giddy London that existed before World War I.

SECRET AGENDA

Churchill, Eisenhower and De Gaulle liked the Ritz so much they booked a suite so that they could plot the invasion of Normandy and be assured of topnotch room service.

The Ritz's location on Piccadilly is another reason for its popularity over the years since it overlooks the verdant expanse of **Green Park** which goes on for about 60 acres in the middle of some of the priciest real estate in London. You can stroll through, listen to the birds and after a short commune with nature, be ready to hit Piccadilly once again.

Near **Hyde Park** corner, on the north side of the street is **Apsley House**, the home of the **Duke of Wellington**. It houses the **Wellington Museum**. The Duke's claim to fame was as the man who defeated **Napoleon** long before Beef Wellington ever made it onto a menu. Ironically, Napoleon, who himself later became a famous pastry, is represented here by an 11-foot nude statue. Go figure! For anyone with a need to view the short one without his Speedos this is the place to come.

Hyde Park corner itself has to be reached by a labyrinth of underground tunnels that twist and curve in a rather demented fashion. Once you emerge from the subterranean depths, you will be facing the most confused traffic patterns in London, as well as the **Wellington Arch**, with its bronze sculpture of **Victory's Chariot** riding atop it. (See "Top Sights," page 11.)

Wellington Arch features a bronze sculpture of Victory's chariot.

JUST AROUND THE CORNER AGENDA ADVENTURES/ PICCADILLY

Half Moon Street is very literary, aside from its wonderfully romantic name. Shelly, Samuel Johnson, Boswell and Hazlitt, called it home. Best of all, Bertie Wooster and Jeeves were ensconced here by P. G. Wodehouse.

Agenda Shopping/Piccadilly

Sogo

Piccadilly Circus, SW1, ☎ *0171-333-9000.*
A little bit of Tokyo on Piccadilly. The largest department store in Japan decided to open this mini version so visitors from home could buy their Aquascutum's in a familiar atmosphere. The Rising Sun also shines on **Lagerfeld**, **Berbury**, **Dunhill** and **Wedgewood**.

Cording's

19 Piccadilly, ☎ *0171-734-0830.*

It doesn't look like much on the outside, but it's been selling rough and tumble outerware, sensible boots and enough tweeds to keep any Heathcliff happy since 1839.

Hatchards
187 Piccadilly, ☎ *0171-439-9921.*
Bookworms turn into butterflies as soon as they cross the threshold. Their travel section is one of the best in town (of course Fielding readers are already prepared). Three floors filled with everything from Shelley to Danielle Steele.

Swaine, Adeney, Brigg & Sons
185 Piccadilly, ☎ *0171-734-4277.*
The queen loved them so much she bestowed not one, but two Royal Warrants. One for whips and gloves (we will refrain here from pointing out the obvious!) and one for umbrellas. It sounds more like Freud's favorite shop than the queens.

Fortnum & Mason
181 Piccadilly, ☎ *0171-734-8040.*
(See "Department Stores," page 148)

BURLINGTON ARCADE

Since there are over 30 luxury shops to put a curl in your credit cards, we'll mention just a few of the high-life highlights. Remember, the Arcade closes at 5:30 p.m.

N. Peal
☎ *0171-493-0714.*
Cashmeres with the emphasis on the first syllable. Peal's is hands down *the* place for the most luscious cashmere in London.

St. Petersburg Collection
☎ *0171-495-2883.*
The genius of Carl Faberge is being revived by his grandson Theo, who has created his own designs for new Faberge eggs and other future museum pieces.

Michael Ross
☎ *0171-493-0714.*
Wedding rings are a blissful specialty here as well as other unique antique jewelry.

Penhaligon
☎ *0171-629-1416.*
They've had the sweet smell of success since 1870, not to mention Royal Warrants from the Duke of Edinburgh and the Prince of Wales. The perfumes here have been turning heads for years, and so has the beautiful packaging.

Sutty
☎ *0171-495-3099.*
Bone China creations that are handpainted by Michael Sutty and sold here. They've been collected by the royal family and other dignitaries for years.

W & H Gidden
☎ *0171-734-2788.*

Primarily known as a specialist in equestrian leathers, this branch sells fine small leathers, such as purses, briefcases and card cases. The quality is definitely "like buttah."

Irish Linen Company

☎ *0171-493-8949.*

The kind of napkins and tablecloths that are made to compliment Georgian tea services. Don't even think of taking these to the laundromat!

Agenda Best Bites/Piccadilly

The Criterion

222 Piccadilly, ☎ *0171-925-0909. Credit cards. Moderate.*

This is a dazzler that dates back to 1874. Its extravagant decor had become quite seedy until it was given a face-lift that revealed a breathtaking gilded mosaic ceiling. The room itself is 120-feet long and done in marble with rattan chairs and tables. Right in the middle a huge clock hangs over the room to remind you the century is ticking away. The menu is a mix of Italian, American, British and God knows what else, but it all seems to work in an informal way. One of the best choices, is the tomato and bread soup.

Cafe Sogo

Sogo, Piccadilly, ☎ *0171-333-9000. Credit cards. Moderate.*

Anyway you slice it sushi is the perfect on-the-run repast for anyone beating a path up Piccadilly. Tucked into Sogo's is a very neat sushi bar; just don't request them to make it well done.

The Granary

39 Albermarle Street, ☎ *0171-493-2978. Credit cards. Inexpensive.*

Right across from Brown's Hotel is one of the most wholesome, appealing little restaurants in London. It's always packed with shoppers and "pinstripes" elbowing their way around the cafeteria-style counter. Cheerful servers heap plates with salads, comforting casseroles and veggie treats. The "pudds" are particularly decadent.

The Fountain at Fortnum's

181 Piccadilly, ☎ *0171-734-8040. Credit cards. Moderate.*

Have a yen for a hot fudge sundae? In the basement of Fortnum and Mason's, **The Fountain** dispenses all manner of confections, including sodas, lemonade and more mature choices like sandwiches and grills. It's a great spot for breakfast or after theater drop-in. Maybe life *is* a fountain.

Wren at St. James

197 Piccadilly, ☎ *0171-437-9419. Cash. Inexpensive.*

The best homemade soups on Piccadilly, in a truly divine setting. This sweet restaurant is part of St. James Church and caters to vegetarians who watch their peas and cucumbers.

Royal Academy Restaurant

Burlington House, Piccadilly, ☎ *0171-439-7438. Credit cards. Moderate.*

Very staid, sensible surroundings to have a sensible lunch after trudging through the Academy.

Langan's Brasserie

Stratton Street, ☎ *0171-493-6437. Credit cards. Expensive.*

Closer in feeling to LA than London, there is always a whiff of fame in the air. Very trendy, very edgy and very expensive. The food is good, but if you're just a wannabe, they may not let you in. If your name hasn't become a household word, be prepared for a long wait and a table near the kitchen. Still, it's always lively and the menu has lots of favorites like bubble and squeak and bangers and mash. Michael Caine has a vested interest here, so there's always the hope he'll be sitting in the corner.

Burger King

Piccadilly Circus.

Just a minute! Calm down! We haven't taken leave of our Whoppers. It happens that Burger King overlooks, from its second floor window, one of the best views in London. You seem to be suspended over the neon, the traffic and the crowds of Piccadilly. It's the very best way to experience the color and vitality of the Circus. All this can be yours for the price of a Coke.

Covent Garden

Covent Garden's Mall attracts hordes to its upscale shops.

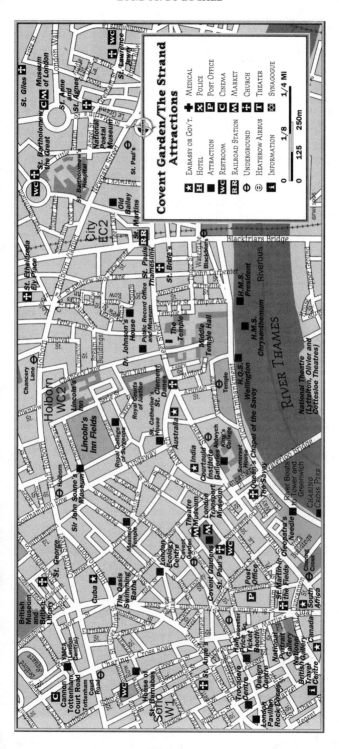

Covent Garden/The Strand Attractions

⊠	EMBASSY OR GOV'T.
🅷	HOTEL
■	ATTRACTION
🆆🅲	RESTROOM
🆁🆁	RAILROAD STATION
⊖	UNDERGROUND
⊜	HEATHROW AIRBUS
🅸	INFORMATION
✚	MEDICAL
🆇	POLICE
🅿	POST OFFICE
🅲	CINEMA
🅼	MARKET
✝	CHURCH
🆃	THEATER
✡	SYNAGOGUE

0   1/8   1/4 MI
0 125 250m

You'll have no trouble finding Covent Garden; just follow the crowds who stream through the upscale shops and the Mall, with its splendid glass roof. Originally, the area was the Convent garden for Westminster Abbey, but the lilting cockney accents slurred convent into covent, which made it the logical place for Professor Higgins to meet the owner of the most celebrated cockney accent in the world, Eliza Dolittle. The Garden was the official exchange for fruits and vegetables from the 1800s right up until 1974. The old flower market stood right behind it. But the streets around Covent Garden were famous for something that gave Londoners far more pleasure than a cabbage or a bunch of grapes. It was the theaters that dotted the area and brought the "swells" down from Mayfair to mingle with the poor flower girls. The most famous of all was the Drury Lane, where **Nell Gwynn** made her debut and Edmond Kean gave an obscure playwright named **William Shakespeare**, a much needed revival. The Drury burned to the ground three times, but it's still going strong in its latest reincarnation. Now its the home of S.R.O. musicals such as *A Chorus Line* and *Miss Saigon*. Most of the other theaters tend to be located right next door on the **Strand**. But after-theater strollers are still drawn here just the way Higgins was. Another theatrical landmark in Covent Garden is the **Opera House**, which is home to the **Royal Opera Company and Ballet**. Performers the past have included Caruso and Callas. A **Theater Museum**, whose collection showcases Britain's stage history from William Shakespeare to present day is close by.

The newest part of Covent Garden is the glass enclosed market building, really a nouveau mall which houses dozens of shops, restaurants and on most days, a crafts exhibition and sale. Every Monday there is an antique's market, which tends to be much more upscale than the hurly burly of Portobello or Beromondsey. Right in back of the market building is the smaller **Jubilee Market**, which is a treasure trove of "junque." Dealers here are definitely low-end, but you can pick up great old medals or bric-a-brac at cut rate pence. Next door is the **London Transport Museum** (see "Museums," page 214), The London Transport system might not make your heart go pittypat, but the shop is great fun.

The whole area around Covent Garden is as irresistible as the market place itself. The boutiques are crammed with imports from Asia, soft cashmeres, chocolates, expensive shoes and fragrant oils and spices. There is always some form of street entertainment going on during the weekend, Punch and Judy shows for the kids, (the first Punch and Judy show was performed here in 1662), street singers and musicians, and the ever-present Mimes.

The little street just off the market that has the most interesting concentration of shops and restaurants is **Neal's Yard**, originally lined with warehouses, today, a mecca for the health food crowd in London. Try to arrive in the Yard as close to the hour as possible. You'll be treated to the world's most unique water clock, which sprouts colorful flowers every time it chimes.

Agenda Shopping/Covent Garden

Covent Garden Market
Monsoon, ☎ *0171-499-2578.*
Colorful Thai silks and batiks, fashioned into casual clothes.

Benedicks
☎ *0171-836-1846.*
World famous for their after-dinner mints, and also their nifty chocolates.

Culpeper Herbalists
☎ *0171-379-6698.*
All the creams, scents, spices, perfumes, soaps and other sybaritic sensations, are made from herbs that Culpeper grows in Suffolk.

Penguin Bookshop
☎ *0171-379-7650.*
Their usual collection of the best in publishing and a generous selection of Puffins for the kids.

Dolls House
☎ *0171-379-7243.*
Most of the beauties here make "Barbie" look like the crass upstart she is.

Benjamin Pollack's Toy Shop
☎ *0171-379-7866.*
One of the best displays of teddies in London (and we don't mean lingerie). Lots of other charming toys as well.

Accessorize
☎ *0171-240-2107.*
Everything color coordinated within each section, with scarves, bags, jewelry, belts and shoes. A very 90s concept.

The Streets Around the Market

Neal Street East
5 Neal Street, ☎ *0171-240-0135.*
Inscrutable, Oriental and totally irresistible. From clothes, to writing paper, to books, to bed linen, right down to pin cushions. Some really unique gifts.

The Tea House
15A Neal Street, ☎ *0171-240-7539.*
The folks who gave us the Boston tea party would have met their match here. Tea as far as the eye can see, over 40 different varieties with teapots to match. The shop has a section called "Teaphernalia," which takes all the strain out of brewing.

Neal's Yard Dairy
17 Shorts Garden, ☎ *0171-836-5199.*
If you haven't explored the wonderful world of British cheeses, this is the place to start. Just walking into the place makes your heart rise like a souffle. The very friendly, patient staff will put you on intimate

terms with enough varieties of cheddar to mold you into an expert.
You'll never be blue if you leave with a wedge of Stilton.

Plumline

55 Neal Street, ☎ *0171-379-7856.*
Far out shoes for far out feet. Not for the Gucci loafer set. You need
a brave fashion outlook, but you know you'll never see these in Thom
McAnn.

Red or Dead

33 Neal Street, ☎ *0171-379-7571.*
They have very little to do with Russia, but everything to do with
avant-garde fashion. The shoes here have platforms that would make
Carmen Miranda green with envy.

Neal's Yard Bakery

18 Shorts Gardens, ☎ *0171-836-5199.*
The aroma of the brilliant breads in this tiny bakery makes it almost
impossible to pass them by. Try a small loaf to snack on as you browse
through the streets. They also serve vegetable juices and light lunches
upstairs.

Naturally British

13 New Row, ☎ *0171-240-0551.*
Everything here is designed by British artists and craftsmen. Usually
one of a kind, things here make extraordinary gifts.

Droopey & Browns

99 St. Martin's Lane, ☎ *0171-379-4514.*
Is that a name out of Dickens, or what? All manner of formal gowns
to take you through a night at the opera, a command performance, or
even your own wedding. These are very theatrical confections and
certainly can fulfill a fantasy or two for a traveling Cinderella.

Bell, Book and Radmall

4 Cecil Street, ☎ *0171-240-2161.*
First editions kept under lock and key. Only the serious book collector is welcome here so if you're looking for the latest Judith Krantz,
just keep moving.

Agenda Best Bites/Covent Garden

Pret a Manger

77-78 St. Martin's Lane, ☎ *0171-379-5335. Cash. Inexpensive.*
There are several of these around the city and they're always a welcome sight. They specialize in very freshly made "gourmet" sandwiches with sun-dried tomatoes, prosciutto and other designer
sandwich stuffings. They even have very presentable sushi and of
course, lots of bottled water and juice. The prices are fair and the surroundings cheerful—what more can anyone ask?

Cafe Flo

51 St. Martin's Lane, ☎ *0171-836-8289. Credit cards. Moderate.*

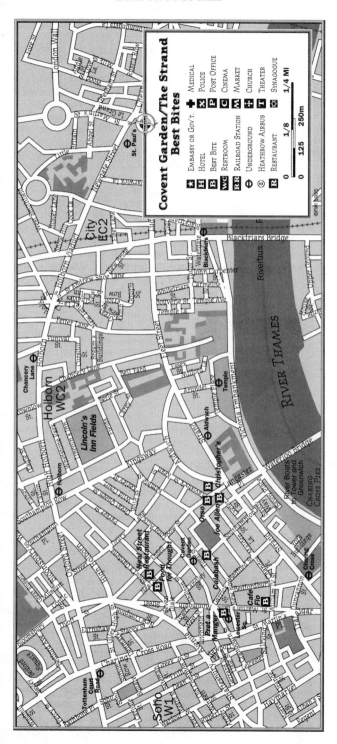

Covent Garden/The Strand
Best Bites

★	EMBASSY OR GOV'T.	✚	MEDICAL
H	HOTEL	✖	POLICE
B	BEST BITE	P	POST OFFICE
WC	RESTROOM	C	CINEMA
RR	RAILROAD STATION	M	MARKET
Φ	UNDERGROUND	✚	CHURCH
⊖	HEATHROW AIRBUS	T	THEATER
R	RESTAURANT	✳	SYNAGOGUE

0   1/8   1/4 MI
0   125   250m

"Flo" has a string of these places around London and they are all good, dependable brasseries, where you can tuck into a steak-frites or a hearty onion soup with no problem. And it's a bargain, mon dieu!

Now & Zen

4A Upper St. Martin's Lane, ☎ 0171-497-0376. Credit cards. Moderate.
Three floors of wonderfully prepared Asian food that runs the gamut from Japanese to Thai. Even better is the fact that the Zen philosophy of life extends to eat-all-you-can set menus. Isn't that Zenderful.

Joe Allen

13 Exeter Street, ☎ 0171-836-0651. Credit cards. Moderate.
If you've never been to the one in New York then you should definitely drop in here for one of their terrific burgers. The restaurant is always jammed after the theater, but at lunch, it's very clubby and relaxed.

Luigi's

15 Tavistock Street, ☎ 0171-240-1795. Credit cards. Moderate.
Good Italian food served up with a helping of celebs on the side. This friendly place is a hangout for the actors, dancers and musicians who come in after work to scarf down the cannelloni, which is the specialty of the casa.

Lamb and Flag

33 Rose Street, ☎ 0171-497-9504. Cash. Moderate.
Would you go to a pub that was formerly called the Bucket of Blood, (Bloody boxing matches were held here)? You might if you were stepping right back to 1679. Naturally, later on they changed its name to something more benign and today they "knock out" some really good food.

Calabash

Africa Center, 38 King Street, ☎ 0171-836-1976. Credit cards. Moderate.
Out of Africa and into Covent Garden makes for some very exotic surroundings. Masks and colorful fabrics cover the walls, and the menu reads like a map of the Dark Continent. Calabash features dishes from Senegal, Sierra Leone and Nigeria. Even more unique, the wines that accompany them come from Africa as well.

Orso

27 Willington Street, ☎ 0171-240-5269. Credit cards. Moderate.
Right next to Joe Allen's, and just as packed with after-theater diners. However, they cook with a decidedly Italian accent here. A perfect bite after the show would be the paper-thin tiny pizzas topped with cheese and black olives, or any of the buttery veal entrees. The conversation is as lively as the menu.

Christopher's American Grill

18 Wellington Street, ☎ 0171-240-4222. Credit cards. Expensive.
The owner, who spent a great deal of time in Chicago, was so bedazzled with the food in the Colonies that he decided to open a steakhouse á la The Palm. These people have no shame—Haagen-Daz is featured on the dessert card.

Food for Thought

31 Neal Street, ☎ 0171-836-0239. Cash. Inexpensive.

Tiny, with a line always waiting, and a very modest price. "FFT" is a veggie addict's dream come true. The stir-fries are unusual combinations, and the soup and salads couple fruits and herbs in a most original manner. Their famous dessert, a Scrunch, could be a meal by itself (oats, fruit, yogurt and heavy cream).

Neal Street Restaurant

26 Neal Street, ☎ *0171-836-8368. Credit cards. Expensive.*
Years ago, Sir Terence Conran opened the Neal Street with an eye to clean lines, famous artists on the walls and modern Italian cuisine on the plates. So it is today, although now it's owned by Antonio Carluccio, who is said to be possessed by mushroom mania. He uses them in everything except the yummy desserts.

The Strand

The Strand is by far the most versatile boulevard in London. It is truly all things to all people. It has elegant hotels, exciting theaters, venerable restaurants, historic churches, important museums and finally down on Fleet Street, the fascinating old haunts of those "inkstained wretches," the gentlemen of the press. Before they moved to the Docklands, almost all of the most important newspapers of the country called Fleet Street home.

The Strand starts at **Charing Cross Road**, which is famous for its eclectic bookshops (see Books, page 139), both current and "memorialized." Helen Hanff's charming book, *84 Charing Cross Road,* based on her witty correspondence with the manager there, brought hundreds of people to No. 84 for a literary pilgrimage. Alas, the bookshop is long gone and best remembered in Hanff's "valentine." **Charing Cross Station**, at the top of the Strand, is a heroic structure where over 100,000 travelers come and go by British Rail every day. It also houses the **Charing Cross** hotel, which is a wonderful, old, rambling place, built in 1865.

Before you continue down the Strand, turn off at **Craven Street**, which will lead you down to the **Thames** and the **Embankment**. Ben Franklin lived at No. 36 before he had to hurry home to attend the American Revolution. The embankment is a balm to the spirit, with its wonderful views, and calmer pace. An added bonus is a genuine Egyptian artifact on the banks of the **Thames**. **Cleopatra's Needle** was given as a gift to Britain by the viceroy of Egypt (talk about being a sport) in 1800 and it is the twin of the one that stands in New York's Central Park.

AGENDA SCENIC ADVISORY

One of the most romantic walks from the **Embankment** *is across* **Waterloo Bridge***. If you do it in reverse after an evening at the* **National Theater***, the views of* **Westminster** *and* **Big Ben***, illuminated in the darkness, are breathtaking.*

AGENDA SCENIC ADVISORY

As you stroll back up to the Strand, you'll see the posh **Savoy Hotel** *and the* **Savoy Theater***, right next door (see "Hotels," page 40) The Strand is the closest thing to Broadway, since, in addition to the* **Savoy Theater***,* **The Aldwych***,* **The Strand***,* **The Fortune** *and the* **Duchess Theaters** *come one right after the other down the street. If you catch a matinee at one of them, you can have tea in the* **Palm Court** *of the* **Waldorf Hotel***, another charmer on the Strand (see "Teas," page 179). A very impressive example of "the quality of mercy" is the huge* **Royal Courts of Justice***, which take up 514 righteous feet of the Strand with seven miles of hallways, and 1000 rooms. What a condo this place would make.*

At the bottom of the Strand, **Fleet Street** *mourns the loss of all its famous newspapers and with them the heady mix of writers and publishers that made the street vibrate with spirit and energy. It all started back in the 15th century, when Wynkin (were his brothers names Blinkin & Nod?) de Worde put together the country's very first printing press. It wasn't long before printed pages turned into books and newspapers. For better or worse, British publishing was born. Even though the papers, led by the* **Times***, moved to the* **Docklands***, the name* **Fleet Street** *is still the term used to identify the newspaper business.*

Agenda Shopping/The Strand

Silver Moon

68 Charing Cross Road, ☎ *0171-836-7906.*
Books specializing in women's issues, with a large selection devoted to feminist literature.

Foyles

119 Charing Cross Road, ☎ *0171-437-5660.*
Acres and acres and acres of titles, sometimes in no particular order. This multi-flavored book browser's delight has things that would never be found in a saner bookstore environment, but at Foyles, anything goes. For bookworms with no control, they'll ship everything home for a pittance.

Steven Scott Stamps

77 Strand, ☎ *0171-836-7611.*
A very varied inventory for the affluent, as well as the budget collector. And their knowledge and patience is endless.

The Russian Shop

99 Strand, ☎ *0171-4497-9104.*

Lenin may be out of fashion in Mother Russia today, but its exquisite lacquerware is still going strong. You have the pick of the crop in this very classy shop, along with nesting dolls and accessories.

Stanley Gibbons International

399 Strand, ☎ *0171-836-8444.*

In business since the 1800s, Gibbons is considered the world's largest stamp shop. No mere "lick and promise operation," they're a magnet for serious collectors, but young hobbyists are welcome too.

Twinings

216 Strand, ☎ *0171-353-3511.*

Lots of tea and sympathy here for people steeped in the tradition of tea. The shop itself goes back to 1716, when Thomas Twining opened it as (horrors) a coffee house. The queen fills her tea caddy here and so can you.

Agenda Best Bites/Strand

The Savoy Hotel

Strand

The Grill Room

at the Savoy Hotel
☎ *0171-836-4343.*
(See "Restaurants," page 177)

The River Room

at the Savoy Hotel
☎ *0171-936-4343.*
(See "Restaurants," page 180)

Wig and Pen Club

229-230 Strand, ☎ *0171-583-7255. Credit cards. Moderate.*
Atmosphere with a capital A. This is a private club for "haute" lawyers and members of the press who gather here to embroider their legal loopholes over lunch. The most interesting legality of all is that foreign visitors can have an instant one-day membership. It's definitely worth doing, not only for the elbow-rubbing, but also the building was the only one on the Strand to survive the great fire of 1666. Attention must be paid.

The George Public House

213 Strand, ☎ *0171-3353-9238. Credit cards. Inexpensive.*
Another favorite of "legal eagles" and writers such as Oliver Goldsmith, who penned *The Vicar of Wakefield.* It's ancient and cozy with dark wood, beams, and a very good buffet lunch. Weekdays only.

Printer's Pie

60 Fleet Street, ☎ *0171-353-8861. Credit cards. Inexpensive.*
Most of the Printers have moved away, but the pies linger on, and very good they are too. Twenty blackbirds would love this place. shepherd's, steak and kidney, chicken pot and other assorted pies are baked all in a row.

AGENDA ADMONITION

Simpson's-in-the-Strand

100 Strand, ☎ *0171-876-9112. Credit cards. Moderate.*

Quite frankly, Simpson's, though the most frequently cited example of traditional English food, is in fact *our* prime example of limp vegetables, overdone roast beef and soggy Yorkshire Pudding! It's everything that used to be wrong with British cooking; however, it is an institution in London, so we advise using caution, but not crossing it off the list entirely. If you have no other alternative, and find yourself in front of Simpson's at lunchtime, order a steak and kidney or shepherd's pie, no matter how ceremonious the roast beef trolley looks. At least anything that comes directly from the oven will be hot. The best of all possible experiences here would be one of Simpson's extraordinary breakfasts (see "Breakfast," page 180). If you start your day on The Strand early, you can have your crumpet and eat-it-too.

Ye Olde Cheshire Cheese

145 Fleet Street, ☎ *0171-353-6170. Credit cards. Moderate.*

Dates back to before the Great Fire of 1666, burned to the ground, was rebuilt, and after seeing the reign of 16 different monarchs, goes on serving meat pies and ale to a never-ending stream of admirers. It is the most beloved of all London pubs, and even if you think going isn't "cool," you're wrong. It was "real cool" for Dr. Samuel Johnson, who got some of his best C words here (it's a wonder that his dictionary ever got finished). Centuries later, Mark Twain was able to lift his glass to Tom and Huck, here. Yes—Dickens, was here too!

St. James

St. James Park is the playground of the pinstriped.

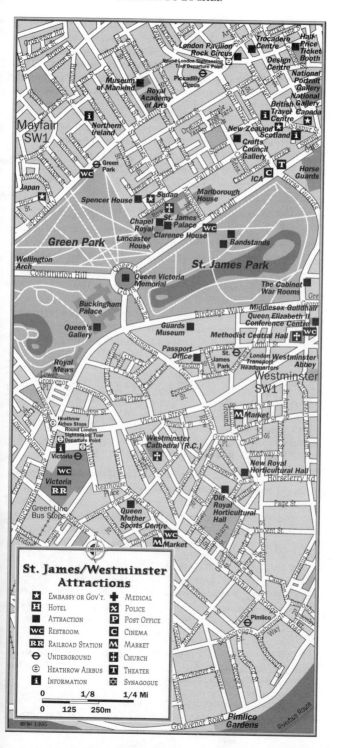

St. James/Westminster Attractions

★	EMBASSY OR GOV'T.	✚	MEDICAL
H	HOTEL	✕	POLICE
■	ATTRACTION	P	POST OFFICE
WC	RESTROOM	C	CINEMA
RR	RAILROAD STATION	M	MARKET
⊖	UNDERGROUND	✚	CHURCH
⊜	HEATHROW AIRBUS	T	THEATER
i	INFORMATION	✡	SYNAGOGUE

0		1/8	1/4 Mi
0	125	250m	

©PWI 1995

This is home base for the bastions of pinstriped suits that add formality and tradition to London. St. James is the masculine counterpart to **Mayfair's** feminine, stylish grace. One of the reasons for that is the profusion of gentlemen's (read: mens') clubs that are found on almost every street. They are the fortresses of the rich and privileged, and the only way to get through the door is to be no less than that. St. James is the center of "swank."

When is a mall not a mall? When there isn't a Bloomingdale's or Saks in sight, and it leads from St. James straight to Buckingham Palace. The Mall (say Mal) is a very grand avenue, running from **Trafalgar Square** to the palace gates. Not since the "yellow brick road" has a path led to such a magical place. It's the route the gleaming, golden coach of her majesty takes to weddings, the opening of Parliament, trooping the colors and perhaps having the royal pizza delivered. In any case, it is St. James' most celebrated route. The Mall is also opened for the queen's garden parties and teas.

St. James is the district of London which is synonymous with royalty. The **Court of St. James** was the glittering scene to make at **St. James Palace** from Henry VIII right up to Princess Victoria. However, Victoria decided to pack up and move to Buckingham Palace when she became queen. She must have known she couldn't start the Victorian era from a palace that was as run down and drafty as St. James. It stands today at the end of St. James Street, in all it's Tudor glory. The gatehouse is its most interesting feature, with twin turrets and a clock tower. Christopher Wren tried his best to jazz the palace up in 1703, but it still looks stoic and depressing. Today, St. James still plays a part in the Empire; foreign emissaries must present their credentials at the Court of St. James, before being received. The only part of the palace that is worth visiting is the Chapel Royal that Henry VIII built in the 1500s. Under its coffered ceiling, some of the happiest royal weddings took place. William and Mary were married there, as well as Queen Victoria and George V and Queen Mary. It's a shame when Prince Charles decided to tie the knot, the queen put a deposit down on St. Paul's instead. (Sundays 8:30–11:15 a.m.)

On the west side of **St. James Palace** stands **Clarence House**, the residence of London's most beloved royal, The Queen Mum. She sometimes comes to the front gate to greet her subjects, who worship her. They've never forgotten the support she gave to her people during the Blitz. When she's at home, a bagpiper plays a tune at nine in the morning. Anyone else would just set their alarm. Is she a class act or what?

The palace that everyone wants to play is the one the royal family lives in now. (See "Top Sights," page 4) One may well say, "uneasy is the head that wears the crown," but aside from her "annus horribilus," Queen Elizabeth still radiates confidence and charm. However, if things continue to be diabolical she may be the last one to whom we will happily shout, "long live the queen."

Frankly, we would gladly pass up the palace to visit the **Royal Mews**, which does not house the palace cats, but its golden state coaches. They don't turn into pumpkins either! (☎ *0171-930-4832*)

The shopping streets of St. James are elegant and mega-expensive. As Mayfair is devoted to designer originals and the ladies who lunch, so St. James is dedicated to the "men of distinction."

AGENDA'S ACES OF CLUBS

The Atheneum Club
> *107 Pall Mall.*
Members included Charles Darwin.

Traveller's Club
> *106 Pall Mall.*
Members included Duke of Wellington, Tallyrand.

Reform Club
> *104-5 Pall Mall.*
Members included anyone who supported the Reform Bill of 1832.

Royal Automobile Club
> *89 Pall Mall.*
Members included G. B. Shaw, Burgess and MacLean.

Boodles
> *28 St. James Street.*
Members are anonymous.

Brooks
> *60 St. James Street.*
Members included Beau Brummell.

The Carlton
> *69 St. James Street.*
Members included Gladstone.

White's
> *37-38 St. James Street.*
Members include Prince Charles, Evelyn Waugh.

Agenda Shopping/St. James

Design Centre
> *28 Haymarket,* ☎ *0171-839-8000.*
The best that British design can offer under the auspices of the Design Council. If *you* have designs on the latest potato peeler, they'll tell you where you can buy it. They also have a bookshop.

Alfred Dunhill
> *30 Duke Street,* ☎ *0171-499-9566.*
From a simple tobacconist to a world famous status symbol of affluence. Since 1907, the Dunhill motto has been "It must be useful, it must work dependably..." Over the years, they have kept that promise with pens, watches, wallets, elegant sportswear and of course, the finest pipe tobacco and cigars in the world. Even if you are a non-smoker, you'll be fascinated by the walk-in humidor.

Fox & Lewis

19 St. James Street, ☎ *0171-930-3787.*
Speaking of cigars, this was where Sir Winston got his Cubans.

Lobb's

9 St. James Street, ☎ *0171-930-3664.*
Handmade shoes, which are so masterfully done you'll never mind footing the bill here. Some of the satisfied feet that have walked out shod in Lobb's best have been, Queen Victoria's, King George VI's, Churchill's, Laurence Olivier's, Cole Porter's and Katherine Hepburn's. No one ever heard of Dr. Scholl at Lobb's.

Lock & Co.

6 St. James Street, ☎ *0171-930-8874.*
What did Lord Nelson, the Duke of Wellington and Paul McCartney all have in common? Hats from Lock's. This store has been measuring cool heads since 1759.

Berry Bros and Rudd

3 St. James Street, ☎ *0171-839-9033.*
Oenophiles will find Berry Bros. a time machine back to Dickensian London. No lover of fine wines should leave the city without a stop here. Their vintage ports will get you through any storm that turns up.

Christie's

8 King Street, ☎ *0171-839-1611.*
The flip side of Sotheby's, in St. James. There are fabled wine auctions held from time to time, and the usual art and antiques. Worth a sit in, even if bidding is a little too forbidding.

Pink's

35 Dover Street, ☎ *0171-493-6775.*
They'll give you the shirt off their backs. Known for being *de rigueur* for young dandies and trend setters, their fine cotton poplin shirts have set a few trends themselves. The phrase "in the pink" started right here.

Paxton & Whitfield

93 Jermyn Street, ☎ *0171-930-0250.*
The most picturesque cheese shop in London. A Victorian facade, which leads to such an array of cheeses that the cheshire cat would laugh out loud. The best of regional British cheesemakers, they offer more than 250 varieties. The queen drops in now and then for a wedge of Stilton.

Floris

89 Jermyn Street, ☎ *0171-930-2885.*
Their perfumes are all over the U.S. by now, but there's nothing like visiting the Jermyn Street shop. They've been blending perfumes for Royalty since 1730.

Turnbull & Asser

71-72 Jermyn Street, ☎ *0171-930-0502.*
Made-to-measure shirts for the gentry since 1885. A shirt takes about as long to be born here as a baby. First, a model is constructed, then changes are made, discussions back and forth about collar style, cuff style, shirttail proportion and other world-shaking details. The mini-

mum order for custom work is six shirts, but they can be sent back for repair and sprucing forever.

Agenda Best Bites/St. James

Le Gavroche

43 Upper Brook Street, ☎ *0171-408-0881. Credit cards. VERY expensive.*

The Roux brothers dynasty started in this basement restaurant and went on to influence most of the young chefs, not only in London, but around the world. Albert, who was chef for the Rothschilds, runs Le Gavroche like a very precise machine that needs frequent lubrication with the best olive oil and triple cream. This is classic cuisine, as formal as St. James itself, and a great comfort to the made-to-measure set.

Green's

36 Duke Street, ☎ *0171-930-4566. Credit cards. Expensive.*

More like a private club, Green's Oyster bar is perfect for the "pinstripes." Everyone knows everyone at lunch and Simon Parker-Bowles (don't dare ask him about his sister-in-law Camilla), could charm a snail from its shell. The oysters, briney and perfect, are the traditional favorites. There's cod roe pate, Raj fishcakes, and gooseberry fool, speaking of which, do not expect to see Prince Charles there anytime soon.

Les Saveurs

37A Curzon Street, ☎ *0171-491-8919. Credit cards. Expensive.*

This small, fine French restaurant is a jewel in a town with no shortage of terrific French food. The young chef draws a young crowd who want a place to relax. The food is inventive and delightful to look at. Try the licorice ice cream for dessert.

Wilton's

55 Jermyn Street, ☎ *0171-629-9955. Credit cards. Expensive.*

Right in back of Piccadilly, on Jermyn Street, is one of the pillars of the British Establishment, Wiltons. And it is more than entitled to its reputation, since it's been serving the creme de la clotted creme since 1742. Today, the leading politicos and pinstripes crowd make room for their daily dose of Dover Sole and trifle. It is an institution and charges accordingly. On the other hand, it's really "True Brit."

Red Lion

Crown Passage (Off King St), ☎ *0171-930-4141. Credit cards. Moderate.*

More Pub than restaurant, this is a "working stiff" place, which is a rarity for St. James. It's gorgeously Victorian with dark wood and mirrors. After you leave St. James's Palace, the perfect place to step back in time for a plate of fish and chips, with an Ale chaser.

Overton's

5 St. James Street, ☎ *0171-839-3774. Credit cards. Moderate.*

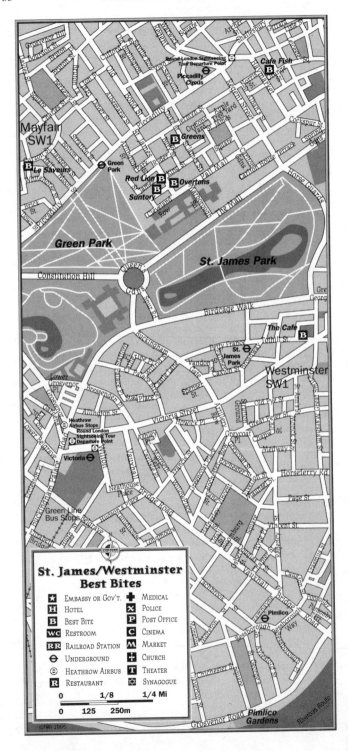

Right in the middle of all those staid British clubs is a fish house that proves the members don't always lunch at those rarified social institutions. By the look of the crowd here tucking into Dover sole and smoked salmon, they're all at Overtons.

Suntory

72-73 St. James Street, ☎ *0171-409-0201. Credit cards. VERY expensive.*
This is the Tiffany's of Japanese restaurants in London. Bring negotiable securities! However, Suntory which owns the huge spirits empire in Japan, have opened this stunning restaurant to showcase the emperor's favorite cuisine. They have a wonderful Teppan-Yaki room presided over by master chefs who's knives fly with the precision of a Ninja. Everyone sits around the Teppan (a deep cooking well) watching the meat and vegetables being sliced and hoping they won't be part of the surgery.

Cafe Fish

39 Panton Street, ☎ *0171-930-3999. Credit cards. Moderate.*
So much brain-food is served here you're likely to leave with a 200 IQ. Everything that goes on at the busy little cafe is "very fishy." They have more than 50 different specialties to choose from. They poach, they fry, they grill, they saute and they even soup (bouillabaisse, of course). The perfect place to get into the swim.

Westminster

To best understand Westminster, is to understand **The Palace of Westminster**, where the **Royal Court** moved from **The City of London**. The power of the Throne in medieval times and the power of the British Government today, is the story of Westminster. It's the Pomp and Circumstance, Rule Britannia, and Colonel Bogie March, all rolled into one emotional outlet. The palace ultimately became the **Houses of Parliament**, where the British democratic system is still evolving, but **Westminster Abbey**, right next door, is traditionally where the British Monarchs are crowned. Kings, queens, prime ministers, and of course the Church have all shared in the governing of England from this small piece of land that was a marshy swamp in 1042.

Whitehall, often spoken of in the same breath as Westminster, is a broad boulevard, lined with governmental buildings, much as **The Treasury**, **The Admiralty**, **The Ministry of Defense**, and in a small cul-de-sac at the end, **Downing Street** (see "Top Sights," page 17).

Plan to see Westminster during the week. This area, much like **The City**, is deserted on weekends and the **Abbey** is used for regular church services on Sunday. It's worth a second trip back after you explore it during the week to attend a service. The music is splendid and the **Abbey**, being used for the purpose it was originally intended, is a breathtaking sight to behold.

Most of the landmarks of Westminster, such as **Parliament**, **Big Ben**, **Westminster Abbey**, and **Downing Street** have been discussed in "Top Sights" (see page 4).

At the other end of **Parliament Square** is the Byzantine masterpiece, **Westminster Cathedral**. To ensure that it would never be confused with

Westminster Abbey the Cardinal, who approved the plans, opted for a Byzantine design. It took over 12 million bricks to complete and it's a sumptuous example of the medieval architecture of Constantinople.

AGENDA TIP

Westminster Pier is very near Parliament Square, at the Victoria Embankment. There are all kinds of Thames River trips available, which would be a splendid way to top off your look at Parliament. The Thames was the route the Lords took to get to Westminster long before they were able to hail those terrific Black Cabs.

Lords and Commons debate matters of State in Parliament.

Agenda Shopping/Westminster

Whippel & Co., Ltd.

11 Tuxton Street, ☎ *0171-222-4528.*
Basically this dignified shop is devoted to religious garments and accessories for the church, but they are quite willing to take orders for beeswax candles in regular and odd sizes.

National Portrait Gallery Bookshop

Millbank Street, ☎ *0171-306-0055.*
A large collection of books about the famous subjects of the portraits upstairs.

Tate Gallery Shop

Millbank Street, ☎ *0171-821-1313.*
The usual museum kitsch, carry bags, posters and souvenirs. T-shirt collectors will leave with a "masterpiece" covering their chests.

Abby Garden

Abingdon & Great College Street.
What can you buy in a garden? Lavender, that fragrant bloom that goes so well with old lace. They will ship it for you. It's the best aromatherapy in town.

Agenda Best Bites/Westminster

Clarence

53 Whitehall, ☎ *0171-930-4808. Credit cards. Inexpensive.*
A pub right out of the 18th century, gaslights and all. The Ministry of Agriculture is a neighbor, maybe that accounts for the farm implements hanging from the ceiling. They serve decent food and superior ales.

The Cafe

Methodist Central Hall, Stories Gate, ☎ *0171-222-8010. Cash. Inexpensive.*
You don't even have to be a Methodist to have a nice quiet lunch downstairs in the cafe. The building itself is turn-of-the-century handsome, and the food is as straightforward as the religion.

Silver Cross

33 Whitehall, ☎ *0171-930-8350. Credit cards. Inexpensive.*
If you want a really classic English Breakfast served up in a 13th century pub, look no further. The Silver Cross is remarkably preserved and still going strong, serving both the press and the M.P.s they cover.

Footstool

St. John's Church, Smith Square, ☎ *0171-222-2779. Credit cards. Moderate.*

Yet another cryptic restaurant. This one is in the crypt of the little Church of St. John. You'll find yourself rubbing shoulders with both the Conservatives and the Labor Party, who come here to vote on the sensible, tasty lunches.

The City

The Monument commemorates London's Great Fire of 1666.

Dick Wittington was the first person to make a financial killing in **The City of London**, back in 13 something, way before The City became the financial nerve center of the Empire. Wittington's cat thought rats tasted

much better than steak and kidney pie, and this very determined extermina-
tor brought Dick a fist full of farthings, not to mention getting him named
lord mayor of London Town. That brings us back to how London began.

Forget **Mayfair**, forget **Knightsbridge** and **St. James**! None of them, or
any of the other boroughs, is located in The City, which operates as a separate, autonomous "Square Mile." It is was here, in 43 A.D., that ancient
London (Londinium) was settled by the Romans. They built a wall around
their new settlement and Voila!, a city was born.

There are still odd bits and pieces of the original wall at the side of the
Museum of London, but the most substantial reminders of the wall are in
the names given to the access gates: **Cripplegate**, **Ludgate**, etc. (they sound
more like a series of scandals). After the Romans exited and the Saxons
moved in, The City began to grow with commerce and trade, until it became a force to be reckoned with. But not for Edward the Confessor, who
opted to move the court up to the high rent district **of Westminster**. There
was a definite separation, and The City retained its own identity as the Cor-
poration of London, with its own Lord Mayor, police force and elected of-
ficials.

For so small an area, **The City of London** has had more than its share of
disasters. It was here that the Great Fire of 1666 started in a Baker's shop,
and destroyed nearly every street of the "Square Mile." The **Monument**,
(see "Top Sights," page 13) was built by Christopher Wren to commemorate that catastrophe. Even before the fire, most of The City was wiped out
by the Great Plague just a year before.

The confusion between **The City of London** and the city of London is experienced by the visitors; the locals think of The City as "beautiful downtown London," a place to make money and deals, while (or whilst, if you'd
like to speak the king's English), the city is a place for restaurants, shopping
and Di watching! The secret is all in the Cs. Big C is The City, small c, the
London we all know the best. Whew!!!

The City is deserted on the weekend and at night. All the action goes on
during business hours, so plan your visit in time to see the bankers, the pinstripes from Lloyds and the brokers, hurrying through **Threadneedle Street**
on their way to make a fortune. If you continue on Threadneedle Street,
you'll not only pass **The Bank of England** (see "Top Sights," page 8), but
also the **Royal Exchange** and farther down near **Old Broad Street**, **The
Stock Exchange**. The narrow streets and lanes take you back to the London
of Shakespeare and Marlowe, with their tiny pubs and Elizabethan wood-
framed buildings. In stark contrast, the **Lloyd's of London Building**, on
Lime Street, was designed by the architect who did the **Pompidou Center**
in Paris. It has the same high-tech cartoon look, and at night, it can be seen
for miles around, all aglow with eerie purple and green lights.

The very best way to understand the history of The City, as well as the
rest of London, is to visit the **Museum of London**, at *150 London Mall* (see
"Museums," page 215). It covers 2000 years of London's growth with arresting exhibitions that are quite simply, mesmerizing. They even have the
lord mayor's extraordinary golden coach that is kept on display between
state occasions. Aside from Wren's spectacular **St. Paul's Cathedral** (see
"Top Sights," page 15), the other most visited piece of real estate in The
City is the **Barbican Centre**, on **Silk Street**, a rather ugly, fortresslike struc-

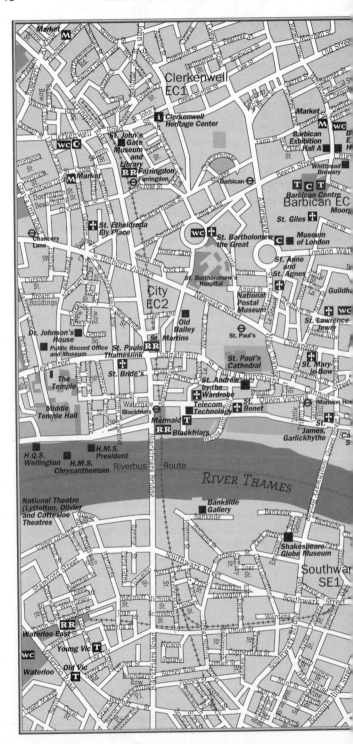

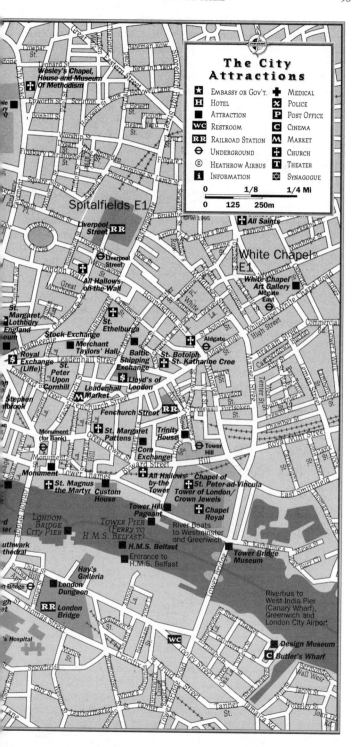

The City Attractions

★	EMBASSY OR GOV'T.	✚	MEDICAL
H	HOTEL	X	POLICE
■	ATTRACTION	P	POST OFFICE
WC	RESTROOM	C	CINEMA
RR	RAILROAD STATION	M	MARKET
⊖	UNDERGROUND	✝	CHURCH
⊜	HEATHROW AIRBUS	T	THEATER
i	INFORMATION	✡	SYNAGOGUE

0   1/8   1/4 Mi

0   125   250m

©FWI 1995

Spitalfields E1

Leonard St.
Wesley's Chapel, House and Museum Of Methodism
Epworth St.
Bonhill St.
Worship St.
Finsbury Christopher St.

Liverpool Street RR
Liverpool Street
London
Great Winchester
All Hallows on-the-Wall

White Chapels E1
All Saints
White Chapel Art Gallery
Aldgate East
Whitechapel High Street
Commercial Rd.

St. Margaret, Lothbury
England Museum
Royal Exchange (Liffe)
St. Peter Upon Cornhill
Stock Exchange
Merchant Taylors' Hall
Leadenhall Street
St. Ethelburga
Baltic Shipping Exchange
St. Botolph
St. Katharine Cree
Aldgate
Aldgate High Street

Lloyd's of London
Leadenhall Market M
Fenchurch Street
Fenchurch Street RR

St. Stephen Walbrook
Monument (for Bank)
Monument
Monument
St. Magnus the Martyr
Custom House

St. Margaret Pattens
Corn Exchange
All Hallows by-the Tower
Trinity House
Tower Hill
Chapel of St. Peter-ad-Vincula
Tower of London/ Crown Jewels
Chapel Royal

Tower Hill Pageant
TOWER PIER (FERRY TO H.M.S. BELFAST)
River Boats to Westminster and Greenwich

LONDON BRIDGE CITY PIER
Southwark Cathedral
H.M.S. Belfast
Entrance to H.M.S. Belfast
Tower Bridge Museum

Blackfriars Bridge
Hay's Galleria
London Dungeon
London Bridge RR
St. Thomas Street
Guy's Hospital
Snowfields

Riverbus to West India Pier (Canary Wharf), Greenwich and London City Airport

Tooley Street
WC
Design Museum
Butler's Wharf C
Bermondsey Wall West
Jacob St.
Tanner St.
Jamaica Rd.
Leathermarket

ture that houses the **Royal Shakespeare Company**. It also is home to the **London Symphony**, an art gallery, two movie houses, a convention center and an apartment complex. Most people who actually make the trek there in the isolation of the evening (everything else is closed), complain about the confusing layout at the **Barbican** and its inhospitable design, unlike the **National Theatre**, whose design and sight lines are absolutely outstanding. A far more enjoyable theater experience can be had at the **Mermaid** on **Puddle Duck** (you would have to love anything whose address is a place called Puddle Duck!). Try to stop in if anything worthwhile is playing.

The most exciting theater experience in London was still being built as we went to press, but it promised to be an incredible sight to behold. In almost the very spot the **Old Globe Theater** presented "young Will's" latest dramas, the raising of the New Globe is taking place. The most fascinating part of the story is that all of this is due to the unceasing dedication of American actor, Sam Wanamaker. His dream was to raise the funds to rebuild the **Globe** so that Shakespeare could be produced exactly the way it was meant to be seen. They've incorporated all of the original architectural methods: goat hair mixed with plaster, hand turned wood, and thatch for the open air roof. We can hardly wait!

Agenda Shopping/The City

Gift Shop/Museum of London

☎ *0171-600-33699.*

Aside from souvenirs and prints, they have hundreds of books about London.

Searle & Co.

1 Royal Exchange, ☎ *0171-626-2456.*

They specialize in jeweled animals that make exclusive pets for people who can't deal with the real things.

Mappin & Webb

2 Queen Victoria Street, ☎ *0171-248-6661.*

These people definitely belong in the financial district, since high-finance is needed to take one of their superb pieces of jewelry home. It's been at this address since 1870.

Agenda Best Bites/The City

Imperial City

Royal Exchange, Cornhill, ☎ *0171-626-3437. Credit cards. Moderate.*
Very elegant Chinese delights under the famous Chef Ken Hom's inscrutable direction. The choices here are eclectic for the usual Chi-

nese menu, but marry the best of Hong Kong with the American touches that make for Home cooking.

Jamaica Wine House

St. Michael's Alley, Cornhill, ☎ *0171-626-9496. Credit cards. Inexpensive.*
It stands in exactly the same spot as the Jamaica Coffee House of the 1600s, where rum and sugar traders used to make their deals. Stop in for a rum toddy, and do some time traveling.

Birley's

5 Bow Lane, ☎ *0171-248-0358. Credit cards. Inexpensive.*
Designer sandwiches made with wonderfully fresh bread. It's a good, quick stop before taking on St. Paul's.

The George & Vulture

3 Castle Court, Cornhill, ☎ *0171-626-9710. Credit cards. Moderate.*
This is the very same place Dickens used as his pub in *Pickwick Papers*. They serve more heroic things than just your average pub lunch. There are impressive roasts and even more impressive pinstripes. Don't miss this one.

The Place Below

St. Mary-Le-Bow, Cheapside, ☎ *0171-329-0789. Cash. Inexpensive.*
This is yet another one of those crypt eateries (there's one in St. Martins off Trafalgar); this one is under St. Mary-le-Bow Church. They make great comfort food, even if you're eating it with the Ghosts of Christmas Past. Their soups are delicious and desserts are straight from the nursery.

Islington and Camden Town

Camden Lock has a carnival atmosphere on weekends.

North London has always been too off the beaten track to draw masses of visitors, who usually prefer anything as long as it is within walking distance of the Tower. But for the true adventurers who want to explore a district of the city that is just on the brink of becoming London's next Chelsea, Islington is very much their cup of tea.

Gentrification has been creeping into this 18th-century enclave of picture postcard squares and wide boulevards since Her Majesty's yuppies

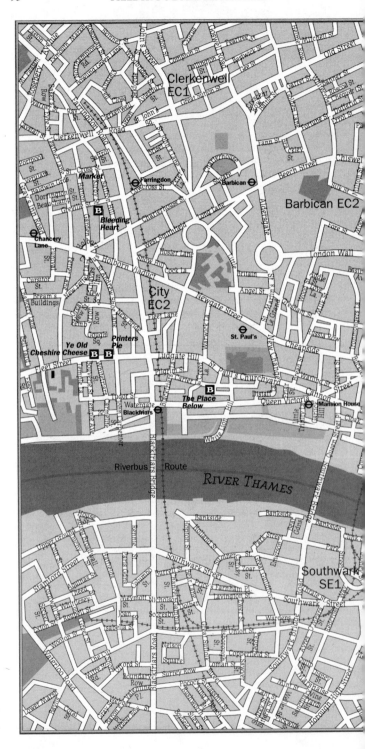

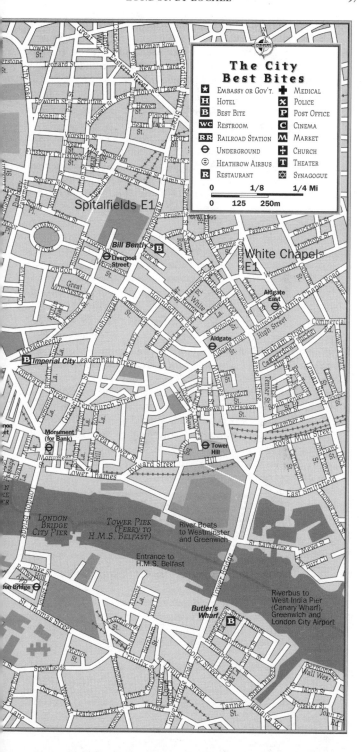

found out about the low real-estate prices. Islington is just 15 minutes away from the city, far enough from the action to give the junior pin-stripers a taste of suburbia. They've made it their mission to buy all the 18th- and 19th- century row houses and turn Islington into an Eden for the young and the affluent. (They're called "Trendy Lefties").

The best place to start exploring is Upper Street which is lined with chic boutiques and restaurants. Its most amazing structure is the monumental Royal Agricultural Hall, built in 1869. It's made of cast iron and glass and it was originally used for cattle shows. It's called the "Aggie" by the locals, but today its become the Business Design Centre, known for displays of commercial interiors. The true magnificence of the Aggie can best be appreciated from the inside. Since the centre is filled with cafes and coffee bars, this might be just the place for a rest-stop. The other major attraction in Islington is **Camden Passage**, one of the best antiques markets in London (see "Markets," page 150). The little winding streets behind Islington Green are filled with upscale antique shops during the week, but on market days (Wed. and Sat.) the stalls spill out into the alleys and streets with an array of collectibles that would make the mouth of any true clutter-bug water. The Passage started business back in 1776 (sound familiar?).

Camden Town, unlike Islington, is becoming an artsy, bohemian village rather like our own Greenwich Village was in the old days. It lies to the North of Islington. It's main street is **Chalk Farm Road**. Artists and craftspeople have been flocking here for cheap lofts and stores. **Regent's Canal**, which runs through the streets off **Camden Lock**, gives a Venetian look to the place; in fact, west of the canal there is a community called "Little Venice." On the weekends, Camden has a carnival atmosphere (see "Markets," page 151), and is jam-packed with hippies, yuppies, and groupies, all looking for the latest in T-shirt trends. Not everything at **Chalk Farm** is for the 18-something set. There are crafts, antiques and pure kitsch. The best way to play it is to follow the madding crowd through the converted stable (the stalls are now filled with dealers), and to the shops that are built around the canal. There are street snacks to keep you fueled up for the hordes of teens you'll have to elbow to get around the place.

JUST AROUND THE CORNER AGENDA ADVENTURES/ ISLINGTON

You can transport yourself from London to Italy by exploring Rosebery Avenue, the area that's known as Little Italy in Islington. There are fragrant cheese shops and markets irresistible enough to make you stop to smell the salami. Worth a try to smuggle one of the hero sandwiches back to the Connaught for a midnight picnic!

Agenda Shopping/
Islington, Camden Town

Compendium

234 Camden High Street, ☎ *0171-485-8944.*
New age thinking going on here with books and tapes on women's issues, politics, "green" philosophy and other fringe benefits.

Glorious Clothing Company

60 Upper Street, ☎ *0171-704-6312.*
They celebrate the best of the 60s and 70s. Up and coming fashion stylists haunt the place.

Gobil's

246 Camden High Street, ☎ *0171-485-9195.*
They make belts on the spot from their collection of buckles and studs, and whatever else they have on hand. Not as classy as Mark Cross or Gucci, but as long as you're here, waist-not, want not.

The Beer Shop

8 Pitfield Street, ☎ *0171-739-3701.*
These people not only roll out the barrel, they can also roll out hundreds of bottled brewskis from around the world. If foam goes to your head, you might want to check them out.

Agenda Best Bites/
Islington, Camden Town

Alfredo's

4-6 Essex Road, ☎ *0171-226-3496. Credit cards. Inexpensive.*
Pies and mash are what the locals come in for. Very old art deco surroundings that make the "pudds" with custard taste, even better.

Bar Gansa

2 Inverness Street, ☎ *0171-267-8909. Credit cards. Moderate.*
What could be wackier—tapas bar right in the middle of the Camden Market—but it works. The best part is that you can snack and be ready to go back to the "wars" without spending too many pesos.

Cafe Flo

334 Upper Street, ☎ *0171-226-7916. Credit cards. Moderate.*
We've already talked about the one in Covent Garden, but the mythical Flo is a welcome sight in Islington. All of her tried and true bistro goodies are here along with a few hybrids like deep-fried potato skins and vegetable strudel.

Casa Franco

134-137 Upper Street, ☎ *0171-226-8994. Credit Cards. Moderate.*

A converted warehouse is the center for trendy Italian food on Upper St. It's almost always filled with The City movers and shakers who tuck into Franco's designer Pizzas and pastas.

The Upper Street Fish Shop

324 Upper Street, ☎ 0171-359-1401. Cash. Inexpensive.
Fish and chips at its most delicious. This is a friendly cafe with crunching and munching going on from noon till late evening. There is also poached fish, if you have "fear of frying."

Granita

127 Upper Street, ☎ 0171-226-3222. Credit cards. Moderate.
London is all a-buzz about this new, modern Italian restaurant, with a minimum of decor and the maximum of creativity on the menu. As soon as you sit down to the tub of French butter and homemade breads, you know the kitchen cares. The rest of the preparations do not disappoint. Try the spinach cake with mushrooms and goat cheese.

Anna's Place

90 Mildmay Park, ☎ 0171-249-9379. Cash. Moderate.
If the urge for a Swedish meatball overcomes you, Anna's Place would be the place for you. The room fairly gleams with a Scandinavian polish, and so does the food. Aside from the terrific meatballs, try taking a herring to lunch or even a graved lox. Desserts are a welcome relief from the endless "puds," no matter how "British" they are, so opt for the Swedish waffles with berries and cream.

Camden Brasserie

216 Camden High Street, ☎ 0171-482-2114. Credit cards. Moderate.
Not a classical brasserie. Instead, comforting French "soul food" such as Toulouse sausages with mashed sweet potatoes, or Scotch salmon with a tart Hollandaise. Very popular in Camden.

Belgo

72 Chalk Farm Road, ☎ 0171-267-0718. Credit cards. Moderate.
Eclectic surroundings that come dangerously close to being weird, but the food is the best of Belgium, which to us means mussels to the max. They do moules mariniers and moules provencales with lusty, garlicky sauces that make you want to leave for Brussels on the next plane.

Docklands

London's busy docks were the entryway for all the commodities upon which the city depended. Today they are no longer used for commerce. Instead, they have become whole new residential communities with restaurants, magnificent views and the promise of even greater usage in the next century. Right now, these areas are the new frontiers of the city and it's anyone's guess as to the multi-directions they may take.

St. Katherine's Dock, which dates from the 16th century, was the beginning point for the redevelopment of the area, with a marina, shops and a beautiful river walk to the **Tower of London**. It's also the location for London's **World Trade Centre**. On the opposite side of the river and only a bracing walk over **The Tower Bridge** is **Butler's Wharf**, where the riverside warehouses have been turned into upscale apartments and trendy new restaurants. The winding streets are cobblestoned and lead to **The Design Museum** (see "Museums," page 214), with it's delicious **Blueprint Cafe** and breathtaking views of the river. The **Branarm Tea and Coffee Museum** is right next door.

Right beside **St. Katherine's Dock** is the **Tobacco Dock**, which was originally meant to rival **Covent Garden's** shops and restaurants. It took some hard knocks during London's recession, so the verdict is still out on this one. The entire Docklands development is still very much a work in progress.

"Cat & the Canary" pub, Docklands

Agenda Shopping/Docklands

Oils & Spices

36 E. Shad Thames, Butler's Wharf, ☎ *0171-403-3434.*
A very professional array of the best in olive oil and other exotic nut oils, side by side, with bright colored spices that are irresistible for sniffing, as well as buying.

The Food Store

36 D Shad Thames, Butler's Wharf, ☎ *0171-403-3434.*
Breads flavored with pesto and sun dried tomato, the freshest cheeses and charauterie, luscious fruit tarts and even picture perfect veggies, all ready for a picnic or a hotel room pick-me-up.

The Design Museum Store

Butler's Wharf, ☎ *0171-407-6261.*
The most elegant kitchen gadgets, home accessories and jewelry that you would expect from a place called the Design Museum Store. They also have witty postcards and games for kids.

Agenda Best Bites/Docklands

Blueprint Cafe

Design Museum, Shad, Thames, ☎ *0171-378-7031. Credit cards. Expensive.*

Another of Terence Conran's efforts, this bright, white, sundrenched (sometimes) space is a bona fide top drawer restaurant, not just a place for a quick bite while ambling around the exhibits. The menu is sleekly designed for a thoroughly modern British experience. Start with the great tapanade and end with one of their ravishing desserts. If the season allows, there is a terrace overlooking the river that's designed for delightful dining.

Le Port de la Tour

(see "Restaurants," page 167)

The Butler's Wharf Chop House

Butler's Wharf, ☎ *0171-403-3414. Credit cards. Expensive.*

Oysters, good steaks and chops, with a bit of grilled fish, beautifully done, for good measure. It's a great big sprawling place, just the right measure of relaxed dining for a topnotch steakhouse.

Dickens Inn

St. Katherine's Dock, ☎ *0171-488-2208. Credit cards. Moderate.*

This was once an old spice warehouse in the 1700s, and in converting it to a very atmospheric inn, they redid it (for some unknown reason) in the style of the 1800s. What the Dickens is going on here! However, it looks very cozy with lots of wood and exposed brick, so if you stop in for a stout you won't be sorry. They also serve pub stuff and soups in the tavern, while upstairs they have a pizza place. We don't remember Dickens ever having Pip take Estella for a pizza!

Chelsea

Chelsea's Thames Embankment invites strolling.

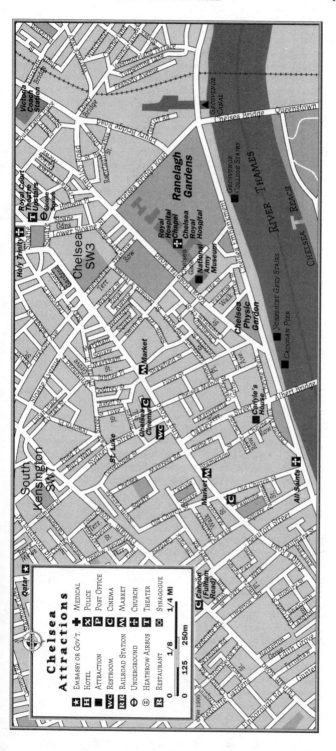

The words that spring to mind when we think of Chelsea are, cozy, intimate, affluent, privileged and bizarre. The last adjective doesn't seem to be comfortable with the others and that characterizes the essence of Chelsea. It was originally laid out like a small village, but through the years, some of the biggest changes in London's staid, reserved image, started right here. Chelsea swung into the sixties with hip contributions to the sedate mindset of the city. Mods, Rockers, Punk-chic and most of all the stylish rebellion of the young that is still going on today.

Chelsea was always the scene of intellectual ferment, with a bit of decadence on the side. A community that welcomed the avant-garde. **Oscar Wilde**, **George Eliot**, **James Whistler**, **Mark Twain**, **Dante Rossetti** and **Henry James**, all lived in Chelsea. Free thinkers among artists and writers have always found Chelsea a safe port when they've stirred up a little good, clean, controversy. In the 50s, that angry young man, John Osborne, had *Look Back in Anger*, produced at the **Royal Court Theater** in Chelsea. Ever since the 19th century, Bohemian abandon has been a way of life here.

The main artery of Chelsea is **Kings Road**, called that because the king used it to travel to the Palace at Hampton Court. It wasn't a public thoroughfare until the 1800s. Today, it's the Broadway of Chelsea, lined with movies, shops, restaurants and bumper to bumper traffic. The newest off-the-wall fashions show up in the rarified boutiques that dot **Kings Road**, with alarming speed. The kids that gravitate here with almost religious fervor on the weekends haunt them for the "new look" that's going to shock the rest of the city. The rest of London may be dancing the waltz, but Kings Road is definitely doing the hustle.

Chelsea is also an upscale antiques showcase, for the City. There are a number of antique dealers in the tiny side streets as well as the main drag, so if you O.D. on "today" you can always slip back to the more gracious past.

King's Road starts at **Sloane Square**, which is the boundary between Chelsea and **Knightsbridge**. The Square is the home of the **Royal Court Theater**, **Peter Jones**, Chelsea's very trendy department store and last but certainly, not least, "**The Sloane Rangers**," those terribly well-dressed, terribly well-connected ("daddy is a Viscount, you see") terribly well bred, terribly au courant, and sometimes terribly boring, young social butterflies, who congregate here for fun. The most famous and definitely *not* boring, alumni **Sloane Ranger** was **Diana Spencer**, while she was waiting for her Prince to come (we'll bet she's sorry she didn't wait a bit longer). **Sloane Street** itself, runs from the Square to **Brompton Road** in **Knightsbridge**, and is the closest **London** comes to **Madison Avenue**. It's lined with power designers, such a **Ungaro**, **Chanel**, **Max Mara**, **Valentino** and **Kenzo**. Bring many £s if you decide to sample their wears.

The very military looking outpost along **Kings Road** is in reality, the **Duke of York's Headquarters**. Neither the Duke nor **Fergie** appear here very often. But "Headquarters" is really a barracks that houses regiments of the **Territorial Army** (who must love to shop in their spare time).

The Chelsea Royal Hospital is by far the grandest structure in this odd little village. It was designed by **Christopher Wren** in 1670 and modeled after the **Hotel des Invalides**, in Paris. **The Royal Hospital** was used to house and feed war veterans. And that's exactly how it is used today. Over

400 Chelsea Pensioners live here. You can see them strolling on **Kings Row** in their smart blue uniforms, or in summer, Scarlet Tunics, looking wonderfully dignified. If you'd like a tour of the hospital, one of the Pensioners will take you around and tell you about the old days. A few pence for this service is regarded as one of the spoils of war.

No visit to Chelsea is complete without a stroll along the **Embankment**, at the edge of the **Thames**. This is without a doubt the poshest and most exclusive part of the whole area. **Cheyne Walk** is where the **Embankment** meets Royal Hospital road, and the priceless rows of Georgian townhouses that have been owned by the Who's Who of the world, past and present. There are those wonderful little "blue plaques" that give you historical inside information.

AGENDA BULLETIN

*Beware the annual Chelsea flower show lest you wind up sleeping in **Hyde Park**. The entire city goes daff-o-delirious, and hotel rooms are as scarce as Easter Lilies in December. However, if you're into haute horticulture, plan your trip to London for late May. The queen herself opens the show, and it lasts four days. So, if you can, take time to smell the roses.*

Agenda Shopping/Chelsea

John Sandoe Books

10 Blacklands Terrace, ☎ *0171-589-9473.*
A landmark bookstore for literary London. You just can't stump them with an obscure title. They might even know where Rushdie is hiding.

David Mellor

4 Sloane Square, ☎ *0171-730-4259.*
Tableware, cookware and most anything to make your kitchen more stylish. They also stock rare olive oils and of course, sun-dried tomatoes.

India Jane

140 Sloane Street, ☎ *0171-730-1070.*
You can guess where all their merchandise comes from, but you'd never guess how affordable (in London, not an overused adjective) it all is. There is always something here to fill that tiny corner of the suitcase that would just be used for your socks anyway.

The General Trading Company

144 Sloane Street, ☎ *0171-730-0411.*
This is obviously the royal family's favorite department store. It holds 4 Royal Warrants (seals of Royal Trade) and Princess Di was registered here. What better recommendation could you ask from one chic, elegant, creative, unique store? It's really a group of townhouses that ramble together so you can roam through their housewares, lin-

ens, imports, china and crystal departments. They also have a terrific cafe in the basement, which is well-worth a drop-in.

Johnny Moke

396 Kings Road, ☎ *0171-351-2232.*
High-stepping souls will beat a path to Johnny Moke for his shoe expertise. They're witty and well-made, in fact they can be custom-made if you want a rainbow of the same style.

Designer's Guild

271-277 Kings Road, ☎ *0171-351-5775.*
Even though you may not be prepared to schlep a sofa home with you, this extravagant display of fabrics, wallpaper, pottery and cush-ions, is definitely tempting.

Manolo Blahnik

49 Old Church Street, ☎ *0171-352-8622.*
He always puts your best foot forward. Cobbler to the stars and roy-als, his line reeks of sex and success. Don't bother unless you're very well-heeled.

Designer's Sale Studio

241 Kings Road, ☎ *0171-351-4171.*
Major bargains on designers labels. They carry discontinued lines, and sometimes prices are cut by half (which, in the case of Armani, means £3,000,000 instead of £6,000,000).

Hampstead Bazaar

38 Kings Road, ☎ *0171-431-3343.*
Beautiful knits and prints from Italy. Designs with flair and elegance. Great imported jewelry too.

Quincy

137 Kings Road, ☎ *0171-351-5367.*
The last fashion word for the man of *au courant* distinction. Clothes can be garden party formal, or the most meticulously cut jeans in the Empire.

Chenil Galleries

181-183 Kings Road, ☎ *0171-351-5350.*
An art deco collection in an art deco setting. The gallery itself has a domed ceiling with a mural, telling the history of Chenil and his ded-ication to the arts. Today, the dealers show very distinctive examples of the period from silver and mirrors, to toys and furniture.

Hetherington

289 Kings Road, ☎ *0171-351-0880.*
A very discreet clientele comes here for their gowns and even their wedding gowns. Sasha Hetherington turns out glamorous clothes with prices to match.

David Tron

275 Kings Road, ☎ *0171-352-5918.*
He specializes in antiques of the 17th and 18th century. For the seri-ous collector only.

Givans

207 Kings Road, ☎ *0171-352-6352.*
If you've always wanted real Irish linen to cuddle up with, Givans has linen sheets, comforter covers, table cloths and a selection of extrava-gant robes.

Agenda Best Bites/Chelsea

Chelsea Potter

119 Kings Road, ☎ *0171-352-9479. Credit cards. Inexpensive.*
No one sells bowls and pots here. This is, in fact, a restaurant that's always crowded with denizens of Chelsea or shoppers who can get a reasonable lunch.

Chelsea Kitchen

98 Kings Road, ☎ *0171-589-1330. Cash. Inexpensive.*
This is a spot that can trace its success all the way back to the swinging sixties. Their claim to fame is wholesome food at the right price. Try the casseroles. They are particularly homey.

Mijanou

143 Ebury Street, ☎ *0171-730-4099. Credit cards. Expensive.*
Some of the top politicos in town show up at the very cozy Mijanou. It may be small but Sonia Blech's capacity for imaginative cooking is unlimited. If she has Salty Cakes on the menu (bread made of cheese, ham, olives and herbs) don't leave without trying them, or the jellied fois gras or her famous "Nutcase" filled with chocolate mousse and nuts.

Alberro & Grana

Chelsea Cloisters, 89 Sloane Ave, ☎ *0171-225-1048. Credit cards. Expensive.*
The chef here came straight from Madrid and brought with him the kind of rich, full-flavored food that makes Spain so sunny. The crowd that wolfs down the black pudding and spicy sausages is friendly and loud, mainly because the tapas bar in front draws mobs of people with their succulent Madrileños' mouthfuls.

Aubergine

11 Park Walk, ☎ *0171-352-3449. Credit cards. Expensive.*
One of the hottest restaurants in London right now, with the faithful willing to wait weeks for a reservation. In truth, the food is quite wonderful and presented with great style. Modern British, here is really French with an Italian accent. If you've only got two or three days in town, don't feel left out; it looks like Aubergine will be around for a long time.

The Canteen

Harbour Yard, Chelsea Harbor, ☎ *0171-357-7330. Credit cards. Expensive.*
The combination that is important here has little to do with the food; it's the one that includes Michael Caine and his partner, controversial chef (read: heavy on attitude), Marco Pierre White. Together they've hatched this very breezy, trendy place. The food is fine, but it's the celebs who stir the pot here.

Ed's Easy Diner

362 Kings Road, ☎ *0171-352-1956. Credit cards. Moderate.*

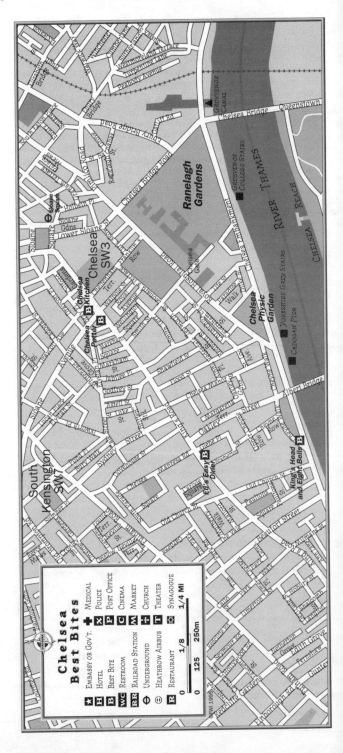

Should Americans go to an American-style diner in London? Sure. Sometimes a hot dog is better than a Valium when you have travel frazzle. Ed's is shiny and jazzy, and the shakes are almost great.

Foxtrot Oscar

79 Royal Hospital Road, ☎ *0171-352-7170. Credit cards. Expensive.*
If you care, the first initial of each name is military code for two very naughty words. That, in effect, sets the tone for this very clubby hamburger joint for pinstripes who want to unwind. The food is good and the crowd is affable, but if you're not a regular, you may feel as if you didn't get a part in the play.

Daphne's

112 Draycott Ave, ☎ *0171-589-4257. Credit cards. Expensive.*
Daphne's is full of fashion people, so it's hard to tell if the food, the people or the decor is the most beautiful. Perhaps the most beautiful of all is Daphne's Finnish owner. The kitchen is "mod" Italian with the risottos the stars of the menu.

King's Head and Eight Bells

50 Cheyne Walk, ☎ *0171-352-1820. Credit cards. Inexpensive.*
As historic as Cheyne Walk itself, this great pub dates back 400 years. You can have a drink, look out on the Thames and pretend you can hear a carriage drawing up outside.

Knightsbridge

Grandeur, glitz and glamour. Those are the 3Gs that best suit Knightsbridge. The motto of **Harrods** (see "Department Stores," page 147), the brightest Jewel in Knightsbridge's crown, best describes the whole inimitable scene—**Omnia, Omnibus, Ubique**: everything for everyone, everywhere. Knightsbridge is not only Princess of Wales country, it is the capitol of "happening" in London.

Brompton Road is the wide boulevard that runs through the center of Knightsbridge. The majestic **Hyde Park Hotel**, **Harrods** and **Harvey Nichols**, a department store more suited to the 90s, are its most visible landmarks. But it is in the small, smart, side streets that the real feeling of wealth and privilege are most dramatically felt. **Beauchamp Place** and **Walton Street** are filled with luxury boutiques and restaurants; **Basil Street** has elegant small hotels (The **Capitol**, **L'Hotel**, **The Basil Street Hotel**) and townhouses. **Sloane Street** is the mega-expensive route from Knightsbridge, over to **Chelsea**, filled with designer boutiques, including **Armani** and everybody's cup of **Coco**, **Chanel's**.

To best understand the aura of affluence in Knightsbridge, take the time to wander in and out of these small, elegant satellite streets, which radiate out from **Harrods**, all the way down to **Brompton Cross**. That's where the **Michelin Building** will stop you dead in your tracks. An art nouveau masterpiece, built in 1911, that was once the headquarters of Michelin in London, it was rescued by **Sir Terence Conran**, restored and turned into one of London's most exclusive restaurants, **Bibendum** (see "Restaurants," page 156). Even if you don't book a table, it's great fun just to take a look at this extraordinary example of turn-of-the-century joie de vivre. It's also the home of **The Conran Shop**, Sir Terence's high-tech den of design. In terms of home decor, it is quite simply the most creative collection in town. They

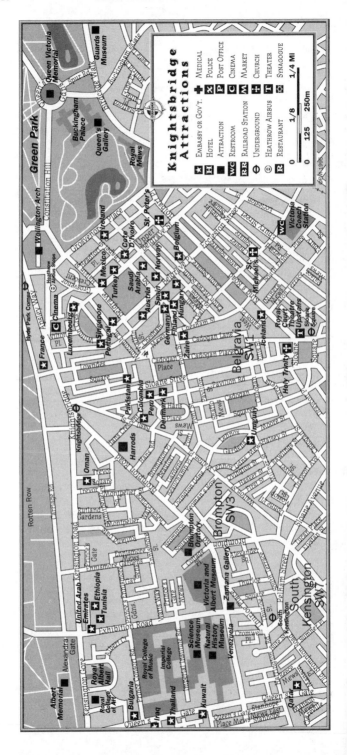

have everything from one-of-a-kind antiques, to the latest kitchen equipment. Across the street is the beginning of **Fulham Road**, more credit card adventures and endless exquisite Mews houses to admire.

Knightsbridge is filled with designer shops and gourmet markets.

Agenda Shopping/Knightsbridge

Janet Reger

    2 Beauchamp Place, ☎ *0171-584-9360.*
Lacy undies for racy ladies. The most luxurious unmentionables, with prices to be whispered with discretion.

Conran Shop

    Michelin House, 81 Fulham Road, ☎ *0171-589-7401.*

Imports and accessories, home furnishings and baggage, design and decorative arts. Everything here is the best you'll find around. Sir Terence makes sure!

Theo Fennell

177 Fulham Road, ☎ *0171-352-7313.*
The last word in original jewelry. Fennell is a jeweler for all seasons, and all socialites. He's known for his silver miniatures of London's favorite sights, such as phone booths and postboxes. Great portable memories.

Harvey Nicols

(see "Department Stores," page 147)

Harrods

(see "Department Stores," page 147)

Van Peterson

117 Walton Street, ☎ *0171-589-2155.*
You'll lose your heart in the Peterson's sweet boutique, but you can find a nifty replacement among their collection of heart-shaped everything.

Deliss

41 Beauchamp Place, ☎ *0171-584-3321.*
The elves who toil at this up-market shoemaker's work their magic in elephant and crocodile, as well as other beastly hides.

The Italian Paper Shop

11 Brompton Arcade, ☎ *0171-589-1668.*
Marble patterned paper for notebooks, desk accessories and stationary. They're made in Florence by El Papiro, who has outlets all over the world.

Old England

18 Beauchamp Place, ☎ *0171-584-1100.*
Beautifully made cashmere and silk designs with skirts and tops coupled to make dressy combinations. The prices are substantial, but the quality is worth every pence.

Walton Street Stationary Company

97 Walton Street, ☎ *0171-589-0777.*
Very elegant, personal stationary and engraving done here for the Knightsbridge set. You can place an order and they will ship it on to you.

Bruce Oldfield

27 Beauchamp Place, ☎ *0171-584-1363.*
Both civilian and royal celebs flock here with tons of pounds and leave with ne-plus-ultra gowns. Made to order so that they will cling in all the right places.

Kanga

8 Beauchamp Place, ☎ *0171-581-1185.*
An old "friend" of Prince Chuck, Lady Tryon was nicknamed Kanga by him and it instantly became her label. Delicate little frothy dresses are her other trademark. The clothes are perfect to pack for short hops.

Reject China Shops

34-35 Beauchamp Place, ☎ *0171-581-0737.*

There are many of these around town. They're fun for rummaging around in the occasional bargains and clutter. Don't feel too rejected if you don't find any marked-down Waterford.

The Map House

54 Beauchamp Place, ☎ *0171-589-4325.*
They'll keep you right on course while you browse through the antique maps, charts and prints in their fascinating collection. Just the place to plan a trip around the world.

Scotch House

2 Brompton Road, ☎ *0171-581-2151.*
In truth, this place looks as interesting as any of those "wares of the country" mishmashes that are both exhausting and exasperating. However, Scotch House is known for its enormous stock of cashmeres and woolens of fine quality. There's a terrific kids department as well. You can really paint the town plaid.

Joseph

77 Fulham Road, ☎ *0171-823-9500.*
Breakthrough clothes from Kenzo, Dolce and Gabbana and anyone else that means the best of Britain. The shop itself looks severely minimalist and has one floor for her and one for him. You feel dressed to kill, even before you leave.

Agenda Best Bites/Knightsbridge

Pearl of Knightsbridge

22 Brompton Road, ☎ *0171-225-3888. Credit cards. Expensive.*
Just the place after a hard day at Harrods. The Dim Sum are delicate and the other choices are far more sophisticated than your usual Cantonese canteen. The baby ribs in hot vinegar are a tangy delight. The room is black, white and very smart.

Bill Bentley's

31 Beauchamp Place, ☎ *0171-589-5080. Credit cards. Expensive.*
A very formal fish restaurant, with fresh, briney, oysters and grills, done perfectly. If you choose to have the oysters in the downstairs bar with a wonderful glass of wine to match, you may never bring body to the sole upstairs.

Emporio Armani Express

191 Brompton Road, ☎ *0171-823-8818. Credit cards. Moderate.*
You'll never overeat at Armani's. How could you, watching a video of an anorexic model gliding around in one of his smashing outfits. Try to make your elegant smoked salmon sandwich last through illicit thoughts of dessert. Play your cards right and someday there might be one of the big A's in your closet.

Walton's of Walton Street

121 Walton Street, ☎ *0171-584-0204. Credit cards. Expensive.*
Aside from its redundant name, the cuisine at this exclusive Knightsbridge "landmark" is quite good and always crowded with the Harrod

Hordes, who revel in Walton's plush interior. There's more fabric around the room than at a Persian Bazaar, but if you don't dwell on the upholstery, you can put together a pretty fine meal. Try lunch; you won't have to mortgage the house.

San Martino

103 Walton Street, ☎ *0171-589-3833. Credit cards. Expensive.*
The owner of San Martino is as warm and affable as the menu in this little gem on Walton Street. Influenced by Tuscany, the flavors are robust and striking. Try the spaghetti, cooked in a paper bag. There's a secret to it, so don't even ask.

Turner's

87-89 Walton Street, ☎ *0171-584-6711. Credit cards. VERY expensive.*
Owned by Brian Turner, a T.V. celeb chef in Britain, he hosts the restaurant with the same charm he uses on the show. It's a great treat to be part of such an expansive (albeit expensive) atmosphere. He serves a deceptively simple menu that is classically presented. The filet of beef melts away and is served with caramelized potatoes in a crust.

St. Quentin

243 Brompton Road, ☎ *0171-581-5131. Credit cards. VERY expensive.*
The same people who own Grill St. Quentin (see "Restaurants," page 162), own this handsome brasserie. It has a long zinc bar à la Paris and a good bowl of moules marinier, to go with it. There are velvet banquets and boeuf bourguignonne. What more could anyone want?

Khun Akorn

136 Brompton Road, ☎ *0171-225-2680. Credit cards. Expensive.*
Thai food, especially from Bangkok, scents the air with lemon grass and coriander. The fish cakes are meltingly rich, served with a fiery dipping sauce. You can cool down with the sculptured, exotic fruits and coconut ice cream.

Luba's Bistro

6 Yoman's Row, ☎ *0171-589-2950. Credit cards. Moderate.*
Luba's is always fun. It's a BYOB place (you can bring wine) and the Russian specialties are comforting, (even before detente). The long wooden tables make for comrades as well as camaraderie.

Le Metro

L'Hotel, 28 Basil Street, ☎ *0171-589-6286. Credit cards. Moderate.*
This is a terrific wine bar in the basement of this "smart" little hotel. They serve wonderful cheeses and salads, great soups and very careful attention is paid to the wine selection available by the glass.

Basil Street Hotel

Buffet and Salad Bar
8 Basil Street, ☎ *0171-581-3311. Credit cards. Moderate.*
What could be more convenient than a good, solid, hot and cold buffet, a few steps from Harrods. The food is serviceable and it's an all-you-can-eat bargain, at that. The carved meats are the way to go, and desserts are very cheery. Service is fast enough for your charge card to barely cool down.

Patisserie Valerie

215 Brompton Road, ☎ *0171-823-9971. Credit cards. Moderate.*

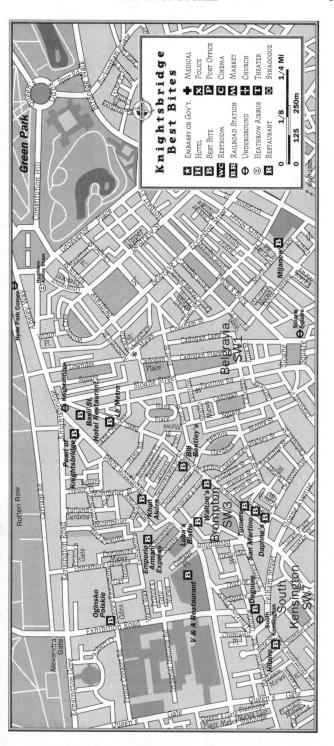

Knightsbridge Best Bites

★	EMBASSY OR GOV'T.
H	HOTEL
B	BEST BITE
WC	RESTROOM
RR	RAILROAD STATION
⊖	UNDERGROUND
⊜	HEATHROW AIRBUS
R	RESTAURANT
✚	MEDICAL
⊠	POLICE
P	POST OFFICE
C	CINEMA
M	MARKET
✚	CHURCH
T	THEATER
⊠	SYNAGOGUE

0 125 250m
0 1/8 1/4 MI

Yummy desserts and good sandwiches make this a fab shopping resource. It's comfortable, and the service is caring.

Georgian Room

Harrod's, 135 Brompton Road, ☎ *0171-730-1234. Credit cards. Moderate.*

If you just can't bear to leave the premises, then the Georgian Room will produce a good cream tea, decent sandwiches and salads, all amid a green velvet milieu. It's very proper and prim, so don't try to buy the banquets.

Kensington

Organ grinders still entertain on Portobello Road.

Queen Victoria called **Kensington** home. She was born in **Kensington Palace** and only when she became the monarch of the Empire, did she decide to move over to **Buckingham Palace**, in the high rent district. Instead of languishing from its loss, Kensington became the borough of the young, the hip and most importantly, the shopper. Two of its main streets, **Kensington High Street** and **Kensington Church Street** are both devoted to endless shopping possibilities. The former is the place where designers on the brink dress most of the London's disco denizens, the later is the "serious" antique collector's stamping grounds.

But some of us do not live by shopping alone. Kensington (actually, **South Kensington**) is also known as **museum Country**, which starts at the point **Brompton** meets **Cromwell Road**. Aside from the **Victoria and Albert** (see "Top Sights," page 18), there is the vast **National History Museum**, which looks much more like a royal residence than a museum, and the **Science Museum**, which aside from the showcase it provides for the scientific contributions the British have made, it's a real delight for children. It is a very hands-on, learn through "touch me" types of displays that are heaven for kids.

AGENDA DENTAL DETAIL

*Napoleon's toothbrush is on display at the **Museum of Medicine**, within the **Science Museum**. He may have lost the Battle of Waterloo, but his dentist gave him a gold star.*

Back at the **palace (Kensington)**, Victoria may have moved out, but there are still enough tiaras in residence to make it "Princess Central." Both Princess Margaret and Princess Di (although there may be a moving van in her future before too long) among others, have apartments there. In fact, Di used to be seen pushing a stroller in **Kensington Gardens**, back in B.C. (before Camilla). The Gardens themselves are lushly green and full of song birds and flowers. You can drop in at the palace, but only the rooms open to the public, so don't count on seeing the royal residents on their exercycles. Stop by the **Court Dress Collection**. You can get a look at Princess Di's wedding dress which is in much better shape than her marriage. The most endearing of all the rooms is young Princess Victoria's bedchamber. What must it have been like to be told at 18 that you were suddenly the queen of England?

Another of Victoria's valentines to Prince Albert was the **Royal Albert Hall**. It's enormous, Roman style in design and can hold 8000 people. Luckily, Albert loved it and to this day, they are filling it with concertgoers and sports fans year round. In the Summer, they have Promenade concerts, which are much like our own Boston Pops.

Notting Hill and **Holland Park** are to the North of Kensington and are both becoming attractions in their own rights. **Portobello Road** (see "Markets," page 150), has brought new, exotic boutiques and restaurants to the "Hill" as well as the fine antique shops that are open even when the Market is not. **Holland Park** is "millionaire's row," and that in itself has made it the last word for London "gentry."

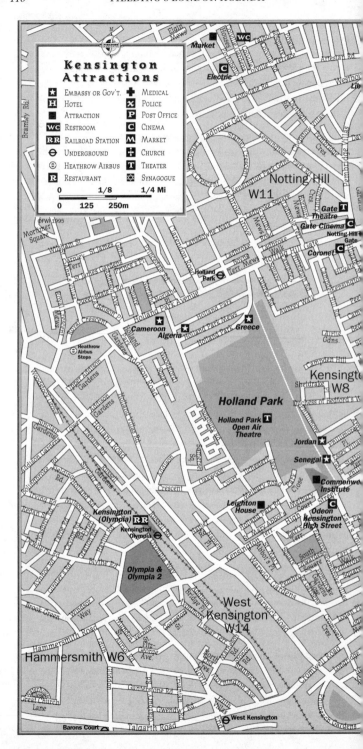

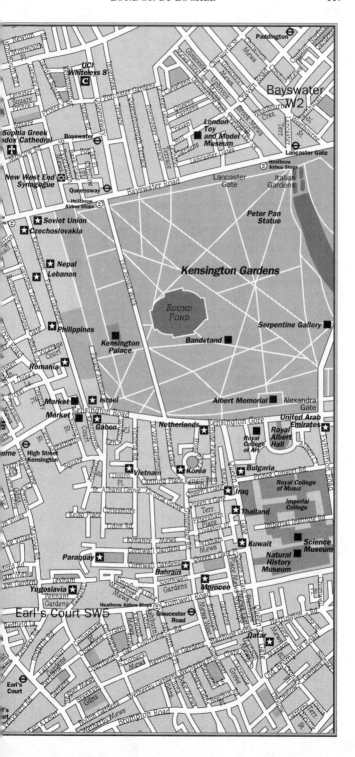

Agenda Shopping/Kensington

Museum Shop

Victoria & Albert Museum, Cromwell Road, ☎ *0171-589-5070.*
The same wonderful array of decorative objects that form the basis of
the V&A's approach to its collection. Prices are high, but so is quality
and design.

Hyper-Hyper

26-40 Kensington High Street, ☎ *0171-938-4343.*
You're sure to Hyper-Ventilate just trying to get around this sprawling maze of stalls. New, young British designers contribute "Outre,"
sometimes zany, styles that show up in Discos all over town.

Daniel James

70 Kensington High Street, ☎ *0171-937-4207.*
These shirts will suit you to a T. The selection of colors, patterns and
detail take them out of the run of the mill T-shirt category and make
them eligible to be works of art.

Kensington Market

49-53 Kensington High Street, No phone.
A mishmash of wall-to-wall oddities. Army surplus, imports from
India and China, secondhand clothes, and if you get bored, you can
have a tatoo done. Terminally tacky, but fun.

Children's Book Centre

237 Kensington High Street, ☎ *0171-937-7497.*
You don't have to read between the lines here to know kids love this
place. A big playroom, with books all over just begging to be
thumbed.

Japanese Gallery

66D Kensington Church Street, ☎ *0171-229-2934.*
Japanese woodblock prints of extraordinary quality, along with Noh
masks and anything else a 90s Mikado might want.

Jonathan Howe

66B & 66D Kensington Church Street, ☎ *0171-221-5658.*
Pottery that dates from medieval times, up to the British arts and
crafts period. They also have rare pieces of Staffordshire that are
bound to rattle any collector.

Kensington Church St. Antiques Centre

58-60 Kensington Church Street, ☎ *0171-376-0425.*
There are 14 shops under this roof, specializing in French art glass,
arts and crafts pottery, vintage fashion, jewelry and art works. It may
take you hours to get through all of the goodies that are tucked away
here.

Agenda Best Bites/Kensington

Persepolis

39 Kensington High Street, ☎ *0171-937-3555. Credit cards. Moderate.*
The flavors of Persia in this very reserved establishment come through
loud and clear from the kitchen. The chicken with walnuts and the
baklava would have made even the Ayatollah smile (maybe).

Hilaire

68 Old Brompton Road, ☎ *0171-584-8993. Credit cards. Expensive.*
Don't let the seasick green of the place put you off (hopefully, by
now, they've chosen a restful mauve) the food can be very stylish, and
the word around town is "tres" flattering. The tagliatelle with chorizo
is a flash of Mediterranean sunlight. Plum sorbet or the creme brule
to end with, makes you feel Hilaireous.

Boyd's

135 Kensington Church Street, ☎ *0171-727-5452. Credit cards. Expensive.*
This is an airy, bright place, with a conservatory look and very fine
food. Grills are perfect and salad, served with a spicy Chinese vinai-
grette, is delicious. If you're feeling expansive try the pheasant in
black currant sauce. Very classy.

Sticky Fingers

1A Phillimore Gardens, ☎ *0171-938-5388. Credit cards. Moderate.*
Kids are going to love this place. Even big kids! Bill Wyman of the
Rolling Stones opened it as a mini-rock museum with burgers. The
staff is laid back and friendly, so we guess they don't even mind sticky
fingers.

V and A Restaurant

Victoria and Albert Museum, ☎ *0171-581-2159. Credit cards. Inexpensive.*
They sometimes match the specials to the exhibits, but even if they
don't, the food here is more than a cut above the usual museum cafe
steam table.

Ognisko Polskie

53 Exhibition Road, ☎ *0171-589-4670. Credit cards. Moderate.*
The stuffed cabbage here is greatski. We think that if you can pronounce its name, you should be given a 10 percent discount, but even
if you can't, you'll have no trouble pointing to the steaming bowls of
pierogi (dumplings) around the room. The incendiary drink du jour
is the Polish vodka.

Daquise

20 Thurloe Street, ☎ *0171-589-6117. Credit cards. Inexpensive.*
You take your choice here: good, simple, Polish soul food or delicious
cakes and pastries for a sit-down after "museum madness." Either
way, you'll leave smiling.

Texas Lone Star West

117-119 Queensway, ☎ *0171-727-2980. Credit cards. Inexpensive.*

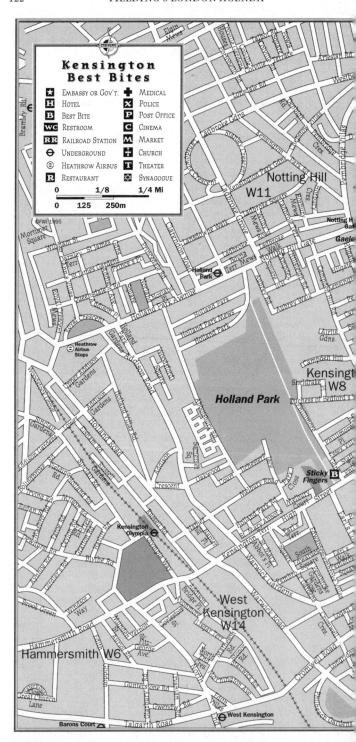

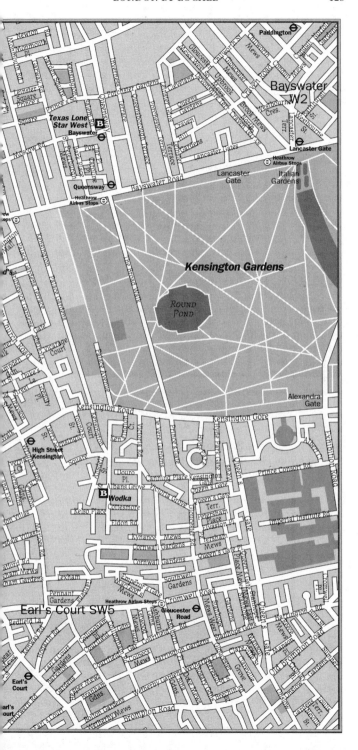

Ribs in London! Sure, and they have other Tex-Mex indigestibles, as well as country music.

Gaeles

2 Farmer Street, ☎ *0171-727-7969. Cash. Inexpensive.*
There is an ongoing fight with "fish and chippies" about the superiority of Gaeles over the Sea Shell (see "Restaurants," page 172), and vis versa. Here's the scoop—it doesn't matter! The fish is fresh and crisp and the chips terrific, so we are telling you "life is too short!"

Wodka

12 St. Albans Grove, ☎ *0171-937-6513. Credit cards. Expensive.*
This is sleek, modern, sophisticated Poland, with wild boar sausages, blinis with Herring and over 15 different kinds of Vodka. You probably won't know what you're eating anyway.

Bloomsbury

The British Museum is two and a half miles of treasure including the Rosetta Stone.

Aside from Eliza Doolittle wanting with all her heart to have a room here, Bloomsbury is not known for its housing, but for its intellect. Eliza must not have been afraid of Virginia Woolf because both Virginia and her husband Leonard made their home in Bloomsbury. It was also the setting for the Bloomsbury Group, that very august bunch of literary lights (such as T.S. Eliot, D. H. Lawrence, Katherine Mansfield and E.M. Forster, who met in the Woolf's parlor, for a large helping of "terminal angst" with their crumpets.

AGENDA MEMORIAL

Sylvia Plath committed suicide at No. 23 Fitzroy Road.

The whole area is laid out around gracious, tree-lined squares suggesting a college campus, which indeed it almost is. The University of London adds to the historical academe of Bloomsbury, with its own cerebral contributions into the 21st century. Aside from the University, the other most important center of scholarly learning is the **British Museum** (see "Museums,"

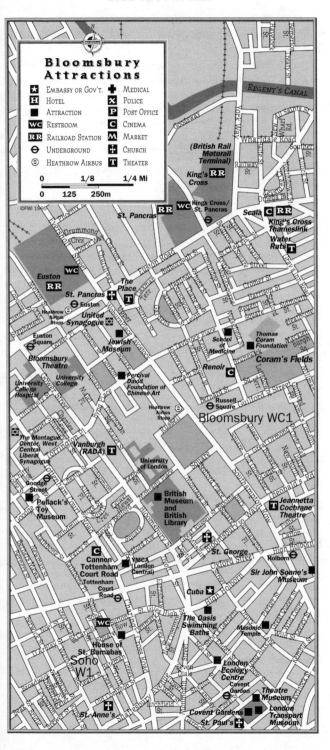

Bloomsbury Attractions

★	EMBASSY OR GOV'T.	✚	MEDICAL
H	HOTEL	✖	POLICE
■	ATTRACTION	P	POST OFFICE
WC	RESTROOM	C	CINEMA
RR	RAILROAD STATION	M	MARKET
⊖	UNDERGROUND	✝	CHURCH
⊜	HEATHROW AIRBUS	T	THEATER

0   1/8   1/4 Mi
0   125   250m

©FWI 1995

REGENT'S CANAL

(British Rail Motorail Terminal)

King's Cross RR

St. Pancras RR

Kings Cross/St. Pancras WC

Scala C RR

King's Cross Thameslink

Water Rats T

Wharfdale Road

Euston WC RR

St. Pancras ✝

The Place T

Heathrow Airbus Stops ⊜ Euston

United Synagogue ✡

Euston Square ⊖

Jewish Museum ■

School of Medicine ■

Thomas Coram Foundation ■

Coram's Fields

Bloomsbury Theatre

University College

Renoir C

Percival David Foundation of Chinese Art ■

Heathrow Airbus Stops ⊜

Russell Square ⊖

Bloomsbury WC1

University College Hospital

The Montague Center, West Central Liberal Synagogue

Vanburgh (RADA) T

University of London

Goodge Street ⊖

Pollack's Toy Museum ■

British Museum and British Library ■

Jeannetta Cochrane Theatre T

Cannon Tottenham Court Road C

YMCA (London Central) ■

St. George ✝

Holborn ⊖

Sir John Soane's Museum ■

Tottenham Court Road ⊖

Cuba ★

The Oasis Swimming Baths ■

Masonic Temple ■

WC

House of St. Barnabas ■

Soho W1

Seven Dials

London Ecology Centre ■

Covent Garden

Theatre Museum ■

London Transport Museum ■

St. Anne's ✝

Covent Gardens ■

St. Paul's ✝

page 213). The streets around the museum are filled with art galleries, bookshops, and coffee houses, overflowing with earnest-looking students having earnest conversations.

Not far away from "Bloomsbury Central" is the small, quiet street that Charles Dickens lived on long enough to write *Oliver Twist*, *Nicholas Nickleby*, and *Pickwick Papers*. He seems to have lived on every street in London, judging from the endless blue plaques all over town, but *48 Doughty Street* is where his home, now a museum, can be visited (see "Museums," page 214). It's a wonder he was able to get anything longer than a pamphlet written, with all that moving around.

If you go on from **Dickens'** house past **Conduit Street**, you will be in the most Dickensian part of London, sometimes referred to as Legal London.

There is no doubt that these narrow, winding streets will take you back in time to the London that springs from the pages of *David Copperfield* and *Great Expectations*. The greatest expectations to come out of this section were the legal and court systems practiced by the Barristers, who in those days, lived in the four "Inns of Court." Thomas More, Oliver Cromwell and Ghandi all spent time studying here. The **Old Bailey** is nearby and is yet another scene immortalized by Dickens, when Fagin was sentenced to death there in *Oliver Twist*. It's now called the **Central Criminal Court**, but that isn't half as colorful or evocative of the past.

Agenda Shopping/Bloomsbury

The British Museum Shop
Main floor, ☎ *0171-636-1555.*
The last word in museum collections, they have jewelry paintings, sculpture, glass and some of the best posters around.

Aanello & Davide
92 Charing Cross Road, ☎ *0171-836-5019.*
Cobblers to the ballet and theater set, they have professional as well as civilian styles. The place looks like it could have made *The Red Shoes*.

Print Room
37 Museum Street, ☎ *0171-430-0159.*
If you'd like to take home the best in British prints and caricatures, they have an astonishing assortment. It's the best way to celebrate a visit to London.

S. J. Shrubsole
43 Museum Street, ☎ *0171-4405-2712.*
The silver lining here is their old Sheffield plate and sterling.

London Silver Vaults
53-64 Chancery Lane, ☎ *0171-242-3844.*
This is where the silver is buried in London, 42 feet underground, under lock, key and the watchful eyes of countless security guards. If you're just browsing, forget it, but if you have enough sterling for the sterling, you can find almost anything. There are 30 of the finest silver

dealers in London with nothing to do but to flex their polishing cloths and wait on you.

Westway & Westway
92-93 Great Russell Street, ☎ *0171-636-1718.*
More wool than at a sheep-shearing convention. Scottish cashmeres, blankets, clothing and other cuddly, cozy, fuzzy stuff. Supposedly, the largest selection in town.

Her Majesty's Stationery Office
49 High Holborn Street, ☎ *0171-873-0011.*
These people can map out everything for you. They stock charts, guides, travel books and British countryside maps. There are also pretty diaries and cards for gifts.

Hatton Garden
Chancery Lane, ☎ *0171-242-6452*
This is an area rather than a single shop, much like New York's diamond district. The streets that lead off **Hatton Garden** itself are devoted to precious metals and gemstones sold usually by Orthodox Jewish merchants. There are some stores that specialize in antique jewelry and occasionally, a true bargain is possible, but bargain *is* the operative word here. If that's not your strong suit, you'd best stick to Bond Street or the Markets.

Jarndyce Antiquariun Booksellers
46 Great Russell Street, ☎ *0171-631-4220.*
It's a far far better thing they do by selling first editions of Dickens as well as other books of the period.

Agenda Best Bites/Bloomsbury

Museum Street Cafe
47 Museum Street, ☎ *0171-405-3211. Cash. Moderate.*
Appearances are definitely deceiving here. The place looks like nothing more than your average sandwich shop or take-out joint, but in truth, it is one of the best new restaurants in London. They have a wonderful command of simple food, although they prefer to call the menu "British Modern." The grills are perfect, succulently done and the bread is home-made. After trying to conquer the British Museum, you deserve the best.

Wagamama
4 Streatham St (see "Restaurants," page 173)

Museum Tavern
49 Great Russell Street, ☎ *0171-242-8987. Credit cards. Inexpensive.*
Right opposite the museum and very elegantly Victorian. It's crowded with students and writers who come for the good, cheap, pub menu, both hot and cold. It was a favorite of Karl Marx, who was particularly fond of "Socializing."

Plough
27 Museum Street, ☎ *0171-636-7954. Credit cards. Inexpensive.*

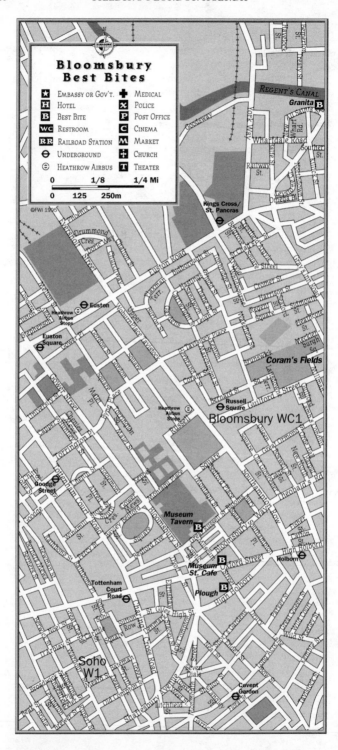

It's yet another pub that attracts publishers and writers in the literary tradition of the neighborhood. It has tables outside in summer and good pub food.

Bleeding Heart Yard

Chancery Lane, ☎ *0171-242-8238. Credit cards. Inexpensive.*
Because this pub was featured in *Little Dorrit*, it has first editions of all of Dickens' work on shelves around the room. It's almost as good as having a drink with Charles himself. However today, the small pub has evolved into a brasserie, as well as just a place to have an ale. The food is very good and the atmosphere is worth the visit.

Marylebone/Regents Park

Regents Park is 500 acres of pastoral beauty.

There are three top attractions that dominate this very sedate, elegant part of London, and they are totally unrelated one to the other in temperament, significance or appeal. They are **Madame Tussaud** (See "Top Sights," page 13), the most visited tourist sight in London, **221B Baker Street**, the "home" of Sherlock Holmes, and the London **Zoo** in **Regent's Park**. But, amazingly enough, one never gets the feeling that Marylebone is overrun with tourists in Bermuda shorts, flashing their bulbs and littering the streets with gum wrappers. There is a calm, sedate grace about the small cafes that line **Marylebone High Street** and Chiltern Street. Even Marylebone Road, with its business traffic and tour buses, still has the feeling of Regency London.

The name Marylebone comes from the Church of the area, **St. Mary le Bourne** (river). If you run that all together, you get something like Marr-a-le-bon, which is how they pronounce it.

The three most famous streets off Marylebone Road are **Baker Street**, **Harley Street** and for all the romantics who hold it most dear, **Wimpole Street**.

Harley Street is filled with stunning Georgian townhouses, famous as the address of London's most fashionable doctors, all in the private sector, without attachments to the National Health Care Plan. They have their "surgeries" (offices) up and down **Harley**, which is often clogged with

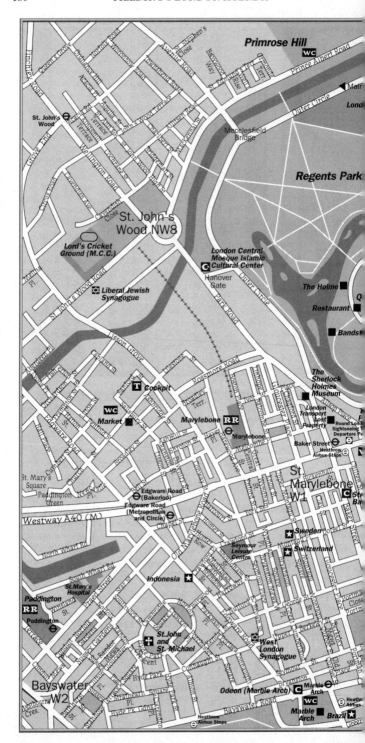

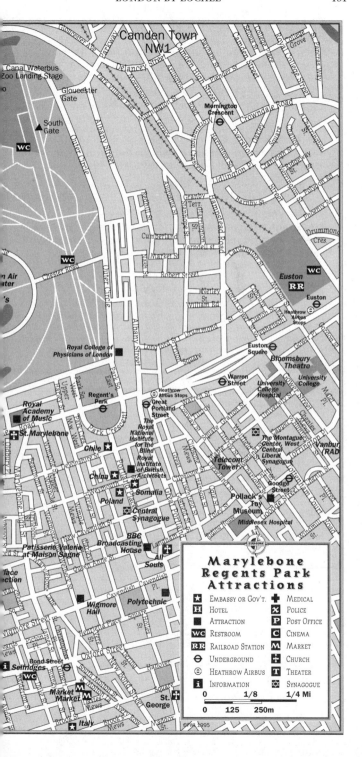

Camden Town
NW1

Regent's Canal Waterbus
London Zoo Landing Stage

Gloucester
Gate

South
Gate

WC

Mornington
Crescent ⊖

Open Air
Theater

WC

Euston **WC**

Euston **RR**

Euston ⊖

Heathrow
Airbus
Stops

Royal College of
Physicians of London

Euston ⊖
Square

Bloomsbury
Theatre

Warren ⊖
Street

University
College
Hospital

University
College

Royal
Academy
of Music

Regent's
Park

Heathrow
Airbus Stops

Great
Portland
Street ⊖

🕂 St.Marylebone

Chile ★

The
Royal
National
Institute
for the
Blind

Royal
Institute
of British
Architects

The Montague
Center, West
Central
Liberal
Synagogue

Vanbur
(RAD

China ★

Telecom
Tower ▪

Goodge ⊖
Street

Poland ★

Somalia ★

Pollack's
Toy
Museum

Central
Synagogue

BBC
Broadcasting
House

Patisserie Valerie
at Maison Sagne

Middlesex Hospital

All
Souls 🕂

Wigmore
Hall

Polytechnic

Place
ection

Selfridges ℹ

WC

Market ▪ **M M**
Market

Bond Street ⊖

St.
George 🕂

Italy ★

Marylebone
Regents Park
Attractions

★ EMBASSY OR GOV'T.	🕂	MEDICAL
H HOTEL	**X**	POLICE
▪ ATTRACTION	**P**	POST OFFICE
WC RESTROOM	**C**	CINEMA
RR RAILROAD STATION	**M**	MARKET
⊖ UNDERGROUND	🕂	CHURCH
⊖ HEATHROW AIRBUS	**T**	THEATER
ℹ INFORMATION	✡	SYNAGOGUE

0   1/8   1/4 Mi

0   125   250m

©FW 1995

Rolls' and Bentleys. *No. 50 Wimpole Street* was the scene of the world's second most famous elopement (after Romeo and Juliet's) much to Papa Barret's chagrin. And of course **Baker Street** is even today the place Holmes' footsteps can be heard heading for 221B, on a dark and foggy night. The Holmes' museum is really at *237 Baker*, but everyone charmingly plays the game and someone dressed up like his housekeeper conducts tours through the house (see "Museums," page 216). It's elementary that every mystery buff will be helpless to resist.

Madame Toussaud's in all its dripless glory, sits on the same sight as The London Planetarium, whose **Space Trail** exhibition and star extravaganza is the reason to drop in and get rid of all that waxy buildup.

Regent's Park was laid out by John Nash in 1811 to be 500 acres of pastoral beauty. He developed residential terraces lined with stucco and columns that give them the look of a huge wedding cake. The park has a canal that runs about eight miles and passes through the **Zoo**, giving you a ship-to-shore view of the animals(see "Top Sights," page 12). There is also an open-air theater in the park that performs Shakespeare in summer.

Agenda Shopping/Marylebone

Daunt

83 Marylebone High Street, ☎ *0171-224-2295*
Two floors of travel books with over 25,000 titles. Everything that pertains to travel has found a place in Daunt's index files.

Villandry

89 Marylebone High Street, ☎ *0171-487-3816*
Dear to every Francophile's heart, this "haute gourmet" gathering place has a full range of goodies à la Parisienne. Chocolates, breads flown in daily along with cheeses and pastries. They also have the best of London's comestibles. Sherlock gets all his pâté here.

Button Queen

19 Marylebone Lane, ☎ *0171-935-1505*
You'll not only button up your overcoat here, but this place has buttons for everything else you own, or intend to make. They have everything from plastic to Wedgewood buttons.

Agenda Best Bites/Marylebone

The Winter Garden

Regent Hotel, 222 Marylebone Road, ☎ *0171-631-8000. Credit cards. Moderate.*
An awe-inspiring space in the atrium of the new Regent Hotel (see "Hotels," page 39). This is not the main dining room, which is still

working out its opening kinks, but a unique setting for light snacks or tea. It's bound to become a top meeting spot in town.

Stephen Bull

5-7 Blandford Street, ☎ *0171-486-9696. Credit cards. VERY Expensive.*
The decor is smart and the food even smarter. For example, crabmeat and black beans wrapped in wontons, served in a tart coriander sauce, or neck of lamb with pasta. All very original and appealing. Try the goat cheese souffle, it's heaven!

The Muscadet

25 Paddington Street, ☎ *0171-935-2883. Credit cards. Moderate.*
A bistro with a blackboard! What could be more comforting. All the usual suspects appear—mussels, Dover sole, pâté, a terrine of the jour, and the homemade dessert sorbets are just right for the end.

Villandry Dining Room

89 Marylebone High Street, ☎ *0171-224-3799. Credit cards. Moderate.*
They're cheek to jowl here because it's the perfect "drop-in" place for lunch. The dining room is in the back of the Villandry gourmet shop, so the menu reflects what's just arrived out in front. Their salads and soups are very sophisticated and their desserts very decadent. Well, zey are French, No?!

Lemonia

89 Regent's Park Road, ☎ *0171-589-7454. Credit cards. Inexpensive.*
This place is the closest you'll ever come to having dinner with a Greek family you've never met before, in London. The staff welcomes everyone as if they've been waiting for you. Very good Greek home-style cooking. The taramasalata is pungent and creamy, and the tabbouleh is fragrant with mint. Anything with lamb is the way to go here.

Garbo's

42 Crawford Street, ☎ *0171-262-6582. Credit cards. Moderate.*
As long as you don't "vant-to-be-alone," stop by for their minismorgasbord at lunch, beloved by workers at the Swedish Embassy nearby. They make a "mean" meatball and great pea soup. Except for the people, Greta would have loved it!

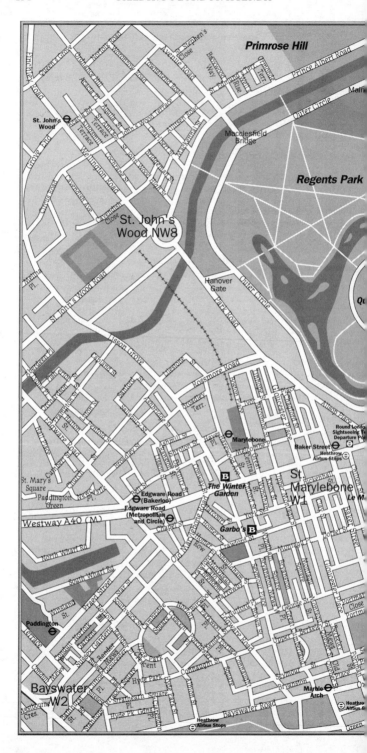

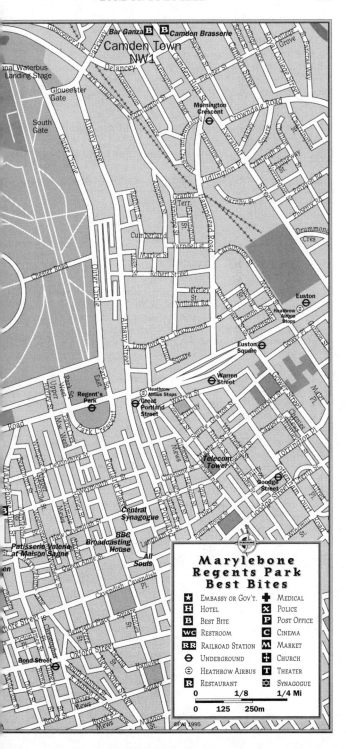

LONDON SHOPPING AGENDA

Egyptian Hall is one of Harrods' exciting gift emporiums.

The Best Around Town

London shopping is like being in love and never having to say you're sorry. You simply will not be able (or most of you) to resist the elegance of its boutiques, the "Stiff upper lips" of its department stores, and the treasures in its markets. However, that does not necessarily mean living the rest of your life as an impoverished, indentured servant. While it's true it won't take very long to spend a royal ransom in London's memorable West End luxury emporiums, notably those with Royal Warrants, you can also find wonderful bits of the past as well as imports from "The Empire" that will keep the memory of London alive whenever you look at them.

Most major sights and buildings usually have very good souvenir possibilities, so try to get the "kitsch" shopping out of the way to clear more time for the serious "conspicuous consumption" that makes any self-respecting shopaholic's heart beat faster. And since you're paying a pretty

Shilling just to *be* in London these days, it would seem to make sense to focus on goodies that the Brits are famous for. Unless it falls into the category of Antiques, try to save every red pence for China, Crystal, Woolens, or Cashmeres, Old English floral soaps and oils, or even a superior aged Cheddar or two. We think you should put the Danish Modern on hold for your next trip to Copenhagen.

The Romance of Royal Warrants

If you do find yourself mesmerized by the glamour of a Royal Warrant over a shopkeepers door, it's vital to understand that these royal stamps of approval are the choices of the royal family (and we know from recent events how some of those are working out), not necessarily yours. The Warrants are granted by the queen, the Queen Mother, the Duke of Edinburgh, and the Prince of Wales. To acquire a Warrant, the shop has to have been patronized by one of the above for at least three years. If you have all four Warrants (Harrods, Hatchards, The General Trading Company) you can pass go and collect 2 billion pounds!

We have listed some of our shopping favorites, both warranted and unwarranted that do not appear in the London "Locales" sections:

Antiques

As a dealer in Kensington once said, they're not making antiques like they used to.

Sotheby's Auction House
34 New Bond Street, ☎ ☎ *0171-493-8080.*

Christie's Auction House
55 Old Brompton Road, ☎ *0171-321-3321.*
These are the Auction Houses against which all others are measured. Today, they have branches throughout the world, but both houses started in London—Sotheby's in 1744, Christie's, a bit later in 1766. If you'd like to try your hand at some "big time" bidding, call ahead for upcoming sales so that you can play the auction game with the best of them.

Stanley Leslie
15 Beauchamp Place, ☎ *0171-589-2333.*
You'll have to cross his palm with quite a bit of silver before he crosses yours with some of his Georgian and Victorian sterling and plate. Very high quality in a great big selection.

Partridge Ltd.
144-46 New Bond Street, ☎ *0171-629-0834.*
Known for their splendid collection of 18th-century furniture and decorative antiques.

Grosvenor Prints
28-32 Shelton Street, Covent Garden, ☎ *0171-836-197.*
It would take weeks to go through their stupendous stock of over 100,000 antique prints. Botanicals, animals, florals, you name it, they have it.

Rachel Brand
21 Kensington Place, ☎ *0171-737-1151.*
This is the shop most dealers from the U.S. stop into for top notch examples of antique English furniture of very fine quality.

Lewis Kaplan Association.

50 Fulham Road, ☎ *0171-589-3108.*
30s magic is all over this place. Exquisite Daum art glass and deco furniture. Jewels by Cartier and Lalique as well.

John Bly

27 Burry Street, ☎ *0171-930-1292.*
No relation to the Captain (we think), but the Blys have been dealing in 18th-century furniture since 1888. John himself is a local celeb and BBC television star because of his "Antiques Road Show," which collectors watch faithfully.

Norman Adams

8-10 Hans Road, ☎ *0171-589-5266.*
The mirrors on his walls are the fairest mirrors of them all, along with barometers and chandeliers. The whole place reflects good taste.

Klaber and Klaber

2A Bedford Gardens, ☎ *0171-727-4573.*
One of the very best English porcelain shops in London. They also showcase small enamel boxes with charming motifs.

Books

London is a city of bookshops. True to it's legacy of producing some of the greatest writers the world has ever known, books form an important part of the average Londoner's life. Bookstore browsing here is one of the national sports.

A. Zwemmer

24 Litchfield Street, ☎ *0171-240-4158.*
Two floors of books devoted both to artists and the visual arts. The other Zwemmer in Charing Cross Road concentrates on photography.

Waterstone's

121-125 Charing Cross Road, ☎ *0171-434-4291.*
One of several branches that are very much a part of Literary London. There are book signings, readings by new authors and a generally relaxed atmosphere for thumbing through the stacks.

Bernard Quaritsch

5-8 Lower John Street, ☎ *0171-734-2983.*
So serious a book shop that each department is run by its very own director. The store goes back to the 1800s and has a splendid collection of antique volumes, in fact the largest in London. There are gorgeous medieval manuscripts.

Ulysses

40 Museum Street, ☎ *0171-831-1600.*
The specialty here is modern first editions, which are very fairly priced. They don't stand on ceremony either, since there's a sofa downstairs for a novel touch.

Sam Fogg

18 Old Bond Street, ☎ *0171-495-2333.*
They're known for their Renaissance illuminated manuscripts, which collectors find ever more illuminating today. They will also make your credit card cry for mercy.

BBC World

Bush House, Strand, ☎ *0171-257-2576.*

Scripts and other publications about programming for the radio buff.
There are also cassettes of favorite shows from the past. These make
terrific gifts.

China and Glass

Lawley's

154 Regent Street, ☎ *0171-734-2621.*
Almost the size of a small department store, with everything you'd
ever want to see in Wedgewood, Royal Doulton and Waterford crystal. And it's all very elegantly displayed.

Gered

173-174 Piccadilly, ☎ *0171-629-2614.*
Another temple dedicated to Wedgewood amongst other china darlings. They will ship anything, anywhere and they don't even mind
taking a personal check, although the conversion can be messy. Flash
your plastic instead.

Bridgewater

739 Fulham Road, ☎ *0171-371-9033.*
Emma Bridgewater has her own remarkable china that revives
Spongeware, very popular with the Victorians, and then uses it in
every conceivable size and shape. She will even personalize things on
special order.

Lalique Ltd.

162 New Bond Street, ☎ *0171-499-8228.*
If you keep seeing France in your crystal ball, then you'd better head
for Lalique, for a touch of glass.

Clothing

Fashion is flourishing everywhere in London. There's the "industrial"
chic of Bond Street, and the funk of Chelsea. There are those trendy little
shops in Knightsbridge and the pinstripes are drawn like lemmings to Savile
Row. The best news is, you never really know where you'll stumble upon a
new young Laura Ashley or Tommy Helfiger. Not to mention the designer
boutiques in London's extravagant department stores. So, ready, set, shop!

Berk

46 Burlington Arcade, Piccadilly, ☎ *0171-493-0028.*
Fine cashmere's in every color of the rainbow. You'll see all the top
brands but before you put your shillings on the line, be sure to look
at other places. The quest for cashmere is serious work.

Comme des Garçons

59 Brook Street, ☎ *0171-493-1258.*
Superb Japanese design for both the Samurai and the Samurette. The
designs are stark and elegant. You had better like the color black.

Hilditch & Key

37, 73 Jermyn Street, ☎ *0171-930-4707.*
They've made the finest men's shirts since 1899. The shop at 37
branched out into tailored clothes for women, at 73, up the street;
they do "bespoke" (to order) shirts in a wide variety of fabrics.

Laura Ashley

256-258 Regent Street, ☎ *0171-437-9760.*
She started right here in London and even though she built a worldwide empire, her trademark Victorian dresses look even more romantic here. They're perfect for someone's first prom dress.

Pandora

16-22 Cheval Place, ☎ *0171-589-5289.*
Very cloak and dagger, this place. It's really the "Second Hand Rose" of London, but these gently worn frocks come from secret addresses and the owners identities are closely guarded. Could one of the former owners be the P of W? Shhh.

Kilgour, French & Stanbury

8 Savile Row, ☎ *0171-734-6905.*
Savile Row, but this time for "her." They still do "bespoke" for men, but they turn out real cutting-edge tailoring for the ladies who *power* lunch.

The Duffer of St. George

27 D'Arblay Street, ☎ *0171-439-0996.*
Very "cool" casual clothes for the man who dances the night away in the clubs. They also have leather jackets and snooty T-shirts.

R.M. Williams

179-81 Regent Street, ☎ *0171-434-0061.*
If you're dying to look like a Crocodile Dundee groupie, you're in luck. Williams has a complete line of Dryzabone raincoats and mole-skin trousers that will get you a front seat in the outback.

Space NK

41 Earlham Street, ☎ *0171-379-7030.*
New, young designers in a "moderne" milieu. The fashions are very new and whatever is going on today, is going on first at NK.

Jewelry

When most people think about the jewelry scene in London, they envision baubles that Elizabeth I wore in her wig, or perhaps the royal tiaras that have industrial strength sparkle, in the Tower. But aside from the antique jewelry all over the city, there are wonderful contemporary designs as well. And if you feel like a diet rich in carats, head for Hattan Garden in Holborn. That's London's diamond district (see "The City," page 90).

Morra

22 New Bond Street, ☎ *0171-629-0160.*
There's a stylish mix here of contemporary and antique "trinkets," which go for a pretty price. Nouveau, deco and vintage Cartier ready to be worn to the ball.

Ermitage

14 Hay Hill, ☎ *0171-499-5459.*
Naturally, their collection of Faberge and antique Russian jewels would make any czarina weep with joy. They even have pieces that belonged to the Court of Nicholas. Bring lots of rubles.

Andre Bogaert

5 South Molton Street, ☎ *0171-493-4869.*
Designs for the 90s and beyond, in gold and silver. He also creates 18-carat pieces with an overlay of Vermeil, almost a lost art.

Fior

31 New Bond Street, ☎ *0171-493-0101.*
Their Royal Warrant comes far afield, from the prince of the Netherlands, who obviously adores their bejeweled bangles and beads. They have a glittering selection of costume pieces.

Boodle & Dunthorne

128-130 Regent Street, ☎ *0171-437-5050.*

For 200 years, they've been known affectionately as "Boodles." They have diamonds at a fair price, showcase new young designers and will hand-paint enamel pieces with your very own designs.

Food Shops

Harrods' poultry and game department is legendary.

Aside from London's famous department store food halls, the streets are filled with other gems for cheeses, cold meats and deep-dish meat pies. Do not leave without trying a wedge of aged Cheddar—cholesterol be damned!

AGENDA ADVICE—CHEESE-IT!

Stilton–king of British Cheeses, creamy mellow flavor with blue marbled holes.

Cheddar–white or yellow, tangy, sharp or mild, with a melting crumble.

Double Gloucester–deep in color, sweeter than Cheddar, mild.

Caerphilly–developed in Wales, matures faster than cheddar, with a mild, rich, full flavor.

Cheshire–looks like cheddar, but is much brighter, lighter, and falls into small flakes.

AGENDA ADAGE

DON'T BUY IT BEFORE YOU TRY IT!!

Partridges of Sloane Street

Sloane Street, ☎ *0171-730-0651.*
Great takeout from their extravagant selection of pâtés, terrines and hot and cold casseroles. They have tempting fresh bread and the pastries are picture-perfect. Just the place for picnic supplies.

Carluccio's

28 Neal Street, ☎ *0171-240-1487.*
Fresh baked focaccia is just the tip of the parmigiana here. Italian salamis, mortadellas and all the other gourmet fixings for a very classy hero. Just step inside and inhale.

Paxton & Whitfield

93 Jermyn Street, ☎ *0171-930-0259.*
The queen buys her cheeses here, and there are 250 different kinds from which she can choose.

Neal's Yard Dairy

17 Shorts Gardens, ☎ *0171-379-7646.*
They go directly to farms nearby so they can keep an eagle eye on the cheesemakers. Then they store it under optimum conditions, and you get the delicious results.

International Cheese Centre

21 Goodge Street, ☎ *0171-631-4191.*
Their selection is extraordinary, sometimes as many as 400 cheeses, mostly English farmhouse. You'll never get the "blues" here.

Jeroboam's

24 Bute Street, ☎ *0171-225-2232.*
Very elegant cheese shop in a very elegant neighborhood. Definitely as haut gourmet as you can get. They have cheeses from all over, but a fine selection from Britain and Ireland.

Food Halls at Harrods

(see page 147)

Food Hall on 5, Harvey Nichols

(see page 147)

Food Hall Fortnum & Mason

(see page 148)

Confections

Charbonnel et Walker

1 Royal Arcade, 18 Old Bond Street, ☎ *0171-491-0939.*
They may sound French, but they are as British as a "banger."
They've been sweetening the pot here since 1875. They're known for
their gorgeous gift-wraps and tempting treats inside.

Benedicks

7 Aldwych, Covent Garden, ☎ *0171-836-1846.*
Their most famous melt-in-the-mouth refreshment is hand-dipped
fancy chocolate mints.

Prestat

14 Prince's Arcade, Piccadilly, ☎ *0171-629-4838.*
We dare you not to try the brandy-soaked Marello cherries or their
truffles (chocolate) made from a recipe that goes back to pre-French
Revolution.

Rocco

321 Kings Road, ☎ *0171-352-5857.*
This place is a chocoholic's Waterloo, run by the foremost authority
on chocolate in London. When she's not writing books on the sweetest of subjects, Chantal Coady is dipping bars of Grand Crum from
the rarest of cocos. If you're a real grownup about your pursuit of the
sweet life, this is the place to come.

For the Home

In the land of stately homes, chintz and a rather large Victorian hangover, there are endless possibilities to Anglicize your abode.

The Conran Shop, Michelin House

81 Fulham Road.
(see page 111)

India Jane

140 Sloane Street
(see page 105)

The General Trading Company

144 Sloane Street
(see page 105)

Designers Guild

271 Kings Road
(see page 106)

Elizabeth David

3 North Row, Covent Gardens, ☎ *0171-836-9167.*
The world famous British chef and cooking teacher has her own shop
where her very favorite pots, pans, cutlery and baking equipment are
a treat for all the David wannabes.

Habitat

196 Tottenham Court Road.
This once was Sir Terence Conran's down-market version of his Conran Shop in Fulham Road. It's no longer part of the Conran empire,
but it still has very good home design and accessories at very good
prices.

Garrard & Co.

112, Regent Street, ☎ *0171-734-7020.*
Time goes by so quickly as you admire their handsome clock collection. Some were created by Britain's greatest clockmakers. They have longcase (grandfather) as well as mantle, table and wall varieties.

Nina Campbell

9 Walton Street, ☎ *0171-225-1011.*
Wonderful gifts and tabletop accessories by the interior designer who made the Capital Hotel so pretty. There's always something to squeeze into your carry-on here.

Ogetti

135 Fulham Road, ☎ *0171-581-8088.*
High tech, sleek Italian designs for the home. Everything is done with smashing minimalist flare and everything is totally individual.

Those Foolish Things

151 Queensway, ☎ *0171-792-1121.*
This shop is out of the loop, but their things are so charming we couldn't resist. They have handpainted animal doorstops, and tea cosies that celebrate *Alice in Wonderland.*

Pineider

16 Royal Arcade Bond Street, ☎ *0171-584-8328.*
Elegant Italian papers and stationery, just right for love poems.

Laura Ashley

256 Regent Street, ☎ *0171-437-9760.*
London is from whence she sprung and now you can buy her signature florals anywhere, but it's still such a treat to walk through her garden-like shop.

Les Olivades

7 Walton Street, ☎ *0171-409-2938.*
If you can't go on to Provence, this shop is the next best thing. They have luscious selections of Provencal print fabrics, table ware, curtains and all kinds of accessories, including dried flowers and scent.

Perfume, Soaps & Toiletries

Joe Malone

154 Walton Street, ☎ *0171-581-1101.*
The War of the Roses would never have been fought if they could have gotten a whiff of Red Roses, their fragrance that comes in oils, perfumes and sachet.

J. Floris

89 Jermyn Street, ☎ *0171-930-2885.*
Floris has been blending their scents in the same place since 1730. They specialize in a whole garden of florals, including honeysuckle. All the perfumes come in soaps, oils, sachet, powders and an antique cut glass bottle or two. The queen and the Prince of Wales both use Floris (hopefully, not the same scent).

Santa Maria Noella

117 Walton Street, ☎ *0171-584-8328.*
These soaps, colognes, creams and extracts were originally whipped up by Dominican friars in 1221. They are still prepared much the same way here and in their sister store in Florence.

Crabtree & Evelyn

30 James Street, ☎ *0171-379-0964.*
Even though their products are sold all over the world, you feel especially pampered as you cross their threshold. The soaps and bath products are guaranteed to soothe.

Penhaligon's

41 Wellington Street, ☎ *0171-836-2150.*
(see page 68)

Trumper's

9 Curzon Street, ☎ *0171-499-1850.*
(see page 53)

Toys and Games

Virgin Games Centre

100 Oxford Street, ☎ *0171-637-7911.*
Not at all what the name suggests! You can take kids here for a whole floor of computer and non-computer games and diversions.

Just Games

71 Brewer Street, ☎ *0171-734-6124.*
All your favorites with a good mix of what's new on the market.

Frog Hollow

15 Victoria Grove, ☎ *0171-581-5493.*
This is most certainly Miss Piggy's favorite shop in London. Aside from a huge collection of the tiny green darlings, they have lots of books, toys and games.

Absolute Balls

61 Broadwick, ☎ *0171-437-0985.*
This is not an exclamation! This is a witty and delightful setting to experience the wonderful world of juggling. The owner swears that aside from children adoring it, executives take juggling up as a stress-reduction hobby.

Benjamin Pollack's Toy Shop

44 The Market, Covent Gardens, ☎ *0171-379-7866.*
Charming, Victorian model theaters, antique dolls, puppets and a few very fine teddies to round out the stock. He has great things for the little ones at home (of course you remember them).

Hamley's

188-96 Regent Street, ☎ *0171-734-3161.*
(see page 53)

Early Learning Centre

225 Kensington High Street, ☎ *0171-937-0419.*
These are very fine learning tools for the younger child. The educational toys are appropriate for babies and children up to preteen. There's a great play area for tots.

The Kite Store

69 Neal Street, ☎ *0171-836-1666.*
All manner of kites in bright colors, ready-made or do-it-yourself. They come in wonderful shapes and sizes. If someone tells you to "go fly a kite," you'll know just where to start.

Arts and Crafts

London Brass Rubbing Centre

Street. Martin-in-the-Fields Church, ☎ *0171-437-6023.*

If you don't get to do a rubbing at Westminster Abby, you can come here where hobbyists work away making some great impressions.

Luxury Needlepoint

324 King Street, 0181-724-1314.
Tapestries to work on or to order ready-made. A full selection of supplies and accessories.

Green & Stone

259 Kings Road, ☎ 0171-352-0837.
For 60 years they've been selling everything for the artist, including Victorian easels and brushes.

Department Stores

Harrods

Brompton Road, Knightsbridge, ☎ 0171-730-1234.
If Harrods had been around during the reign of Elizabeth I, she wouldn't have been half as upset about her affair with Essex—she would have just coached over to the big H and gotten herself a new dress or a new bag, or a new hairdo (God, she needed one), or booked a trip around the Empire. Quite simply, this bastion of Victorian stability stands like a national monument on Brompton Road, attracting more tourists than Buckingham Palace. Harrods olive green and gold carrier bags (a.k.a., shopping bags), are all over the city, being sported by everyone from chimney sweeps, to the royals. Harrods is all things to all people.

If you haven't been to Harrods Food Halls, then you've left out one of the most important entries in your London agenda. The Halls are decorated with mosaic tiles and endless exquisite arrangements of smoked fish, pâtés, terrines, cheeses, meat and pastas. The Wine Shop is one of the best in London and they even have designer sandwiches to carry away. Some people never leave the Food Halls to explore the rest of Harrods; they are simply too transported by the gourmania spread out in front of them.

The rest of Harrods has over 4000 in staff to do everything from deliver your dog to their kennels, to get you a ticket to the hottest musical in town. The highlights to hit, as you wander through this exciting emporium, aside from the Food Halls, are the glamorous Perfume Hall, The Egyptian Hall, with just the right gifts for your Mummy, The Way In shop with "happening" clothes, and the small leathers department, which has historical significance for us since it was the sight of our first Filofax acquisitions. Talk about expanding your horizons.

This remarkable temple of glitz has a fabled sale every January that literally brings people from around the world. They mark down everything from socks to sables. It's the Olympics of shopping!

Harvey Nichols

109-125 Knightsbridge, ☎ 0171-235-5000.
Everything that Harrods isn't, Harvey Nichols is. They're younger, more innovative, more 90s than Harrods would wish to be. They both stand on Brompton Road, one a regal reminder of the past, the other with a foot firmly planted in the 21st century. The two stores

cater to completely different markets so they coexist happily as the two most important department stores in London today.

Harvey Nix, as it's referred to by the "now" generation, is devoted to designer labels and top-of-the-market chic for both sexes. They also have exotic imports in their home furnishing department, which is one of the most creative in the city. The only area in which H.N. and Harrods overlap is food. The new Food Halls at H.N. are gorgeous, with ravishing displays of fresh fruits and veggies. The entire fifth floor has been devoted to the appreciation of gastronomy, including their "hot" restaurant, The Fifth Floor at Harvey Nichols (see "Restaurants," page 112).

Liberty

210-220 Regent Street, ☎ *0171-734-1234.*

Of all the department stores in London, Liberty is the most romantic. It's been in business since 1875, when they started to sell the distinctive fabrics that would become world famous. The design of the store itself makes it impossible to pass by. It stands in Tudor-style splendor on Regent Street, just waiting to be explored, as well as experienced. On the inside it is beamed and paneled in oak with heroic staircases and stained glass. The charm of Liberty is that it's arranged in no particular order, as if trunks of exotic merchandise had just come off clipper ships and been unpacked all over the store. There is no way to resist the desire to carry away something made from one of those enchanting Liberty prints. They make that very easy to accomplish since all kinds of gift items are made from the prints, as well as shirts, ties, dresses and fabric by the yard. Liberty is decidedly one of a kind.

Selfridge's

400 Oxford Street, ☎ *0171-495-8321.*

Selfridge's is to London what Macy's is to New York. It doesn't have the chic of Harrods, and it doesn't have the romance of Liberty. It's a no-nonsense resource for a wide range of middle-market goods. Not to say that Selfridge's isn't as much of an institution in London, it's just a department store with less of a personal imprimatur. It has a huge stock of everything and even does key making, shoe repair and dry-cleaning. It's definitely one-stop-shopping in comfortable style.

Marks & Spencer

458 Oxford Street, ☎ *0171-935-7954.*

There's always a bargain at "Marks and Sparks" as it's known to the regulars. The chain is synonymous with sensible cashmeres and woolens at sensible prices. This is not a place that's known to be in the forefront of fashion, but it's comfortable, cheerful and often crowded with sales addicts.

Fortnum & Mason

181 Piccadilly, ☎ *0171-734-8040.*

Fortnum's is an institution with the royal family, as well as everyone else in London. It sparkles with crystal chandeliers and salesmen in tailcoat, helping you choose your marmalade. They are most famous for their grocery department, which delivers to the palace, but most every traveler overlooks the fact that Fortnum's is a "real" department store, with all kinds of elegant merchandise upstairs. Their lingerie collections is particularly luxurious. In general the selection of goods you'll see is old-money conservative, so don't bother to ask if they do navel piercing.

Museum Shops

Before museum shops came along, museums were places to visit, enjoy, but resist the impulse to touch. The museums themselves finally understood what a wonderful bonus it would be for the visitor to take a bit of the museum home (if only a reproduction) Voila!—the museum shop was born.

In British museum shops, the quality of the merchandise is particularly high, sometimes having to be evaluated by crafts councils or the boards of governing directors. In any case, we have always found museum shopping both a wonderful resource for gifts, as well as the perfect alternative to the "overkill" of the department stores. Most of the Museum shops that are listed can be contacted before you arrive, if you'd like a copy of their catalogues.

British Museum
> *Great Russell Street, WC1,* ☎ *0171-636-1555.*

Design Museum
> *Shad Thames, Butler's Wharf, SE1,* ☎ *0171-403-6933.*

London Transport Museum
> *Covent Gardens, WC2,* ☎ *0171-379-6344.*

Museum of London
> *150 London Wall EC2,* ☎ *0171-600-3699.*

Museum of Mankind
> *6 Burlington Gdns, W1,* ☎ *0171-437-2224.*

Museum of the Moving Image
> *South Bank SE1,* ☎ *0171-401-2636.*

Natural History Museum
> *Cromwell Road, SW7,* ☎ *0171-938-9123.*

Science Museum
> *Exhibition Road, SW7,* ☎ *0171-938-8008.*

Theatre Museum
> *Russell Street, Covent Gardens, WC2,* ☎ *0171-836-7891.*

National Gallery
> *Trafalgar Sq, WC2,* ☎ *0171-839-3526.*

National Portrait Gallery
> *2 Street. Martin's Place, WC2,* ☎ *0171-306-0055.*

Royal Academy of Arts
> *Burlington House, Piccadilly,* ☎ *0171-439-7438.*

Tate Gallery
> *Millbank, SW1,* ☎ *0171-887-8000.*

Victoria and Albert Museum
> *Cromwell Road, SW7,* ☎ *0171-938-8500.*

The Markets

Shop till you drop, but this time it's the thrill of the hunt that makes the markets more of a sport than a shopping experience. Visitors and Londoners alike crowd the markets looking for old dreams, new dreams and some-times, nightmares.

Portobello Road Market

Portobello Road, ☎ *0171-371-6960. Sat., 6 a.m.–5 p.m.*
This one is the most famous of all the London antiques markets. It's part carnival, part flea market and of course a showcase for some of the best antique dealers in the city. There are outside stalls, inside stalls, as confining as rabbit warrens, and endless arcades. Some deal-ers even sell from the backs of their trucks. For shoppers who dote on collectibles, it's a dream come true as well as a perfect way to spend a Saturday. The prices can spiral from a pound or two, into the strato-sphere. Bargaining is certainly the order of the day and most dealers are great fun to fight with. If you need a 20th-century coffee break after picking through the past, stop in at the **Oporto Patisserie**, *62 Coldborne Road,* for their terrific Portuguese fish cakes.

Bermondsey Market

(New Caledonia), Long Lane and Bermondsey Street, Fri., 5 a.m.–2 p.m.
What better could you do on a drizzly Friday morning at 5 a.m. but head for Bermondsey. There are more dealers here than you can pos-sibly deal with, but oh, what fun to try. This is a much more serious market than Portobello. There are no street signs, no festival feeling, no "quaint" atmosphere. Dealers come at dawn, before the sun is up, with flashlights to pick over the offerings that come from anywhere (with or without the consent of their former owners). The quality of the collectibles varies from stall to stall, but sometimes there are real "finds" for a song. Bermondsey is known for its Victorian jewelry and silver. It stretches out forever and when the outdoor dealers pack up, there is a whole other indoor market that goes on till much later in the day.

HIDDEN AGENDA

There is a little truck that serves steaming hot tea and deep fried bacon sandwiches made with fresh bread, in the damp, early morning chill. Forget breakfast at Claridges. This is the one you'll never forget!

Camden Passage

Upper Street, Angel, Islington, Wed., 10 a.m.–2 p.m.; Thurs.—books only; Sat, 10 a.m.–5 p.m.
This rather expensive, albeit fascinating market is held in the winding streets of the "Passage" off Upper Street. There are over 350 dealers who have fine antique jewelry and top quality collectibles. The stalls are all around the little pedestrian mall and flow into Angel Arcade, where there are another 20 or so shops selling silver and fine china. Take your time and explore Upper Street (see "Islington," page 95). There are good pubs for lunch, or a quick one before you return to the fray.

Gray's Antiques Market

58 Davies Street, ☎ *0171-629-7034, Mon.–Sat.*
Since Gray's is just off Bond Street and a scone's throw from Clar-idge's, you'd expect it to be expensive—and it is. However, you will

probably be seeing the *crème de la crème* of London's dealers. These antiques are not just limited to the decorative arts of the 18th and 19th century; we're talking ceramics which might date back a thousand years. There is also jewelry with astonishing price tags.

Alfie's

13-25 Church Street, ☎ *0171-723-6066, Mon.–Sat.*
Alfie's is hot right now. All the dealers check it out, even before going to Bermondsey or Portobello. We fell in love with it at first sight. It's housed in a rambling, comfortable building that used to be an old department store. The 200 dealers are upstairs, in hallways, basements and attics, in no apparent order. They sell just about everything from furniture to advertising art (we couldn't resist a Lyons Tea sign). This is the perfect market to burrow into.

Antiquarius

131-141 Kings Road, ☎ *0171-675-6155, Mon.–Sat.*
This market captures the spirit of Chelsea by being all things to all "cool" people. They have the latest trends in collectibles, such as antique leather suitcases, and deco fountain pens. About 120 dealers.

Chelsea Antique Market

253 Kings Road, ☎ *0171-675-6155, Mon.–Sat.*
Don't take the antique part too seriously. This is much more flea market than its "tony" cousin next door. They have movie memorabilia, theatre programs and assorted kitsch.

Camden Lock

Chalk Farm Road, Camden Town, Sat.–Sun.
Wall-to-wall kids grooving their way around this outrageous market that sells new, second hand, antiques and craft oddments. The stalls are arranged haphazardly near the canal at the lock, and up and down Chalk Farm Road. To say this whole area "swings," is definitely a conservative assessment. Chances are you won't find too much to buy unless you're about 14, but it's great to mix and mingle!

Greenwich Antiques Market

Greenwich High Road, Sat. & Sun.
This is a rather "tame" market that has crafts and a smattering of antiques. The best thing about it is, the prices are usually right. (See "Excursions," page 209).

RESTAURANTS

Whether you're craving fish 'n' chips, tea and scones or bangers and ale, London has a restaurant for you.

From soup to nuts, from fish to chips, the restaurants in London today have never been better. They are more stylish, more adventuresome and more energetic than they've been in years. The city that brought you Carnaby Street, Twiggy, Shakespeare, Mick Jagger and thousands of other mind-altering experiences, has now switched on restaurants to make them the latest trend to sweep the town. The very same London that shocked the world by swinging into the sixties is cooking up a storm in the 90s.

If truth be told we have always eaten well in London. The throwbacks all over town who had been serving roast beef that needed a social security card were replaced by young chefs from Paris who cautiously crossed the border years ago to plant the first seeds of "nouvellism." They grew as fast as Jack's beanstalk and today have evolved a more chauvinistic cuisine called "Modern British." It is the renaissance of traditional British food but its been given a new rustic spin. And it borrows from all over: California, Asia, France and even our very "hot" southwest.

And so the moral of the story is that not only can you eat well in London, you can eat brilliantly. We have profiled the restaurants that we regard as quintessential London. They are synonymous with the pulse of the city as well as the personality. By no means are these the only restaurants in London that serve good food. We are, however, drawing upon our years of experience writing about restaurants and chefs to choose the ones that to us, most represent the flavor of London.

In addition to the restaurants featured, we have also listed places to eat in each of the London locales in the book.

Prices

Dining out in London today is super-expensive, even for a lowly plate of fish and chips. The dollar against the pound isn't helping either, but there are a couple of strategies to ease the pain of the $80-$100 dinner, which is all too often the case. If you are able to have lunch instead of dinner at some of the most extravagant choices, you will barely need resuscitation when the check comes. There are usually set price luncheons, but this is rarely the case at dinner. Also there is the option of two courses instead of three which will shed pounds even faster. If all else fails, have a glass of wine and an entree; they will think you're more sophisticated and mysterious than a Romanoff.

Credit Cards

Unless otherwise noted, all restaurants profiled accept a variety of credit cards. Do not expect coffee shops or small ethnic restaurants to take cards, although in London almost everyone does. Just be sure to check.

Alastair Little

49 Frith Street
☎ *0171-734-5183 Credit cards. Expensive.*
If this were a restaurant in Tokyo, it would be easier to fathom the decor. Severe enough to make a hospital room seem cluttered and personal, it nonetheless is where some of the most original food in London is being served. No matter that you have to eat it under neon tubes, in a store front in Soho.

Alastair Little, who sounds like a character in a Dickens novel, certainly cooks to a different drummer. He's been dumped into that very ubiquitous category "British Modern" cooking but he's really an original. His menu is highly personal, changes daily and it would appear Chef Little has a really big appetite for adventure. He spans the globe taking a bit of Italy, a pinch of France, a couple of teaspoons of Hungary, to produce his very own signature cuisine. It's always surprising.

Bouillabaisse is often on the menu with the sweetest shellfish and the hottest rouille, the fish stock as rich as the bank of England. There's a carpaccio of panacetta (Italian bacon), grilled artichokes and truffles! Oysters come with hot spicy sausages and a shallot relish. A dish worthy of a firecracker display is crisp potato pancakes with smoked eel,

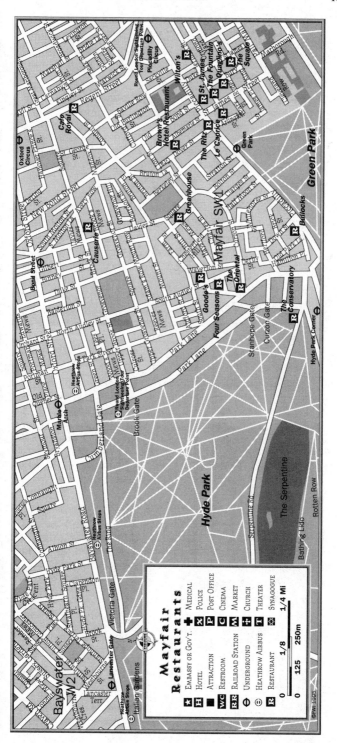

or bright golden caviar and creme fraiche. Then on to pigeon braised with winter vegetables or chicken stuffed with truffles and leeks.

To end brilliantly, sponge cake with raspberries, and figs nestled in a velvet mascarpone. It's *not* a case of too Little too late; he's right in the nick of time.

Bibendum

Michelin House
81 Fulham Road
☎ *0171-581-5817 Credit cards. Very expensive.*

After eating at Bibendum it's easy to see why the Michelin Man is the chubby darling we've grown to love. Not only is the restaurant named for him, but the extraordinary things that come out from the kitchen would make "The Thin Man" bulk-up. Bibendum is the hottest place in London right now. It's one of Sir Terence Conran's high profile watering holes with the chef of the moment, Simon Hopkinson, charting its course. There is hardly time to put fork to mouth as you survey this trendiest of scenes.

Michelin House, once owned by the tire empire, was rescued from the wrecker's ball by Sir Terence and restored to its art deco glamour. There is a collection of striking cartoons on the walls and subdued lighting that lets you sit back and celebrity-watch. The night we were there Liam Neesan and Natasha Richardson looked like they were having the most delicious time. So were we.

The Lobster tart was richer than Sir Terence, with a crumbly,buttery crust. Atop was a perfectly deep-fried lobster claw. Chicken was roasted to produce a lacquer crisp skin and a mellow caramel colored gravy that clung to its accompanying morels like a mink coat. Another of Hopkinson's triumphs was a plate of mussels served in the Thai manner, with coriander, lime juice and chilies. The specialty that brings a tear to the eye is hare soup. Not too many tortoises make reservations here. On the first floor of the building, Bibendum has an Oyster Bar, which is the perfect spot for a little casual pearl hunting. Inexpensive enough not to produce shell-shock.

Blue Elephant

4-6 Fulham Broadway
☎ *0171-385-6595 Credit cards. Expensive.*

Not since Anna got her first look at Siam has there been such a collection of exotic Oriental "kitsch" seen. A real Thai dyed in the wool place. There are bridges that span tiny artificial brooks, palm trees, stilt dwellings that enclose the tables' tropical gardens, a staff in native dress and enough sensory overload to make you see *pink* elephants.

There are other fine Thai restaurants in London but this one is not only delicious, it's too much fun not to visit. The Blue Elephant is a bit of a safari from Mayfair and Knightsbridge, but it's just the right kind of excuse to try out your overview of the underground. Fulham Broadway is just a couple of stops past South Kensington, so it's really not all that remote. By the time you arrive, you'll be ready to tuck into Bangkok street dumplings, fire breathing meat, fish stews and spicy grills. There's also the Royal Banquet Menu for which you'll have to match appetites with the Blue Elephant himself. And speaking of that

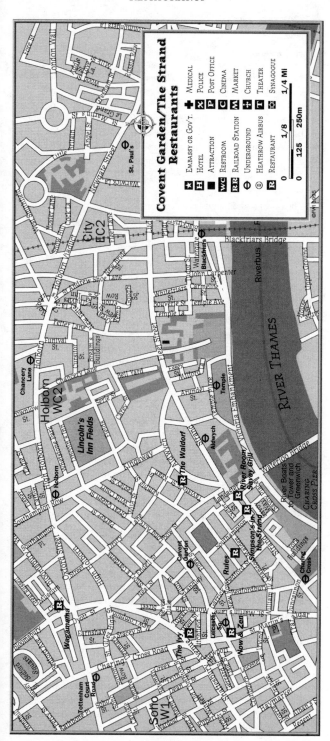

peripatetic pachyderm, after eating here we can't imagine why he's blue.

Bombay Brasserie

Courtfield Road
☎ *0171-370-4040 Credit cards. Expensive.*

One of the most beautiful restaurants in London, the Bombay Brasserie has, since it opened its doors, served a whole panorama of Indian regional food in a breathtaking setting. It has been around for more than a dozen years, but going there for dinner is still an occasion that it's fascinating menu always seems to rise to. The very Victorian Raj atmosphere is highlighted by flickering oil lamps, bamboo furniture, ceiling fans and a glassed-in conservatory for the most romantic of experiences.

The riches of the Moguls is reflected in the incendiary fish stews from Goa, and the special curries from Kashmir. The samosas are the way to begin and the breads are spectacular. Even if you order extravagantly, it's cheaper than a ticket to Bombay.

If the evening hours don't curry favor with you, there is a buffet offered at lunch that would tempt even Ghandi.

Le Caprice

Arlington Street
☎ *0171-629-2239 Credit cards. Expensive.*

Upper class London has had a love affair with Le Caprice ever since it opened. It has all the elements that the "upstairs" crowd covet these days. It's slick, chic, black and white with photographs by David Bailey gracing the walls. It's owned by the same people who have made the Ivy such a smashing success and Le Caprice follows their lead in attracting celebs by the roomful. The Princess of Wales grazes here as does Harold Pinter and a bevy of fashion playthings (Kate Moss was seen almost eating here). The surprise at this glossy example of 90s edge is the menu, which is filled with comfort food from top to bottom. The guests may be "haute" but the cuisine is definitely not! Sausages and mash, eggs Benedict, salmon fish cakes, pastas and creamy risottos, a great steak tartare, and the ever-present grilled tuna for calorie crunchers. Desserts are nursery school goodies such as bread pudding and trifle, but for a wacky spin on trendy sophistication, try the banana ice cream swimming in maple syrup.

Chuney Mary's

535 Kings Road
☎ *0171-351-3113 Credit cards. Moderate.*

To understand the food served here, it is essential to understand that Chuney Mary was a rather mean-spirited term used by chauvinistic Indians to describe a woman who was too fond of western ways. Perhaps to replace the bad taste left by a label of that nature, the owners of Chuney Mary's decided to make their restaurant a stronghold of Anglo-Indian cuisine and dedicated themselves to only delicious delicacies for today's maharajahs.

The setting is wicker and palms with a small conservatory, but again, the English influence gives it the look of a spread from Indian *House Beautiful*. A huge menu is filled with crossover oddities such as Bangalore Bangers and Mash, or a Chicken Country Captain, right out of

a seaside boarding house. But then there are brilliant regional specialties and recipes from the royal palaces to add a little spice to the overwhelming number of choices. Crab cakes from Goa and five-alarm
Madras Prawns, or salmon, done as a traditional Kedgeree, are all
exciting choices for fish fanciers, as are potatoes and chick peas
mashed with yogurt, vegetable dumplings or stewed okra, the best
possible passage to India for the veggie set. True to their Anglo-
Indian heritage, management tries to encourage you to order western
style and have one or two courses. Resist them!

Clarke's

124 Kensington Church Street
☎ *0171-221-9225 Credit cards. Moderate.*
This is California transported to Kensington. Chef Sally Clarke is
clearly an eager disciple of Alice Waters, in Berkley. They both respect
the purity and simplicity of the elements they work with and both
produce a flawless, original cuisine. Even more importantly, if it's not
super-terrific at the market, it never makes it to the menu. In Sally
Clarke's case, she takes the market cuisine concept one step further
and offers a no-choice menu. Whatever Sally wants, Sally cooks. If you
can't live with a loss of menu-independence, you may not be a happy
camper here. But if you leave the driving to Sally, you'll wind up with
a memorable dining experience. She posts her menu's once a week
outside the restaurant just to give everyone a sporting chance to can-
cel before being confronted with their most dreaded food phobia.

All of this high powered creativity takes place in a large basement
room full of fresh flowers and the aroma of olive oil. The kitchen is
open so you can keep an eye on Sally while she keeps an eye on your
dinner. Her watchfulness results in perfect salads, pastas served in the
most delicate of mushroom broth and a cascade of shaved truffles.
Grilled meat or duck comes pastel pink in the center, but seared outside, and with the thinnest of potato crisps. Clarke is a master of flavored oils, chutneys and relishes. She also makes her own buttery
breads and rolls. Her haute may be California, but her dessert mentality is triple British. Dense, wicked, hazelnut chocolate cake, fruit tarts
with cheeses made from fruits as well, and Clarke's own version of
zabaglione. Chocolate truffles are served with coffee, just to complete
the decadence.

The Fifth Floor Restaurant

Harvey Nichols, SW1
☎ *0171-235-5250. Credit cards. Moderate.*
Shop till you drop, but when you drop, do it at the Fifth Floor Restaurant atop Harvey Nichols. The amazing thing about the "F.F.R."
is that it resides inside a department store in Knightsbridge and since
it serves world-class cuisine, this has to be a first. Even in Paris, they
keep their temples of gastronomy separate and apart from anything as
crass as shopping bags and try-on-rooms. The restaurant is part of a
market fantasy that takes up the whole 5th floor. The delicious intent
is to give Harrods' famous Food Halls a run for its pounds.

The high-tech design of the "F.F.R." is witty and very modern with
sky-blue velvet barrel chairs, flashes of chrome and elegantly dressed
tables to let you know in advance that what's being served deserves

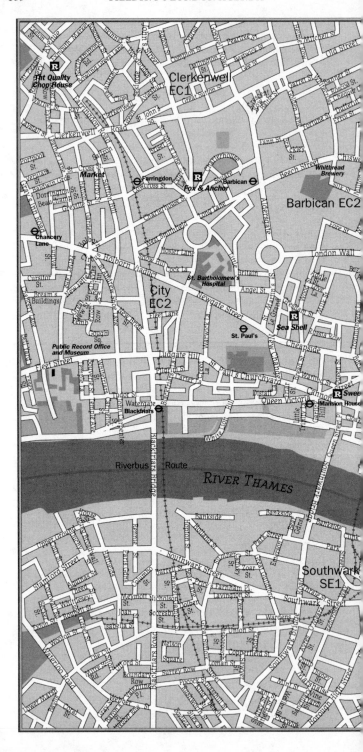

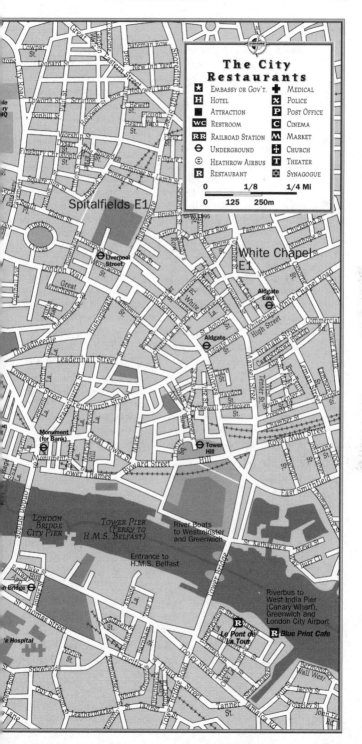

The City Restaurants

⊠	EMBASSY OR GOV'T.	✚	MEDICAL
H	HOTEL	X	POLICE
■	ATTRACTION	P	POST OFFICE
WC	RESTROOM	C	CINEMA
RR	RAILROAD STATION	M	MARKET
⊖	UNDERGROUND	✝	CHURCH
⊜	HEATHROW AIRBUS	T	THEATER
R	RESTAURANT	✡	SYNAGOGUE

0   1/8   1/4 Mi

0   125   250m

Spitalfields E1

White Chapels E1

⊖ Liverpool Street

Aldgate East

⊖ Aldgate

Monument (for Bank)

⊖ Tower Hill

LONDON BRIDGE CITY PIER

TOWER PIER (FERRY TO H.M.S. BELFAST)

River Boats to Westminster and Greenwich

Entrance to H.M.S. Belfast

Riverbus to West India Pier (Canary Wharf), Greenwich and London City Airport

R Le Pont de la Tour

R Blue Print Cafe

's Hospital

the proper setting. So do the people who are singlemindedly cleaning their plates of wonton wrapped prawns punctuated with chili jam, chicken stuffed with gruyere and then tucking into slices of bayonne ham. If you think there's something fishy you're right! Cod is covered with a parsley crust and then sauteed with leeks and cream. French Fries (chips as in fish and…) are slathered in a garlic mayonnaise. All this could lead to a sticky toffee pudding with caramel sauce, or it could lead to avoidance of the fitting rooms after lunch.

The Greenhouse

27A Hay's Mews, W1
☎ *0171-499-3331. Credit Cards. Expensive.*
A bit of the countryside right in Mayfair. The Greenhouse is really an offspring of the dedicated family that runs the wonderful Capitol Hotel and dining room. It's hidden away in a peaceful mews right down the street from the Dorchester. Once inside, it's an oasis of green and floral displays, topiary sculptures and dramatic oil paintings of food on the walls. It is in this bucolic atmosphere that Chef Gary Rhodes is practicing the art of British traditional cooking, while bringing it up to 90s speed with great retro style. He is a traditionalist of the best kind and has resurrected with his own brilliant spin, forgotten favorites such as oxtail stew, homemade black pudding, faggots (just keep reading), which are pigs entrails wrapped in caul fat, mackerel fishcakes and steamed lemon sponge. Perhaps all this is far afield to Yankees searching for a good B.L.T., but the rest of the menu is made up of succulent roasts, fish and some of the most tempting desserts in the city. The steamed jam sponge with custard is ethereal. Sunday Brunch here is an event because all the macaroni and cheese addicts converge to sate themselves before they order the traditional Sunday roast. Since Chef Rhodes is rumored to be hankering for his very own time machine to continue his exploration of culinary times past, you'd better reach for the phone now.

Grill St. Quentin

3 Yeoman's Row
☎ *0171-581-8377. Credit cards. Expensive.*
Location, location, location! What a serendipitous find right in the middle of London's most "happening" nabe. A good brasserie in itself is enough to hoist the flag, but one where you can park your shopping bags after a hard day at Harrods or Harvey Nichols, not to mention the Victoria & Albert museum, which is just a Marron's throw away, is really an important event. This is meant to be London's answer to Paris's La Coupole, which makes it even more fun. The tables are usually filled with Brits chowing down on a huge selection of oysters, a terrific choucroute and plates heaped with Toulouse sausages as dapper young waiters whiz by.

Hugh O'Neill, who also owns Brasserie St. Quentin on Brompton Road, and Les Specialties St. Quentin, is either obsessed with prisons or knows a lot about bistro food. Actually, the "Quentin" he's referring to is not a saint, but the noted British food critic (God help him) Quentin Crewe. O'Neill has infused the Grill with style, wit and a relaxed informality, absolutely *de rigeur* for a genuine brasserie. Almost all of the usual brasserie suspects show up on the attractive

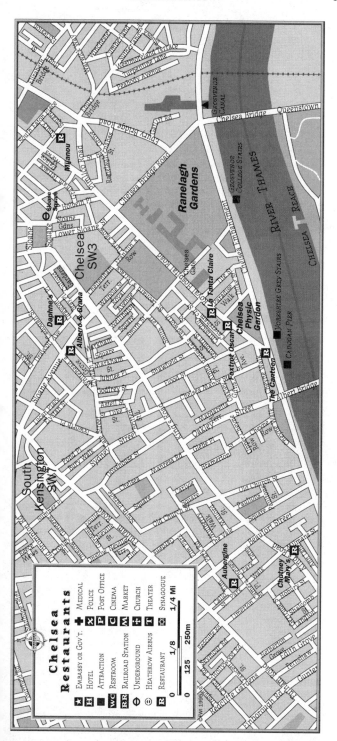

carte du jour: terrine de campagne, steak tartare, smoked herring and a spicy roulade of duck. Entrecote with crunchy fries is definitely the way to go if you don't want to take the "chunnel" to Paris.

The Ivy

1 West Street
☎ *0171-836-4751. Moderate.*
The British Sardi's, with a bit of the Tate gallery thrown in for good measure, this very theater-conscious restaurant is famous for serving thirsty thespians and hungry Hamlets since 1911. There are so many familiar faces in this crowd, it's fun just to have dinner on the off-chance that Maggie Smith might drop by. Even if she doesn't, there are enough splendid examples of contemporary art on the walls to keep you busy until dessert. Some say the ghost of Noel Coward still haunts the place. He'd better make a reservation, the place is always packed.

The Ivy, just off Covent Garden, is all wood paneling, leather banquets and stained glass. Since it's open until midnight, it's the perfect place to go before of after the theater. The menu runs the gamut from bubble and squeak to steak tartare. The traditional English "soul food" seems to fit the clubbiness of the place better than some of their L.A.-influenced transgressions like grilled chicken salad. We'd advise you to go for the gold on the menu such as crunchy fish cakes, a really succulent version of bangers and mash drizzled with a mahogany shallot gravy, or, if you've left your flock back home, the shephard's pie will comfort you. The desserts are pure nursery, with treacle tart, and a custard bread pudding heading the terrific list. The combination of the atmosphere, the food and the very British *joie de vivre* makes the Ivy the kind of place you come back to again and again.

Julie's

135 Portland Road
☎ *0171-229-8331. Credit cards. Moderate.*
When Alice went down the rabbit hole, she would have felt much more at home if she'd tumbled into a rabbit-warren of tiny exotic rooms called Julie's. Wonderland with food is the closest one can come to describing the romantic fantasy of this absolutely unique restaurant in the very upscale Holland Park area of London. Each space has a different name such as The Gothic Room, with cathedral furnishings, the Wedding Room, white and frothy with mirrors draped in ribbons and flowers, and the conservatory with an arched atrium ceiling, wicker furniture and palms to set it all off. Then there is the wine bar with a hint of Morocco. These people definitely do not worship at the feet of the God of "minimal." With all of this drama and romance, there is also food, although sometimes it almost seems an afterthought since it can only take a back seat to restaurant as theater. That said, the food is always done with flair and often great panache. We started with a velvety aubergine (eggplant) mousse, wrapped in spinach, drizzled with a walnut dressing. Then on to perfectly cooked calves' liver with a bright red pepper marmalade and polenta. The rum praline meringue was a show-stopper and that's hard to do at Julie's. Even if you don't go for dinner, at least drop into the wine bar just to feast your eyes.

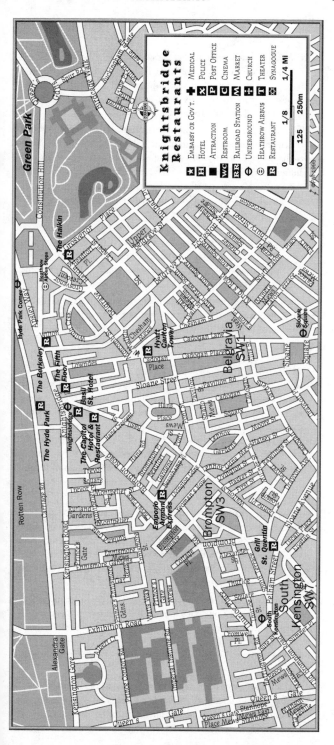

Kensington Place

201-205 Kensington Church St.
☎ *0171-727-3184. Credit cards. Expensive.*

If you like a quiet, calm, reserved atmosphere with your dinner, this is not the place for you, however if you like buzz, laughter, lots of silverware clatter and most of all, innovative, unique food, this is most definitely the place to be. Lots of other people seem to agree because Kensington Place is always packed.

The room is very high-tech with metal chairs, glass, wood and a modern mural running the length of one wall. All of this is very contrary to the neighborhood, which is filled with some of the most expensive antique stores in London. The chef, Rowley Leigh, one of the stars of the British Modern persuasion, has carried out the free-wheeling decor with an even more unconventional approach to "what's for dinner?" The answer is, somewhere between grilled foie gras reclining on a sweet corn pancake, to breast of pheasant with sausage, cabbage and bacon, or sole fillets with noodles and lobster sauce. Another dynamite way to go is the chicken and goat cheese mousse. The menu is filled with surprises such as baked tamatillos (who'd have guessed they had ever heard of a tomatillo in London) with vanilla ice cream.

There's a cross-section of the greats and the near-greats at KP—that's what the "in" crowd calls it—and they all seem to agree: the din is a small price to pay for the dinner.

La Tante Claire

68 Royal Hospital Road
☎ *0171-352-6045. Credit cards. Very expensive.*

If you're one of those people with Michelin stars in your eyes, Tante Claire has three to its credit. Pierre Koffman, the most renowned chef in London since Escoffier, has certainly worked his assiette canardierre off (duck four ways) to get them, too. For years and years, Tante Claire in Chelsea has been the classic French restaurant all others in the city were measured against, and most of them came up short. We are usually loathe to recommend a French "tummy temple" as one of our most quintessential London dining experiences, but Tante Claire simply cannot be ignored.

Now, back to grim reality. Three stars do not make for "budget best" dining. The prices here are astronomical, but pound for pound, Tante Claire rarely disappoints. Chef Koffman is of the old "delicious despot" school so the staff has never even breathed the phrase "laid back." Lunch might be the way to go here since it's a set price and there's no fear of putting the à la carte before the horse.

Koffman's signature dish sounds like an April fool's prank but it is truly brilliant: take one pig's foot, stuff it with foie gras and morels, serve it with a buttery pea puree, then just sit back and inhale. This is not what they ate at Versailles, this if French soul food. It was probably the fact that the peasants had a shortage of pigs feet that started the revolution.

If you're allergic to P.F. you could try the saddle of rabbit with lentils or the pigeon stuffed with truffles and cabbage. If you're still fishing for something else, try the caramelized scallops or the ragout of langoustines. Desserts are classical (tiramisu is never mentioned here), and the apple tarts are the pastries Tante Claire is famous for. A "nutty" alternative is the pistachio mousse served with ice cream to match.

All of this very serious food is served in a surprisingly casual atmosphere. There isn't an inch of red velvet anywhere. Instead, sunny colors and blond woods to bring you back to the countryside. Since you can't eat stars, it is reassuring to know that Tante Claire's cuisine shines all by itself.

Leith's

92 Kensington Park Road
☎ *0171-229-4481. Credit cards. Expensive.*
Prue Leith, of British cooking school fame, has for years, practiced what she preached at her very own restaurant in Notting Hill. Many of the vegetables and herbs that grace her unique menu come from her own farm, so Leith's is a vegan's paradise. But it's also an elegant, chic background for discerning carnivores as well. Head Chef, Alex Floyd, who developed the menu together with Prue, is only a year or two older than the restaurant, but he cooks with the wisdom of a sage as well as an oregano and thyme. The restaurant has a very minimalist attitude with some smashing art on the walls and tables dressed with sophistication. Leith's has style with a capitol *S*.

The hors d'oeuvres trolley is famous for it's extravagant selection of first courses, such as tiny pastries stuffed with goat cheese, crab salad, fois gras with pine nuts, and wild mushrooms à la grecque. If you can't bear to stop, make it your whole dinner; just add pudding and coffee. Or, if you're like us and never met an entree you didn't like, you can press on with pan fried sea bass lolling against a gallate of zucchini, or pale pink lamb with a crisp mustard herb crusting. If you'd rather have a birds-eye view, there's a roast pigeon, covered in crackling phyllo and coupled with braised cabbage.

"Modern British" gives way to sinful pleasure with a chocolate and chestnut souffle crowned with white chocolate ice cream.

The Pont de La Tour

36 Shad Thames
☎ *0171-403-8403. Credit cards. Very expensive.*
Butler's Wharf is right across the Tower Bridge in a new part of London called the Docklands that is still very much in transition. At the moment it is changing from a grim warehouse district to a chic new yuppie haven with great views of the river. Terence Conran realizing its possibilities, has struck again. Singlehandedly he seems to have colonized the cobblestone streets with a tiny Conran duchy made up of new Conran restaurants and food shops. He's out trumping the Donald in stamping his name on everything in sight. One of his most successful endeavors is the dramatic Pont de La Tour, the next best thing to floating down the Thames on a barge. Aside from being a restaurant, its also a smoked fish shop, a bakery and an oyster bar. Conran calls it his Gastrodrome. It has a handsome terrace for outdoor dining when the weather is fine, and inside there are big windows that overlook the river. A sunset reservation is sure to make your heart beat faster. It's rumored that the dining room was intended to

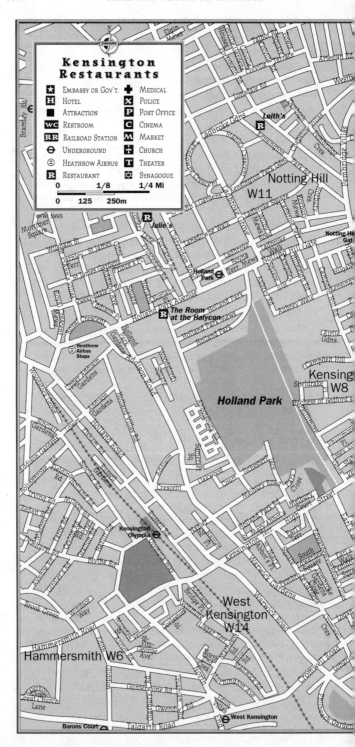

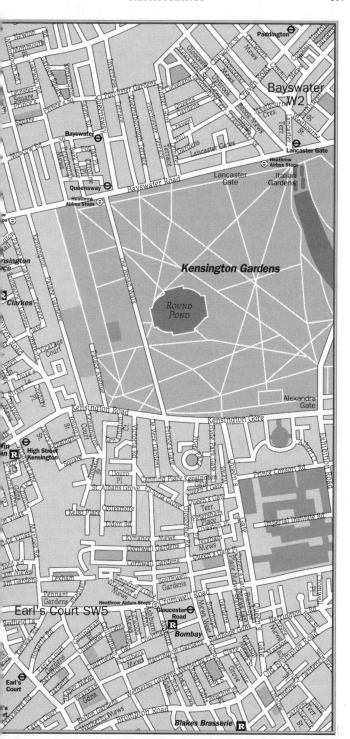

echo the dining room of the ill-fated ocean liner *Normandy*. Not to worry, the only thing likely to sink here is your bank balance.

David Burke, the young Irish chef, has left all signs of corned beef and cabbage far behind and constructed an elegant menu that turns fish cookery into an artistic event. He uses the freshest and most perfect elements to come up with prawn bisque, grilled salmon with basil or a thick slab of fresh tuna decorated with chili and coriander. There are meats as well for the carnivore that loves a river view. The pastry chef, Petra, is far from half-baked herself. The lemon tarte is the perfect astringent for fishy memories.

If you can't spend the time for a formal dinner, just pull up a chair out on the terrace, order the amazing cold fish platter with a glass of chilled champagne, and just watch the Thames roll by.

Now & Zen

4A Upper St. Martin's Lane
☎ *0171-497-0376. Credit cards. Moderate.*
Now & Zen is the Eliza Doolittle of oriental restaurants. One of several in the Zen chain, it has blossomed from the Chinatown concept of bare bones and no frills to an inscrutably opulent glass multifloor structure that is arresting in design and always satisfying in its cuisine. It's perfectly placed in the theater district because it's a top-rated drama all by itself.

For a little cross-cultural diversity, the first floor has a sushi bar with fish that is fresher than James Bond. The cutters are sushi masters of the universe and there are other Japanese delicacies such as cuttlefish cakes and tempura. Upstairs is the perfect place for the Peking duck fanatic, since Now & Zen does a superb version. And that's not all for a set price, you can eat endless little plates of other oriental delights from Thailand as well as China and Japan. They have taken grazing to a whole new plateau of pleasure. On the weekends, the dim sum makes this place nosh nirvana. Even the prisoner of Zenda wouldn't mind being locked up here.

Quaglino's

16 Biru Street
☎ *0171-839-8787. Credit cards. Expensive.*
This is definitely a scene not to be missed. A huge basement space in the elegant St. James locale, with 400 of the most "in demand" tables in London, filled with the movers and shakers of the city, all saying "waiter" at the same time. Quaglino's is another of Sir Terence Conran's mega ventures. He has spent over 2.5 million pounds (many, many dollars) to make a brasserie-type boîte that is most definitely the stomping ground of most of the swingers in London right now. The place seems to have a electricity that is derived by the sheer bravura of its size. Deals are done, affairs are started and the chatter matches the clatter in intensity.

Before we get to the food, a word to the wise. Know in advance that you will be making your entrance down a circular staircase which provides a floor show for the rest of the diners. This is not the place to wear your Bermuda's or have a run in your stocking. Another outrageous design feature is a computer-controlled skylight that is regulated to the time of day and season. Is this a 90s place or what!

Food here is definitely "brasserie-ized," with boudin blanc, chicken with cabbage, great fites, lamb ribs with roasted onions and skate with mash. Do not even think of leaving without spooning up the raspberry pudding with butterscotch sauce.

The only downside to Quaglino's is the bill you may incur when you buy your hearing aid. Four hundred Brits in one place makes the roar of the crowd pretty formidable. Expect to spend most of the evening asking "what?" but don't let that stop you from making the scene. Remember, you can't get one of the best seafood platters ever at the library.

The Quality Chop House

94 Farrington Road
☎ *0171-837-5093. Credit cards. Moderate.*
Anything that has been in existence 120 years deserves a measure of respect and that's just what Charles Fontaine, who used to pot around at Le Caprice, gave it when he rescued The Quality Chop House from its grimy grind to revive it as a true working-man's catering house. In Victorian times, workers were not supposed to relax over a leisurely repast, so the booths here are tall and straight-backed, even if yours objects strenuously. Today, as in the past, (Karl Marx socialized seriously here) it is a beloved haunt of writers (who love to suffer anyway) and newspaper czars, who are fed all their favorite grills and "pudds."

Fontaine has filled the menu with the best British boarding school fare and then he added some of his signature dishes from Le Caprice, such as Bang Bang chicken and his extravagant Caesar salad. That said, the bacon and chips, burgers and mash with onion gravy and the magnificent treacle pudding are all almost impossible to resist. The ambiance is very *Oliver Twist*, so you may have to share a table with one of the very rich orphans who show up daily, but one thing is sure, you'll never need to raise your plate for "more sir."

Rule's

35 Maiden Lane
☎ *0171-836-5314. Credit cards. Expensive.*
When you step into Rule's Edwardian milieu, you are truly stepping back in time. Dickens and Thackery dined here. The waiters appear to be the same staff that opened the place almost 200 years ago. No matter if you're told that Rule's is too "touristy," too "over-the-hill," too "mannered," go! Rule's is the essence of Empire in all its glory. The night we first visited, David Frost was sitting at one of the ruby-red banquettes, embroiled in a discussion with someone very diplomatic that was intense enough to suggest a change of government. Everyone at Rule's seems to take life, and more importantly food, very seriously. Forget all about British Modern cuisine here. These people raise their own game and we're not talking about poker. If you are really lucky, you'll dine at Rule's on a night when some of the guests are sporting their medals and war decorations. If T. E. Lawrence were still with us, he would be having dinner at Rule's.

We can hardly wait to throw cholesterol to the wind here and tuck into one of Rule's buttery pâtés. If we are lucky enough to survive that, we cannot resist the house orange duck, which is shamelessly drenched in a thick orange glaze, laced with Grand Marnier. To make matters worse, it's accompanied by a mountain of potatoes, mashed with butter and double cream. All of this is heart-stopping in more ways than one would think. If you're not feeling ducky, you can have jugged hare or one of the brilliant game pies that Rule's is famous for. As far as we're concerned, dessert is always trifle. The answer to any nanny's prayer, it's layered with pound cake, jam, whipped cream and fruit. If you still have some room left, you can follow in the footsteps of Edward VII and top everything off with a plate of Welsh rarebit. Is it any wonder that the Edwardians never lived to be Victorians?

Sea Shell

49-51 Lisson Grove
☎ *0171-723-8703. Credit cards. Moderate.*
What do most people think about when they think about London? Sure, we know, the palace, the queen, London Bridge, Fog and even though they may not admit it, fish and chips. Everyone saw those old movies with denizens of Soho carrying around newspaper cones filled with crunchy things. We could almost smell them in the theater. At the Sea Shell you can finally taste the real McCoy. This very plain luncheonette-type place, which is close by Victoria Station, has been "frying high" since the 1960s. There's almost always a line of locals waiting patiently for the fried plaice, halibut, or sole, sprinkled liberally with Worcestershire sauce and, heaven help us, dusted with salt. The chips are greaseless beauties that disappear out of the friers as if they had wings. If fear of the cholesterol police proves too difficult to deal with, they will grill all of the above. There's a takeout counter, but most people can't bear to say goodbye to Mr. Chips.

The Square

32 Knight Street, St. James
☎ *0171-839-8787. Credit cards. Very expensive.*
Very establishment, very luxurious and located in very "smart" St. James, the Square seems to be created for livers of the good life. The look of the place is stylish and dressy as are the diners who show up to eat the gorgeously presented food of chef Philip Howard. A disciple of the Roux brothers, he's gone on to carve out a culinary niche for himself that focuses on strongly defined seasonings and unique concepts of old favorites. As for Modern British cooking, Howard is a master of soups and shellfish. His Square meals are always filled with exotic coupling, such as sweet and sour scallops with sauteed squid, a ragout of turbot, leeks and mussels, roast monk fish tails over spaghetti of wild mushrooms, or a bright red mullet soup filled with roast baby fish. If you don't want to swim upstream, there's a lusty roast rabbit lounging on a crisp warm potato pancake. Since the presentations are so dramatic and architectural, your curiosity will make dessert a given. And you won't be disappointed. Have you ever seen "good old" creme brulée served with its sugar shell perched, free form at an angle on top. Maybe the London *Times* won't want to hold the front page, but it got a subdued gasp from us.

Sweetings

39 Queen Victoria Street
☎ *0171-248-3062. NO credit cards. Moderate.*
Even though Sweetings is a Victorian landmark in the financial district, your finances won't be taxed eating here and you'll be trans-

ported back to a kinder, gentler time in London. Let's hear it for *Mary Poppins*. I'm sure most of her charges grew up to come to Sweetings regularly. The Sweeting family opened it in 1906 and it's been tough to get a seat ever since.

Since they don't take reservations, you may have to squeeze into a space at the counter between a couple of swells from the Bank of England. The freshness and simplicity of their denizens of the deep make it all worthwhile. The fish pie is sublime and the oysters are all eager to come out of their shells. They still do haddock with an egg on top. Their traditional dessert puddings have been known to make grown stockbrokers weep. There will always be an England and there will always be a Sweetings. They're really one and the same.

Wagamama

4 Streatham Street
☎ *0171-323-9223. Credit cards. Moderate.*
This is not a code word for Fergie, nor is it the name of the new Rolling Stones album. Wagamama is one of the best Japanese restaurants in London. However, if you don't like to stand on line (queue up, in Blighty) forget it and set off for the Savoy. We have never visited Wagamama without seeing the line spilling out onto the sidewalk. That translates into something very, very good must be going on, and it is. They really used their noodles when they conceived this brilliant raman joint. No red velvet booths here—just long tables where people sit together in front of bowls of the most fantastic noodle soups and rice combinations this side of Tokyo. The choices go on and on: sliced sirloin, chickens, pork with cilantro, soba or raman, or rice, coconut milk, beansprouts and very good dumplings if you need the security blanket of a first course. The speed with which your order is delivered is due to the whole staff being computerized. You just can't help smiling at the good nature of the place. This is definitely not a salon for relaxed dining or exchanging state secrets, but it is one of the few places in London where you can eat for under three figures and have a memorable meal. It's the perfect choice for a day when you're at the British Museum, which is a few blocks away. Try one of the weird fruit juice concoctions after you've finished your Japanese beer. They make up for no dessert.

Wilton's

55 Jermyn Street
☎ *0171-629-9955. Credit cards. Very expensive.*
Expensive, clubby, "teddibly teddibly" British and around in one form or another since 1742. Wilton's is the quintessential upper-class "fish" hangout for the rich and faithful. Edwardian elegance are the words that best describe what a visit to Wilton's will suggest to anyone with enough farthings to pay the very substantial bill. But that's of small consequence to the politicos and MP's that take their "brain food" very seriously.

Wilton's is on Jermyn Street, which is made up of venerable shops, most of which bear the Royal Warrant. You almost expect to see the queen's limo pull up and a really weird hat appear in the window. The very traditional approach to life at Wilton's is echoed in the menu, which sings of dover sole, and grilled salmon, and the most impecca-

ble oysters in town. A few meat pies are permitted and some well-pre-
pared game infiltrates the 250-year-old menu, but the real thrust here
is much more primal. Most of these 50-something sweeties want the
fish plates their nannies fixed for them, and then of course a trifle for
dessert. A few are even brave enough to go on to a savory. Nanny
would be so proud!

Agenda/London's Best Hotel Dining Rooms

Unlike most American cities where the hotel dining room is to be avoided like a dental appointment, London's fine dining heritage historically
began in its hotels, which were the only places "ladies and gentlemen"
could have a meal without a hint of scandal. Restaurants in the city catered
to the working classes or were places to make an improper suggestion or
plan a crime. Even today, with the extraordinary number of excellent restaurant choices in London, the "grand" tradition of dining is found in it's
"grand" hotels.

Blakes Hotel

Off Fulham Road, 33 Roland Gardens
☎ *0171-370-6701. Credit cards. Expensive.*
What's black and white and tastes mysteriously delicious—the restaurant at Blakes. It's all lacquer and screens, and Japanese warrior outfits
in glass cases around the room. The atmosphere more than carries out
the lush drama found in the rest of the hotel. Since Blakes has always
been a mecca for the L.A. set as well as domestic celebs, there is always
someone who's someone, in the room.

The menu echoes and often exceeds this very unique setting. East
most definitely meets West here, to become "signature Blakes." We
couldn't resist the translucent steamed scallops with cumin and fried
seaweed. Buttery langoustine came in a sesame phyllo package with
chile noodles. The Szechwan duck was roasted to an audible crackle
with a roasted salt-and-pepper crust. The evening's show-stopper was
chicken and crab meat molded together and then tied up with a rib-
bon of mori seaweed to look just like a Fabergé egg. This is certainly
not the place to come for a "ham on rye."

Bullocks

Athenium Hotel, 116 Piccadilly
☎ *0171-493-1860. Credit cards. Moderate.*
The very thought of a formal dress code in the dining room of the
Atheneum is most certainly an anathema. No ties, open shirts, my
God, a sweater or two around the room. Is this London or the South
of France. Well, from the look of the room, it's both. Aside from a
terrific Mediterranean menu, Bullocks' strong suit is its dedication to
casual comfort. There is a glass skylight, lots of wood and a red stone
floor. Soft lighting at night makes it romantic and cozy. The menu
carries out the Mediterranean flavor with its own accents. A glistening
grill of Mediterranean veggies is drizzled with a bright saffron aioli.
Duck is pot-roasted in a mahogany, orange sauce and paired with a
lentil ragout. If you're not afraid of the pasta police, there's penne
slathered with a mascarpone sauce, richer than Liz II. Then a quick
trip back to the nursery for bread and butter pudding with marma-

lade, or for the sophisticates in the crowd, a triple tart lime creme brulée. Bullock's is also one of the best places in London to say g'day to a couple of really great Australian wines.

The Capitol Hotel Dining Room

2224 Basil Street, Knightsbridge
☎ *0171-589-5171. Credit cards. Expensive.*

The reputation of the Capitol dining room has for years been as impeccable as the hotel itself. Small, jewel-like, luxurious and devoted to an elegant menu. Even when it went through a change of chefs (today the kitchen is under the innovative guidance of Philip Britton, one of the British Modern mob) the Capitol never missed a beat in continuing to be one of the most popular rooms in town. Today, or at least at press time, it was undergoing expansion so that more of London can beat a path to its very stylish door. The former decor was pastels and silks and frou frou. The new look sans frou frou, is wooden shutters and etched glassed mirrors. David Linley (his mum is Princess Margaret) has designed the furniture and its got a new 90s face.

Chef Britton may look like he should be doing his algebra homework, but in the kitchen, his sage approach to food doesn't just come from his spice jars. He mingles elements together to produce a style that appears delicate but always has a surprise for the palate. Lamb is roasted with red peppers, red onion and basil, steamed baby cod, barely done with a champagne crab sauce, or a golden saute of eggplant with mozzarella and mushroom oil. Definitely food for thought. It might be a capitol idea to end with rice pudding and toffee Bananas.

Causerie

Claridge's Hotel, Brook Street, Mayfair
☎ *0171-629-8860. Credit cards. Moderate.*

A bargain at Claridges, the hotel of Kings! We are not talking about all you can eat at the corner salad bar, or the local surf and turf. We are truly speaking of the Causerie Buffet at Claridges!!! Not since Hamlet had dinner with his uncle has there been a more loaded smorgasbord. And it is not just a passing promotional fancy that some P.R. ding-a-ling thought of. This has been going on for years, attracting the hoiest of paloi. You might just be nudging a Lord or a Sir out of the way so as to spear your pickle. There's a set price at lunch and dinner with as many turns around the table as you have the courage to make.

The buffet is beautifully done with a varied selection of cold salads, smoked fish, pates and terrines all kept wonderfully fresh and appealing. The hot selection could be a roast or something braised and there is always the ever-present veg medley. For a ridiculously low extra charge, they will throw in a cocktail or wine. And best of all, it's open late enough to drop by after the theater for something crisp and crunchy. It's the high life at the lowest of prices (for London, that is).

Connaught Hotel

Carlos Place, Mayfair
☎ *0171-499-7070. Credit cards. Expensive.*

The dining room at the Connaught is in a class by itself. It is THE hotel restaurant all others are compared to, when "typically British" is the means of comparison. To give an idea of the seriousness of intent here—when the new kitchen was installed, it was the Queen Mother who dedicated it. The words "trendy," "in," "hot," will never apply here. This is a bastion of such fine traditions, that even Tevya would be impressed.

The menu here is stamped with the classic imprint of Michael Bourdin, an expatriate of Maxim's, He's responsible for both the very formal diningroom (waiters in tailcoats, crystal, velvet) and the intimate grill room, which is much prettier, but no more relaxed than its grander relative. The menu, may not have The Only game in town, but it has some of the best. They are roasted or grilled to perfection and come with pomme souffle, those crisp little balloon potatoes that were hot stuff in the 70s. Oxtail and kidney pie are also staples, but have a day of the week attached to them (Monday Partridge, Tuesday, Chicken Pot Pie, and so on). Desserts would make Nanny very comfortable with an array of the usual "pudds" but a few sorbets and crisps have crept in as an hommage to the 90s.

The Four Seasons Restaurant
Park Lane
☎ *0171-499-0888. Credit cards. Expensive.*
Haute cuisine is the order of the jour at the Four Seasons and it is both classic as well as creative in the grand design of Chef Jean-Christoppe Novelli. The room has a grand design as well. Lots of crystal and tapestries, tables luxuriously spaced for comfort to the max and it's quiet enough to hear a pignoli-drop.

The Carte de Novelli has extravagant ambitions and they all turn out to be delectably realized. We dare you to try to visualize paper-thin air dried duck slices served with celeriac, mustard seeds and topped with a tiny quail egg. If that doesn't stop you from heading to McDonalds, how about a wild mushroom cake, wrapped in a crepe with herbs and port. The menu goes on and on, never failing to amaze. We couldn't resist the lemon bresse chicken with shitake's poached in coconut milk. If you think Chef Novelli had burnout before he even got to desserts—forget it. How about pan fried brioche with honey and hazelnuts, sitting atop rum-raisin ice cream. Thank God the Four Seasons keeps the health club open late!

The Halkin
5-6 Halkin Street, Mayfair
☎ *0171-333-1234. Credit cards. Expensive.*
An Italian dining room in a British hotel is unheard of. Well, the Halkin restaurant is as much an anachronism as the rest of the hotel. It carries out the sleek, minimalist philosophy that makes the hotel so unusual in a city that thinks minimalist is not having cheese, port and then dessert.

The Halkin has chosen the look of Milan for its dining room, with neutral shades and spare furniture. The decorative accents and colors are added by the gorgeous Milanese risottos and pastas ofChef Marchesi, who earned three Michelin stars back in Milan before he'd even heard of the Halkin. Today, he's producing northern Italian food in its most elegant form. The homemade raviolis can be filled with scallops or rabbit or shrimp. The risotto with gorgonzola would make Pavarotti break into song. Thick tomato-perfumed lentil soup comes with the bones of a roasted breast of quail. For a retro touch, there is a tiramisu that rounds off some of the edges that the Halkin has so brilliantly honed.

The Room at the Halcyon

129 Holland Park Avenue, Holland Park
☎ *0171-721-5411. Credit cards. Expensive.*

Some say he's the best chef in London today, some say he just might be the youngest (24). We say he's the most exciting. Martin Hadden's Halcyon nights are even better than the happiness he creates at lunch. His imagination is what probably will make him one of the great chefs in London when he grows up. In the meantime, sharing his culinary adolescence is a joy.

The room itself is as bright and airy as any restaurant located in Holland Park should be. It's always filled with everyone from Rock stars to gender benders like Ru-Paul, to societies' darlings and other assorted poshest of noshers. It's also a constant rerun for B.B.C. Television, which is close by.

Tarte Taten doesn't end the menu here, it begins it with caramelized shallots in a buttery crust, accompanied by Pan-fried chicken livers and a tiny dome of mashed potatoes. Braised rabbit is coupled with lentils in a pale green sage butter. Poached egg comes nestled in a bed of puff pastry that's filled with a wild mushroom saute, and emerald green asparagus with a golden Hollandaise just so the Vegans will have something to shout about. Of course, no one really shouts at the Halcyon. They just sit back and smile.

The Oriental Restaurant

The Dorchester, 53 Park Lane
☎ *0171-629-8888. Credit cards. Very expensive.*

The Sultan of Brunei, who owns the Dorchester, must have had to give up an oil-well or two just to finance this extravagant room. But even if he had to cut back on groceries at the palace, he must have thought it would be worth it to have a one-star Michelin Chinese restaurant in the most unlikely of locations. The look of the Oriental is spectacular. Black lacquer and pearl screens, silk Oriental hangings, rare tapestries and many splendored rugs, all of this in acres of space. The Oriental even has a special dim sum chef just to roll and pinch. The night we were there, the room was filled with Occidental tourists as well as the usual London luminaries.

The menu is far from Chinatown in its conception, not a moo goo gai pan to be seen. Instead, a clear chicken and vegetable soup with the most elegant diced mushrooms, or finely shredded chicken and duck, with melon and chili-vinegar. The honey-cured barbecue pork glistens and melts away on the tongue. Or, if you've never seen *Jaws*, a lightly braised shark's fin with a velvety lemon glaze. The way to go for dessert is the fresh mango sorbet, just for the heavenly color that delights the spirit as well as the palate.

The Savoy Grill

Hotel Savoy, Strand
☎ *0171-836-4343. Credit cards. Expensive.*

The original chef at the Savoy Grill is a hard act to follow. August Escoffier opened the room in 1899 and his ghost has been known to rattle a few chefs in the kitchen when he thinks something on the menu is just a flash in the pan. Fortunately, that almost never happens because the food at the Savoy has been brought lovingly into the present. When there are innovations on the menu, they are of the gentlest kind, without one coronet being bent out of shape. The Savoy Grill will probably always have a foot in the 1890s and a foot in the 30s. That still leaves a very intelligent mind-set to deal with today.

The whole point of the Savoy Grill originally was to feed D'Oyle Carte's audience at the Savoy Theater next door. As other theaters grew up around the Savoy, the grill became a theatrical mecca. Even today, it's impossible to get a reservation unless you book long in advance, since it is also the meeting place for money and power in the city. Sir Winston didn't have his own table there for nothing.

Most of the daily specials lean to a large helping of Mary Poppins, favorites. Steak and kidney pudding with oysters, boiled bacon and pease pudding, not to mention banana mouse with a ginger snap custard, are enough to make the most stylish of arteries clog.

Agenda/Best Teas in London

Perhaps as revenge for the Boston Tea Party, the British have succeeded in converting "those upstarts" from the colonies to their most beloved of afternoon ceremonies—tea. There is no doubt about it, our British roots are beginning to show. A trip to London would not be complete without a top-of-the-line full British tea, and that means tiny sandwiches, scones, clotted cream, jam and assorted pastries and tarts. Alas, it also means at least three million grams of fat!

Tea is served from 3 p.m. to 6 p.m. There are usually no reservations required (except at the Ritz). We believe that tea before theater replaces dinner and doesn't cost anywhere as much. It also leaves a window of opportunity for a snack après the show.

Brown's Hotel

30-34 Albemarle Street, W1
☎ *0171-493-7020.*
The best in London because of its grace, charm and comfort - the tea is great too. And the people-watching is always a treat in itself. There are generally one or two "Titles" around, a few blokes who look like they are ready to jump into their Grenadier's Guards' uniforms at the drop of a crumpet, lots of shoppers who have picked Piccadilly clean and just want to kick back and rest their shopping bags, and of course, exquisite little old ladies in brogues and tweeds who look like Queen Victoria.

The Ritz

Piccadilly, W1
☎ *0171-493-8181*
A large helping of glitz with your crumpets and clotted cream. Lots of palms, too. In truth, it is a little too gilded and golden for a relaxed tea time. But if you have your heart set on a five o'clock "event," this is the "grandest" of them all. Reservations a must.

The Waldorf

Aldwyth, WC2
☎ 0171-836-2400
Was that Bertie Wooster and Jeeves over there in the corner? There is actually a Tea Dance on Saturday and Sunday to exercise those eclairs away. This is no casual drop-in-and-pull-up-a-sofa meeting place. Chic little dresses and smart cut suits. You wouldn't want to embarrass Bertie.

The Patisserie Valerie

44 Old Compton Street, W1
☎ 0171-437-3466
Always jammed with pastryholics who down them with a vengeance. Do-it-yourself tea assortments for the adventurous.

Fortnum & Mason, The Fountain

181 Piccadilly, W1
☎ 0171-734-8040
Tea in a genteel setting with ice cream on the side. A very informal break in the midst of shopping—to give your charge plates a chance to cool down in a more formal setting.

Fortnum & Mason, The St. James Restaurant

4th floor
This is a lovely room that's perfect for a full Tea which, in their retro version, includes toast served with meat or fish paste, Scotch woodcock (not something with feathers, it's anchovies and scrambled eggs) grilled mushrooms and other savories.

Maison Sagne

105 Marlebone High Street, W1
☎ 0171-935-6240
Very traditional "sweet" shop serving tea and pastry with a French accent, along with those devastating little cucumber thingies.

The Muffin Man

12 Wright's Lan, W8
☎ 0171-937-6652
They really know their corns from their blueberries. They serve set teas all day long. The best part is that the price is very pence-conscious.

Emporio Armani Express

191 Brompton Road, SW3
☎ 0171-823-8818
Just when you've said, "enough Armani already" they go and put a tea room in their boutique. Tea with a definite Italian accent. The only teeny weeny drawback is that they show videos of the collection while you are slathering your crumpet with Devon creme—this is really tea with no sympathy!

The Hyde Park

66 Knightsbridge, SW1
☎ 0171-235-2000
This is where Queen Mother Elizabeth took the little princesses for tea (maybe there was something in the water?). Even without all that royalty, the Park Room is so beautifully British.

The Cadogen

75 Sloane Street, SW1X

☎ *0171-235-7141*

Tea with Oscar Wilde and Lily Langtry. The place to commune with these past guests of the hotel is the Langtry room. Oscar was a pushover for their petit-fours.

The Conservatory

The Lanesborough, Hyde Park Corner
☎ *0171-259-5599*

Tea with a Gilbert and Sullivan hangover? This wonderful room with Orientalia and Victoria kitsch is a confection that rivals any of the ones they serve with tea. Just perfect for your five o'clock fantasies.

Agenda/Best London Breakfasts

British breakfasts, unlike their continental cousins, are meant to nourish the soul as well as the body. Serving an Englishman a croissant and coffee would be like asking Lady Godiva if she'd like a haircut. For centuries the belief that "a Kipper a day keeps the doctor away" has led to the most sumptuous repasts in the A.M.

Blakes Hotel

33 Roland Gardens, Kensington
☎ *0171-370-6701*

Updated British breakfast for the 90s in their exotic dining room, surrounded by enough luminaries to light up the Tower dungeons. The food is sublime and the scene is the one to make, at the moment.

The Connaught

Carlos Place, Mayfair
☎ *0171-499-7070*

Dark polished wood and extra helpings of tradition are served up with the best bacon and sausage in town. The sparkle from the sterling is enough to wake anyone up.

Simpson's-in-the-Strand

100 Strand
☎ *0171-836-9112*

Who would have thought you could turn a cliche into a classic. Since they started to serve breakfast at Simpson's, taste buds are blooming again. And what a breakfast it is. On a plate as big as a manhole cover you'll find: ham, sausage, eggs, baked beans, cheese, black pudding and bacon. The best way to handle it all is to go right back to bed.

River Room

Savoy Hotel, Strand
☎ *0171-836-4343*

The color of the room matches the color of the smoked salmon, being meticulously sliced to accompany your perfect toast or eggs en cocotte. If its a sunny morning, the Thames outside shimmers with light. The Kippers are sauteed in butter and melt on the tongue. How can the day not be wonderful if it starts out in this most luxurious of settings?

Fox and Anchor

115 Charterhouse Street, Barbican
☎ *0171-253-4838*

Located close by the Smithfield meat market, it's not hard to understand why the workers would be drawn to a place that has a license to serve alcohol at 6 A.M. (but only if you can prove you're a worker). Obviously the appetites are properly stimulated because the breakfast is one of the heartiest in London. If you can manage it, you can tuck into multiple eggs, bacon, sausage, boudin noir baked beans and stacks of fried bread. The frantic pace of the market is worth seeing even if you're of the black coffee and dry toast persuasion.

London Rooms with a View or When Is a Restaurant Not a Restaurant?

London is not like New York when it comes to placing restaurants atop skyscrapers or hotels to catch the lights of the city. But there are miles of the Thames that are dear to every Londoner's heart. Occasionally, they will appreciate it from a boat or a bistro. We've listed a few of our favorites that go beyond the question of food, not that some of them would not rate inclusion on any "quintessential" list, but their locations offer a dimension that adds to their appeal. Therefore we've set them apart in a special category.

River Cafe

Thames Wharf Studios, Hammersmith, Rainsville Rd
☎ *0171-381-6217*
What could the Pompidou Center in Paris possibly have to do with the River Cafe—everything, unlikely as it may seem. The cafe was born when Sir Richard Rogers, the architect who designed the Pompidou, moved lock, stock and croissants to Hammersmith. He set up shop in a series of empty warehouses and never considered the possibility that there wouldn't be a B.L.T. to be had for miles. What to do! The answer, quite simply, is to have your wife open a restaurant on the banks of the Thames, with an unbroken view of the river and open green fields on the opposite bank. This is truly a trip out of town without leaving The City.

The menu is dedicated to Tuscany. Fresh made pastas are sauced with anchovies, sage and fragrant olive oil. Buffalo mozzarella overflows from a rich torte. There is a bread soup right out of one of those gorgeous hill towns and the grills are perfectly charred, done before your very eyes in a kitchen that stretches out to 48 feet right behind the shining stainless steel bar. Desserts are extravagant, with chocolate "nemesis" cake true to its name. It is a killer!

My Fair Lady

250 Camden High Street, Camden Town
☎ *0171-485-4433*
Unlike the boat-trips up and down the Thames, this is a much more relaxed Regent canal version that ambles through Regent's Park, the Zoo, Maida Hill tunnel and finally to Robert Browning Island in Little Venice, on a comfortable barge. The trip takes a leisurely three hours and is a wonderful way to take a break from the day to day "sightseeing schlep." You may not see Julie Andrews or smell the open sea, but if you take the luncheon barge, you'll get sunny (maybe) miles of the park and zoo. If you do the evening voyage, you can kick back and listen to the guitarist they bring aboard. The food

is traditional, and Michelin has yet to award them even 1 anchor, so don't expect it to rival the dining room on the QE II, but it's really fine for a lazy look at London. The lunch cruise is about £20—the dinner, about £30.

The Blue Print Cafe

Design Museum, Butlers Wharf
☎ *0171-407-6261*

The Blue Print is another of Sir Terence Conran's dramatic contributions to London's restaurant scene. Since the Design Museum is located right on the Thames, the views are too wonderful not to couple with good food. The Cafe, which is on top of the museum, has two outdoor terraces for your al fresco agenda, or an expanse of minimal decor you would expect at the Design Museum, inside. There are bright colors, glass and even on a gray day (not uncommon in London) the room is flooded with light. The food definitely does not take a back seat to the view, The chef was formerly at Bibendum, Conran's major tummy temple, so the menu runs from straightforward fish, grills, gazpacho, fresh pastas, to an elegant artichoke wearing a tangy goat cheese crust. Far from matching the minimal surroundings, the desserts are maximum luscious.

The Canteen

Chelsea Harbour
☎ *0171-351-7330*

If you love Michael Caine and watching sailboats sway on the water, and dining wonderfully in a restaurant that is overseen by one of the most controversial chefs in London at the moment, you just might want to make a reservation at the Canteen. Chelsea Harbour is becoming one of the trendiest places to live in London, so when Michael Caine bought a condo there, he decided to make sure his neighborhood drop-in had drop-dead food and lots of other celebs to amuse him. Marco Pierre White, the "enfant terrible" of the gourmet grenadiers set, is responsible for the success of the place and the extravagance of the menu. Risotto of squirrel, salmon served with a crust of crabmeat, in a pool of shrimp and lobster sauce, or a velvet vichyssoise with oysters and caviar. More earthbound is cod and chips, but even that is served with a spicy tartare hollandaise. The view of the harbor is so pretty you may forget all about the possibility of raising Caine.

AGENDA
ENTERTAINMENT

Royal Shakespeare Theatre seats 1600 with perfect sight lines.

London has always been obsessed with the performing arts.
You could almost say that the theme of the city is "Let Us Entertain You." As far back as the Elizabethans, there was always a
variety of events to attend. If one didn't spend the evening at the
Bear Pit, there was always something lusty playing at the Globe
or in a pinch, a last-minute Punch and Judy show. The choices
now have, to say the least, multiplied, and the average Londoner
has become more demanding, but the desire to be amused, de-
lighted and most of all enriched, is as strong as it ever was. Anyone who comes to London and doesn't partake of this amazing
artistic banquet will leave without really understanding that
London is its own best production.

Here are the things you'll have to think about to fine-tune
your entertainment agenda. Long gone are the days you could
walk up to the ticket window at the theater or concert hall and
almost be assured of a seat to the same evening's performance.
London has become, in the last few years, less of a spur-of-the-

moment town. Of course, you can use a broker through your hotel, but tickets have escalated so much in London, you may not want to add a stiff commission to the ticket price. A much better approach is to ask your concierge (if you have one) to call the theater or concert hall in your behalf and book all your events as soon as you check in. If you're as neurotic as we are about buttoning down most of your agenda before you leave home, you'll try to get a copy of a major London newspaper (foreign newspapers are sold in most cities) and then make up your "wish list" in advance.

As with restaurants, we believe that calling directly from your home to London using a credit card, and having your tickets delivered to the hotel or held for you at the box office, will ultimately save you precious time once you arrive. In the U.S. you can call **Edwards & Edwards** in New York, ☎ *(212) 944-0190* or ☎ *(800) 223-6108*; **First Call**, in London, ☎ *0171-240-7200*, 15 percent surcharge per ticket. **Ticketmaster**, ☎ *0171-379-4444*; **Theatre Tonight**, ☎ *0171-753-0333.* Credit card booking for the same night of performance, no fee. **Keith Prowse**, ☎ *0171-9001- New York*, ☎ *(212) 398-1420*, ☎ *(800) 669-8687*; **British Airways** (customers only) ☎ *(800) Airways.* They have good seats for all productions, no commissions. **Student Theatre Line**, ☎ *0171-379- 8900*, after 2 p.m. daily, standby prices, student I.D. required.

There are two weekly magazines that are invaluable in planning your entertainment agenda—*Time Out* and *What's On In London*. Both have complete listings of events for the week, as well as restaurant and clubs. They're sold at any London newsstand or at your hotel!

Theatre

Someone (we can't think who) once said "The play's the thing." In London, the play is *everything*. Unlike Broadway, which is alternatively living or dying depending on the vagaries of the season and the economy, theatre in London is a historical fact of life. People have been going to the theater since "Young Will" moved his productions from their tryouts in Stratford, down to the Globe, and The Big Time. Theater is to London what haute cuisine is to Paris. They both nourish the heart and soul of the people.

Today, London is giving Broadway a dazzling run for its money. The mega-hits of the last years have come to the U.S., compliments of Andrew Lloyd Webber, Harold Pinter and Tom Stoppard. The Brits have recolonized the Great White Way and Broadway couldn't be happier, except for an occasional tear or two (where is Cole Porter when you need him?). In London the news is that Fringe Theatre, once the home of experimental grunge, has spawned a whole new movement called Off-West End, that is a more legitimate showcase for new playwrights. Fringe theater still exists and in truth, is more cutting edge than ever, which is a relief for the green-haired, pierced nose set.

The real glitter of the London theater scene still comes from the West End, The National Theatre and the Royal Shakespeare Company. Exciting new productions that are the talk of the town usually come from one of these renowned stage sets.

ECONOMY AGENDA

Half-Price Theatre Tickets

If you don't mind queuing up for an hour or so, you can buy tickets to shows that are not entirely sold out. The tickets are sold at half-price, plus a service charge of £1 or £1.50, depending upon the price of the ticket. The Society of London Theatres (SOLT) has a booth set up in Leicester Square where they begin selling tickets for matinee performances at 12 noon and 2:30-6:30 for evening performances. Both are for same day tickets only. They will accept cash or "Traveler's cheques" and it will give you a chance to "chat-up" the locals who are usually only too willing to help you with your decisions.

Student Standby

West End theatres offer seats to students at standby prices (to be determined by the price of the tickets that are available before the performance, but cheaper than half price), subject to availability. A student identification is required. Call Student Theaterline, ☎ *0171-379-8900, Mon-Fri, from 2 p.m. for daily recorded information.*

The West End

The West End is London's theater district.

This is the very heart, soul and heritage of London Theatre. Today, in an effort to pull the area together and give it a unified identity, it has been named Theaterland. A little too cloying for our taste since The West End conjures up visions of Noel and Gertie, Sir Laurence Olivier and Lily Langtry coming forward to take their bows. What would they have thought about performing in Theatreland! The theatres themselves are Edwardian or Victorian, with ornate architecture, sometimes by Wren or Nash. Even before the curtain goes up, you're transported back to the past. They seem

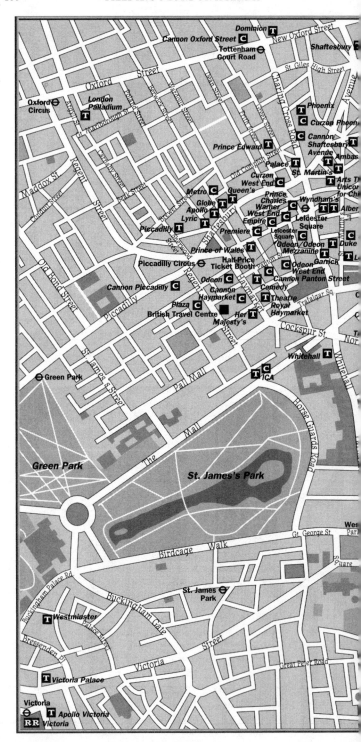

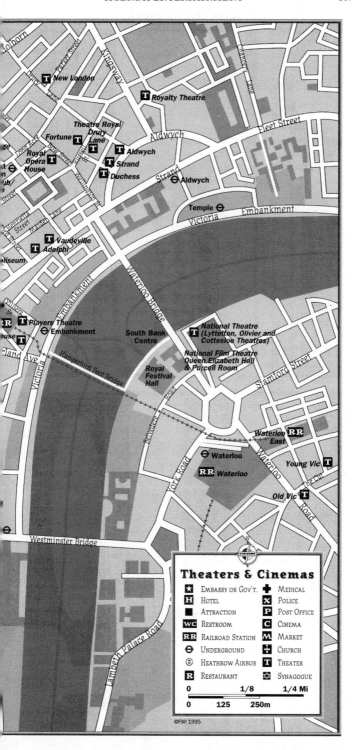

to glow with history. All together, the West End has about 50 theaters, filled with productions that are among the best in the world.

Agenda West End/Theatre Directory

Adelphi
> *Strand, WC2,* ☎ *0171-836-7611.*

Albery
> *St. Martins Lane, WC2,* ☎ *0171-867-1115.*

Aldwych
> *Aldwych, W2,* ☎ *0171-836-6404.*

Ambassadors
> *West Street, WC2H9ND,* ☎ *0171-836-6111.*

Apollo
> *Shaftesbury Avenue, W1V7HD,* ☎ *0171-494-5070.*

Apollo Victoria
> *Wildon Road, SW1V 1LL,* ☎ *0171-416-6042.*

Barbican
> *Barbican, EC2Y 8DS,* ☎ *0171-638-8891.*

Cambridge
> *Earlham Street, WC2H 9HU,* ☎ *0171-379-5299.*

Comedy
> *Panton Street, SW1Y 4DN,* ☎ *0171-494-5080.*

Dominion
> *Tottenham Court Road, W10AG,* ☎ *0171-416-6060.*

Donmar Warehouse
> *41 Earlham Street, WC2H 9LD,* ☎ *0171-867-1150.*

Drury Lane (Theatre Royal)
> *Catherine Street, WC21B 6JF,* ☎ *0171-494-5001.*

Duchess
> *Catherine Street, WC2B 5LA,* ☎ *0171-494-5075.*

Duke of York's
> *St. Martins Lane, WC2N 4BG,* ☎ *0171-836-5122.*

Fortune
> *Russell Street, WC2B 5HH,* ☎ *0171-836-2238.*

Garrick
> *Charing Cross Road, WC2H 0HH,* ☎ *0171-494-5085.*

Globe
> *Shaftesbury Avenue, W1V 8AR,* ☎ *0171-494-5067.*

Haymarket
> *Haymarket, SW1Y 4HT,* ☎ *0171-930-8800.*

Her Majesty's
> *Haymarket, SW1Y 4QR,* ☎ *0171-494-5400.*

London Palladium
> *8 Argyll Street, W1V 1AD,* ☎ *0171-494-5020.*

Lyric
> *Shaftesbury Avenue, W1V 7HA,* ☎ *0171-494-5046.*

Lyric Hammersmith
> *King Street, W60QL,* ☎ *0181-741-2311.*

Mermaid
> *Puddle Dock, EC4 3DR,* ☎ *0171-236-2211.*

New London
> *Drury Lane, WC2,* ☎ *0171-405-0072.*

Old Vic
Waterloo Road, SE1, ☎ 0171-928-7616.

Palace
Shaftsbury Avenue, W1, ☎ 0171-434-0909.

Phoenix
Charing Cross Road, WC2H 0JP, ☎ 0171-867-1044.

Piccadilly
Denman Street, W1V 8DY, ☎ 0171-867-1117.

Players
The Arches, Villiers Street, WC2N 6NQ, ☎ 0171-839-1134.

Playhouse
Northumberland Avenue, WC2N 6NN, ☎ 0171-839-4401.

Prince Edward
Old Compton Street, W1V 8AH, ☎ 0171-734-8951.

Prince of Wales
31 Coventry Street, W1V 8AS, ☎ 0171-839-5972.

Queens
51 Shaftesbury Avenue, W1V 8BA, ☎ 0171-494-5041.

Royal Court
Sloane Square, SW1W 8AS, ☎ 0171-730-1745.
(see also "Theatre Upstairs" under "Fringe")

Royal National Theatre
(Cottesloe, Lyttelton, and Olivier), South Bank Arts Complex, SE1 9PX,
☎ 0171-928-2252.

St. Martin's
West Street, WC2H 9NH, ☎ 0171-836-1443.

Savoy
Strand, WC2R OET, ☎ 0171-836-8888.

Shaftesbury
Shaftesbury Avenue, WC2H 8DP, ☎ 0171-379-5399.

Strand
Aldwych, WC2B 5LD, ☎ 0171-930-8800.

Vaudeville
Strand, WC2R ONH, ☎ 0171-836-9987.

Victoria's Palace
Victoria Street, SW1E 5EA, ☎ 0171-834-1317.

Wyndham's
Charing Cross Road, WC2, ☎ 0171-867-1116.

The Royal Shakespeare Company
Silk Street, EC21, ☎ 0171-638-8891.
Originally based in Stratford-upon-Avon, it moved up to the Barbican
Centre in the 80s. The subsidized group was formed over 100 years
ago and continues to perform Shakespeare in repertory at the Barbican. Even though the theater seats over 1600, the sight lines are perfect and so is the Bard.

The Royal National Theatre
South Bank, SE1, ☎ 0171-928-2252.
Even if you decide not to attend one of their exciting productions, the
theatres themselves (three of them), are so beautifully designed and
the area around them so pleasant, it's the perfect spot for a walk or
coffee at one of the outdoor cafes. Hopefully, you'll experience the
National inside for one of its excellent performances. Originally

started by Lord Oliver, it was under Sir Peter Hall's direction for the years during which it became the respected company it is today. The largest of the theatres is The Olivier, then the Lyttelton, with over 800 seats, and the smallest, The Cottesloe. The sight lines from all these theaters are perfection, so whatever price ticket you buy, will be just fine.

Old Vic

Waterloo Road, SE1 8NB, ☎ *0171-928-7616.*
Classical theatre in a classical setting that dates back to 1818. Most people mistakenly believe that they only perform Shakespeare—not true, they perform contemporary theatre in a really beautiful setting. Incidentally, "Old Vic" comes from Royal Victoria Theatre, which was its original name.

Regent's Park (Inner Circle)

Regent's Park, NW1, 0 ☎ *0171-486-2431.*
In the summer Regent's Park is the place for open air theatre. There's a charming amphitheater close by St. Mary's Rose Garden. The New Shakespeare Company performs Will's top hits as well as other classics, May-Sept. You can even have a cold buffet.

Off-West End

These theater productions fall somewhere between Fringe Theatre and "not quite ready for Prime Time West End." It evolved because people were interested in exploring new theatre but loathe to expose themselves to the weird scene (we think weird is not necessarily bad) that goes hand in hand with the Fringe scene.

Almeida

Almeida Street, N1, ☎ *0171-359-4404.*

The Bush

Shepherd's Bush Green W12, 081-743-3388.

The Cockpit

Gateforth Street, NW8, ☎ *0171-402-5081.*

Hamstead Theatre

Avenue Road, NW3, ☎ *0171-722-9301.*

ICA Theatre

The Mall, SW1, ☎ *0171-930-3647.*

Kings Head

115 Upper Street, N1, ☎ *0171-226-1916.*

Fringe Theatre

This scene is "far out," "off the wall," and totally experimental in the best sense of the word. Performances take place in pubs and cafes and have enriched the music scene even further with a number of excellent new concert halls. And last but certainly not least is, the great church music that is performed in the cathedrals of the city every Sunday morning.

Bloomsbury Theatre

Gordon Street, WC1H OAH, ☎ *0171-387-9629.*

Bush

Shepherds Bush Green, W12 8QD, ☎ *0181-743-3388.*

Chat's Palace

42-4 Brooksby's Walk, E9 6DF, ☎ *0181-986-6714.*

Drill Hall
> *16 Chenies Street, WC1E 7EX,* ☎ *0171-637-8270.*

The Finborough
> *Finborough Arms, Finborough Road, SW10 9ED,* ☎ *0171-373-3842.*

The Gate
> *The Prince Albert, 11 Pembridge Road, W11 3HQ,* ☎ *0171-229-0706.*

Hackney Empire
> *291 Mare Street, E8 1EJ,* ☎ *0181-985-2424.*

Hampstead
> *Swiss Cottage, NW3 3EX,* ☎ *0171-722-9301.*

ICA Theatre
> *The Mall, SW1Y 5AH,* ☎ *0171-930-3647.*

Kings Road
> *115 Upper Street, N1 1QN,* ☎ *0171-226-1916.*

Latchmere
> *503 Battersea Pk Road, SW11 3BW,* ☎ *0171-228-2620.*

Lyric Studio
> *Lyric Theatre, King Street, W6 9JT,* ☎ *0181-741-2311.*

Man in the Moon
> *392 Kings Road, SW3 5UZ,* ☎ *0171-351-2876.*

New End Theatre
> *27 New End, NW3 1JD,* ☎ *0171-794-0022.*

Orange Tree
> *1 Clarence Street, Richmond, TW9 1SA,* ☎ *0181-940-3633.*

Riverside Studios
> *Crisp Road, W6 9RL,* ☎ *0181-748-3354*

Theatre Royal
> *Stratford East, E15 1BN,* ☎ *0181-534-0310.*

Theatre Upstairs
> *Royal Court, Sloane Square, SW1W 8AS,* ☎ *0171-730-2254.*

AGENDA LONGEVITY AWARDS

These are some of the shows that might still be packing them in when you arrive (check for theatres–they move back and forth); Sunset Boulevard–Andrew Lloyd Webber; Cats–Andrew Lloyd Webber; Joseph and the Amazing Technicolor Dreamcoat–Andrew Lloyd Webber; The Phantom of the Opera–Andrew Lloyd Webber. (Do we notice a pattern emerging here?) Starlight Express–You guessed it!; Les Miserable, Miss Saigon–Alain & Claude–Michael Schonberg; and The Mousetrap (all time champ, 42 years)–Agatha Christie.

Music

London likes to think of itself as the music capitol of the World (New York or Vienna might disagree) because of the diversity of the music scene here at any given time. London itself has five symphony orchestras, an Opera Company of renown, and the Royal Ballet has always sparkled with the brightest of stars. In addition, London has always attracted the *crème de la crème* of visiting artists who fill its concert halls year round.

The Barbican Centre

Silk Street, EC2, ☎ *0171-638-8891.*

This confusing, grim looking structure is the home of the London Symphony Orchestra, as well as the English Chamber Orchestra. There are also various music festivals that take place here so be sure to check all its schedules.

Royal Albert Hall

Kensington Gore, SW7, ☎ *0171-589-3203.*

Whenever anyone thinks of symphonic music in London, the Royal Albert Hall comes to mind. It's been here forever and now that The Barbican and the South Bank Centre are both being used by London's major symphonies, the Albert Hall has taken on a new look with "The Prom" concerts that run from July to Sept. They are much like the Boston Pops, with soloists that come from all over. The concerts are beloved by Londoners, so book early.

South Bank Centre

South Bank, Belvedere Road, SE1, ☎ *0171-928-8800.*

This is considered to be the largest arts center in Western Europe and much less of an eyesore than the Barbican. It's also the home of the London Philharmonic. The Philharmonic performs in the Royal Festival Hall, but there are also two other halls that are smaller, the Queen Elizabeth and the charming Purcell Room, used for chamber music. There are some interesting nooks and crannies such as the Voicebox for literary evenings and the Poetry Library, with a collection of more than 4500 volumes. There's no telling how many poems that adds up to. The South Bank is certainly more user-friendly than the Barbican and the Festival Buffet is quite good.

Wigmore Hall

36 Wigmore Street, W1, ☎ *0171-935-2141.*

Charmingly small venue for concerts that don't require space on a grand scale. Musicians love it for its warm, mellow acoustics.

Opera

The London Coliseum

St. Martins Lane, WC2, ☎ *0171-836-3161.*

The Coliseum is London's largest theatre. It has over 2000 seats. Originally, it was a variety house, but today it's the home of the English National Opera, who give their performances in English.

Royal Opera House

Bow Street, Covent Garden, WC2, ☎ *0171-240-1066.*

This is reaching the "top of the charts" for every opera buff in London. It's the Met, La Scala and the Vienna Stats, all rolled into one. The only opera star who hasn't played here is the Phantom. To make it a bit confusing, it's almost always referred to by the locals as "Covent Garden" but that's really just it's address. It's very grand, with its mammoth chandeliers all aglitter, and it's advisable to wear almost everything you've brought in your suitcase. People get out their medals and tiaras for a night at the opera in London.

Dance

Dance Umbrella

Riverside Studios, Crisp Road, Hammersmith, London W6 9RL, 0181-741-4040.

They conduct one of the most prestigious dance festivals in Europe every fall for six weeks. Different events are held all over London. Just call or write for a schedule if that's when you're going to be in town.

Sadler's Wells

Rosebery Avenue, Islington, EC1, ☎ *0171-278-8916.*

If you loved *The Red Shoes* this is the company that Viki wanted most to dance with (poor kid). The Sadler's Wells company moved to Birmingham, but the theatre, which dates from the 1600s is still host to important touring companies from abroad. So far they've all been able to take their toe shoes off, but you never know...

Royal Ballet

Royal Opera House, Bow Street, Covent Gardens, ☎ *0171-240-1911.*

The Royal Ballet shares the house with the Royal Opera and a good thing too, since the most famous ballet company in the U.K. needs a theatre the size of the Opera House to accommodate the masses of people who try to get seats. Ever since Margot Fontayne and Nuryev danced together in the Royal Ballet, the company became as famous as the Bolshoi. They hold some rear amphitheater tickets and standing room space for sale on the day of the performance.

Cinema

London is the perfect place for film buffs. For years Hollywood lived in the shadows of those terribly esoteric black and white dramas that J. Arthur Rank turned out in the 40s and 50s. Back home, the moguls of the moment took their revenge by stealing away all the best British actors and directors, including Sir David Lean, Alfred Hitchcock and Lord Laurence Olivier, to infuse their "movies" with a touch of class. Today, London has a wealth of material on file at The British Film Institute, and a seemingly endless international film library available for study. There is also a very healthy appreciation for independent film makers in London, whose films are shown regularly, if perhaps somewhat inconveniently, out of the very center of the city. If you happen to be in London during the London Film Festival in November, you will be seeing an impressive display of new film makers, as well as the Lions of the industry. West End film houses, for the most part, show all the latest from Tinsel Town, especially in the Movie Palaces off Leicester Square. Tickets are an expensive £6.50–£9.

National Film Theatre

South Bank, Waterloo, SE1, ☎ *0171-928-3232.*

Films from all over the world are shown in this South Bank Cinema complex, including Documentaries.

Lumiere

42 St. Martin's Lane, WC2, ☎ *0171-836-0691.*

New foreign language films in plush luxury. You can reserve ahead in this one.

Minema

45 Knightsbridge, SW1, ☎ *0171-235-4225.*
Independent cinema, showing important films that have won critical acclaim.

ICA Cinema

Nash House, The Mall, SW1, ☎ *0171-930-3647.*
Archival work from around the world during the week. Children's programs on the weekend. A one-day membership is needed here to visit the other exhibits. It is very easy to accomplish.

Prince Charles

Leicester Place, WC2, ☎ *0171-437-8181.*
The best film bargain in London for revivals. Tickets go for about £2.

Renoir

Brunswick Centre, Brunswick Square, WC1, ☎ *0171-837-8402.*
Very offbeat film offerings. Both British and foreign-language independents.

British Film Institute

21 Stephen Street, W1, ☎ *0171-255-1444.*

Museum of the Moving Image

South Bank Arts Centre, ☎ *0171-928-3535.*
Film clips and more memorabilia (See "Museums," page 215)

The London Club Scene

London has one of the liveliest club scene's in Europe. Forget the familiar image of the "staid" pinstripes attending a cricket match or a dog show. They may amuse themselves with typically British pursuits during the a.m., but in the p.m., London fairly explodes with jazz, disco, rock or cabaret. They call it clubbing, which though it sounds rather violent, in fact, means to swing from club to club over the weekend. They literally dance the night away, starting very late and going right through until dawn. Aside from the discos and cabarets, the rock scene here has produced such pop stars as Boy George, The Sex Pistols, Elton John, and the Rolling Stones. We are talking Pop mega-Power!

Cabarets here are what we would call comedy clubs, so don't be disappointed if they don't remind you of the Folies Bergère. And the humor can focus on bodily functions and bathroom fixtures, both of which, for some reason, have always sent British audiences into hysterics. "Stand-up" in London is much raunchier and less political than in the U.S., so if you're expecting Peter Ustinov, you may be disappointed.

Don't be put off by membership requirements at some of the clubs. It really has to do with the type of license they have. Since it's little more than a technicality, it's usually handled by a one-time charge at the door, and presto chango, you're a member. What is somewhat harder to deal with is the astronomical entrance fees that can put a crimp in your carioca. Some of them can run as high as £10 or £12. As if by magic, they drop considerably after 3 a.m. to encourage you to bar hop and pub crawl. If you can linger over your after-dinner coffee or take a nap and set the alarm, you can save almost 50 percent.

Before even thinking about going to a club, check *What's on in London*, a weekly magazine that is a top resource for everything on entertainment.

You'll find out who's appearing while you're in town, at what time and most importantly, if the club still exists. The mortality rate, as you can imagine, is high.

Even after checking the listing, always call ahead. Do you need to be a member? What's the dress code? Is there a minimum? If they serve food, what kind and at what time. Obviously, you're not expecting a gourmet experience, but it's helpful to know that you can skip dinner, go to the theater and have a cold supper just before the jazz gets hot. If you decide to spend the night with a good book, it's nobody's fault but your own!

Jazz

Ronnie Scotts

47 Frith Street, WI, ☎ *0171-439-0747.*
Scotts is a Jazz institution in London. It's been here for years. They get the biggest names in town. Ronnie Scott himself is an important "sax symbol."

The Fridge

Town Hall Parade, Brixton Hill, ☎ *0171-326-5100.*
This is a really big one; 1500 people can jive here. They have theme nights, gay nights and something called "Love Muscle" night. Need we say more?

Bass Clef

35 Coronet Street, ☎ *0171-729-2476.*
It's pretty hard to find but when you finally do, it's worth it. It's considered an exciting center for live Jazz, including African and Latin. Next door is the Tenor Clef, with "higher tone" jazz.

Pizza on the Park

11-13 Knightsbridge, ☎ *0171-235-5273.*
They started with just good pizza, but now they want a bigger slice of the pie. They attract all the hot new groups.

Pizza Express

10 Dean Street, ☎ *0171-437-9595.*
These are the same people who own the above and have the same good pizza and the same good jazz, but they do it in Soho.

100 Club

100 Clifford Street, ☎ *0171-636-0933.*
Dixieland here as well as blues and rock and roll.

Palookaville

13A James Street, Covent Garden, ☎ *0171-240-5857.*
How can you resist that name? It's really a wine bar that has very good jazz musicians that play in the p.m. Very late they have dancing.

Rock Garden

6-7 The Piazza, Covent Garden, ☎ *0171-240-3961.*
A wonderful old vegetable warehouse turned restaurant and jazz club. The specialize in new sound.

Prince of Orange

118 Lower Road, ☎ *0171-237-2224*
A switch for London, the jazz is free for the price of a drink, and very good it is, too. It's really a neighborhood pub that's got rhythm.

Rock

Electric Ballroom

184 Camden High Street, ☎ *0171-485-9006.*
Punk rock is its stock and trade, but every once in a while, they close
their eyes to a little slow dancing.

The Grande

Clapham Junction, St. John Hill, ☎ *0171-284-2200.*
Takes its name very seriously. It's a barn of an old theater that definitely rocks around the clock.

Brixton Academy

211 Stockwell Road, ☎ *0171-326-1022.*
Cutting-edge rock for about 4000 adventurers that crowd the Brixton for an earful of the latest.

Hammersmith Apollo

Queen Caroline Street, ☎ *0181-741-4668.*
Big rock bands used to stop here on tour. They've had the best of the
best in this vintage theater. They still do.

Dublin Castle

94 Parkway, ☎ *0171-485-1773.*
Rockabilly and reggae, both make this pub vibrate with great sound.

Robey

240 Seven Sisters Road, ☎ *0171-263-4581.*
They have at least five different bands, each and every night.

Dance Clubs

Limelight

136 Shaftesbury Avenue, ☎ *0171-434-0572.*
This is no slap-dash operation. It's a converted church that is starkly
dramatic. The perfect place to dance the night away.

Bar Rumba

36 Shaftsbury Avenue, ☎ *0171-287-2715.*
Latin music that's irresistible for some hot turns around the floor.

Stringfellows

16 Upper St. Martin's Lane, ☎ *0171-240-5534.*
Fab place for club watching between dances. Its been "in" for years
and is still great fun.

Hippodrome

1 Cranbourn Street, ☎ *0171-437-4311.*
This one is owned by the same fellows as Stringfellows. They have a
great light show and disco till dawn.

Legends

29 Old Burlington Street, ☎ *0171-437-9933.*
Very classy, very dressy and very expensive. Where the rich meet the
super-rich to dance and relax. Lots of Sloane Rangers floating by.

Madame Jo Jo

8-10 Brewer Street, ☎ *0171-734-2473.*
For the comfortable, uninhibited and free spirited. This is basically a
transvestite club, but is attended by the civilian straights as well. They
have outrageous drag acts, cabaret and dancing. Lots of fun although
the "waitresses" are not all they seem.

Comedy Clubs

Jongleurs

The Cornet, 49 Lavender Gardens, ☎ *0171-924-2766.*
Both the Cornet and Jongleurs are twin clubs, which between them
can handle a crowd of 500. If one is full, you can book the other—
they're interchangeable. They have lots of comedians, dancers and
even mimes (only in London would anyone actually pay to see a
mime).

Comedy Store

Haymarket House, Oxendon Street, ☎ *0171-344-4449.*
If you loved them in the states, you'll love them with a British accent.
New young comic blood and even improvisational groups have great
fun with the human condition.

Orange Boom Boom

De Hems, Macclesfield Street, ☎ *0181-694-1710.*
This is one of those very out of the ordinary places that is too intrigu-
ing to miss. It's a Dutch pub, which hosts all kinds of comedy served
up with Dutch Beer.

Canal Cafe Theatre

The Bridge House, Delamere Terrace, ☎ *0171-289-6054.*
The players here have ongoing news revues that rake the politicos and
royals over the coals regularly.

Bars

Many of London's best bars are in hotels.

The great bars of London are for the most part, in the great hotels of
London. We're not discussing wine bars or pubs at the moment, just places
to have a relaxed, and in some cases nostalgic, experience that is exclusively
tied to a sensational martini or perhaps an icy cold Pimm's #1, served up
with great style by a bartender who knows the difference between shaken
and stirred. We've put together a thirst-quenching list of favorites around
town—Cheers!

The Athenaeum

116 Piccadilly, ☎ *0171-499-3464.*

The whiskey bar is stocked with 56 different malt whiskeys to keep you busy.

The Ritz Bar

The Ritz Hotel, Piccadilly, ☎ *0171-493-8181.*
Most people think only of the formal tea served at the Ritz. We much prefer the bar. Come to think of it, we probably prefer a Ritz bar any-where.

The American Bar

Savoy Hotel, The Strand, ☎ *0171-836-4343.*
You can just see Fred and Ginger clinking martini glasses in its dark, clubby and elite-filled recesses. They swear the martini was invented in the American Bar, but who's to know? If you have any respect for tradition you'll have it with an olive!

The Lanesborough

Hyde Park Corner, ☎ *0171-259-5599.*
The bar here is called the Library, but we assure you there is very little reading going on here. Aside from the literary look, they have a col-lection of rare cognacs that go back hundreds of years. Most of them are at least ready for social security cards.

The American Bar

The Dorchester, Park Lane, ☎ *0171-629-8888.*
Always filled with celebs nibbling the nuts and scarfing down the olives. It's one of the top meeting places at cocktail time, so the crowd is great for ogling.

The Winter Garden

The Regent Hotel, 222 Marylebone Road, ☎ *0171-631-8000.*
You can have your sidecar in the midst of a soaring palm-filled atrium. There's a very discreet piano in the background and first rate snacks. But the story here is the dynamite setting.

Trader Vic's

London Hilton, 22 Park Lane, ☎ *0171-493-7586.*
Man does not live by Pimm's cups alone. If you can't make it to Tahiti, you can get a terrific mai tai or suffering bastard right here, not to mention a possible Pu Pu platter.

The Langtry Bar

Cadogen Hotel, 75 Sloane Street, ☎ *0171-235-7141.*
Lily Langtry and Oscar Wilde regularly met here to toast the arts. It's a wonderful step back to Victorian excesses and perhaps "The Impor-tance of Being Oscar."

The American Bar

The Stafford, St. James Place, ☎ *0171-493-0111.*
This bar is steeped in history, nostalgia and dozens of toys that hang from the ceiling. During the war American and Canadian officers met in the bar and, sadly, some of them never made it home. Today, The Stafford is filled by the locals at lunch and dinner. It's full of laughter and memories. A classic!

Wine Bars

Wine has always been dear to the hearts of most Brits, perhaps because they're just a Sauvignon's throw from France, unlike the colonies, where it took a couple of hundred years to just be able to identify red from white. The wine bar scenes have grown enormously over the last years, and wine by the glass is a wonderful way to try some of the really great ones that are a queen's ransom by the bottle.

Ebury Wine Bar
>   *139 Ebury Street,* ☎ *0171-5447.*

The Metro
>   *28 Basil Street,* ☎ *0171-589-6286.*

The Fire Station
>   *150 Waterloo Road,* ☎ *0171-401-3267.*

Bill Bentley's Wine Bar
>   *31 Beauchamp Pl,* ☎ *0171-589-5080.*

Balls Brothers
>   *2-3 Old Charge Street, St. Paul's,* ☎ *0171-248-8597.*

Bow Wine Vaults
>   *10 Bow Churchyard,* ☎ *0171-248-1121.*

Brahms & Liszt
>   *19 Russell Street,* ☎ *0171-240-3661.*

Shampers
>   *4 Kingly Street,* ☎ *0171-437-1692.*

Bar des Amis du Vin
>   *11-14 Hanover Pl,* ☎ *0171-379-3444.*

Actor's Retreat
>   *46 Lexington Street,* ☎ *0171-437-5708.*

Pubs

Pubs are London's stress relievers.

Ever since medieval times, the pub in England has been a meeting place, a political forum, a game room and even a part-time theater (Shakespeare first presented his plays in pubs, until he hit the Globe circuit.) Before the British ever heard of the word stress, they had started their very own stress reduction centers. Ale, bitters, beer and spirits were their narcotics of choice centuries ago, to deaden the despair of their sometimes horrifying existence. That was then; now pubs are their social clubs, with some of the best food in the city. A pub lunch with good cheese, scotch eggs, meat pies, thick bread and pickles, is about as good as it's going to get for the price. Bottoms up!

George Inn

77 Borough High Street, ☎ *0171-407-2056.*

Originally opened in 1590, the great fire destroyed it, so they just rebuilt it in 1676, right down to the last nail. Shakespeare himself had an après play pint here and Dickens used it as a setting over and over. Talk about thrilling!

The Dove

19 Upper Mall, ☎ *0181-748-5405.*

It overlooks the Thames, so you can have your drink on the terrace, but the inside is where the history of The Dove is. "Rule Brittannia" was written here by James Thomson, who died upstairs after finishing it.

The Anchor

34 Park Street, Bankside, ☎ *0171-407-1577.*

Another one destroyed by the great fire, and rebuilt again in 1750. Dr. Johnson used it for his address while he saved up enough *As* thru *Zs*, to write his dictionary. It's really five tiny bar rooms that have open fireplaces and lots of pub color. It's one of the great ones.

Grenadier

18 Wilton Row, ☎ *0171-235-3074.*

The Duke of Wellington and his troops used to "tuck it in" here, and if that weren't enough, the Grenadiers left for Waterloo from here. It's a military treasure-trove of memorabilia. Today it's famous, appropriately enough, for its Bloody Marys.

Sherlock Holmes

10 Northumberland Street, ☎ *0171-930-2644.*

Don't expect to see Holmes himself or even Moriarty, even though Conan Doyle had Holmes meet Henry Baskerville here when it was called the Northumberland Arms (that's *Baskervilles*, as in *The Hounds of.*) The pub decided if it was good enough for Holmes, they would name it after him and even re-create his complete study, test tubes, microscope and all, upstairs. Elementary for any real fan.

The Lamb

94 Lamb's Conduit Street, ☎ *0171-405-0713.*

A beautiful room in Bloomsbury, with all the Victorian fixings. There's cut glass, plush gilt and photos of old music hall favorites.

Ye Olde Cheshire Cheese

Wine Office Court, 1145 Fleet Street, ☎ *0171-353-6170.*

If you have time for only one, this is it. Another from the 1600s, it's made up of six low-ceilinged rooms with sawdust on the floor, and long oak tables. Dickens spoke of it in *A Tale of Two Cities*. It's the real thing—don't for a minute let people tell you it's a tourist trap. It is! But that makes no difference, it's the real McCoy, and so is the shepherd's pie.

Beach Blanket Babylon

45 Techbury Road, ☎ *0171-229-2907.*

Very hot! Very in! A modern pub for the 90s with packed crowds and a huge bar. It's so 90s they have a large selection of imported beers. You have to admit, the name is catchy.

Lamb & Flag

33 Rose Street, off Garrick Street, ☎ *0171-497-9504.*
Another of Dickens' favorites, it's the only timber-framed Tudor
that's still standing in the West End. It used to be called The Bucket
of Blood because of the fights that took place there. Things have
changed—really!

Nell of Old Drury

29 Catherine Street, ☎ *0171-836-5328.*
This smashing looking pub in Covent Garden is opposite the Theatre
Royal. It was named for Nell Gwynne who was born near Drury Lane.
Here's a real theatre pub with a bell to warn of ending intermissions.

SPORTS AGENDA

Equestrian sports are faves of the British.

Spectator Sports

Be sure to call ahead for times and reservations for events.

Cricket

Lords
> Matches at St. Johns Wood, NW8, ☎ 0171-289-1611.

The Oval
> Kensington Oval, SE11, ☎ 0171-582-6660.

Rugby

Rugby League
> London Crusaders Barnet Copthall Stadium, Great North Way, NW4, ☎ 0181-203-4211.

Soccer

London Football
> Assoc, Oldworth Gro, SE13, ☎ 0181-690-9626.

Arsenal F.C.
> Highbury Stadium, Cornell Rd, WO5, ☎ 0171-226-0304.

Chelsea F.C.
> Stamford Bridge, Fulham Rd, SW6.

Racing

Ascot
>   High St., Ascot, ☎ 0344-22211.

Epsom
>   Racecourse Paddock, Epsom, ☎ 0372-727811.

Windsor
>   Maidenhead Rd, Windsor, ☎ 0753-865234.

Polo

The Guards Polo Club
>   Smiths Lawn, Windsor Great Park, Englefield Queen, Egham, ☎ 0784-43-7797

Tennis

All England Lawn Tennis Club
>   Church Rd, SW19 (☎ 0181-944-1066, Wimbledon Park)

Participant Sports

Tennis

Queens Club
>   Palliser Rd, W14, ☎ 0171-385-3421.

Lawn Tennis Assoc.
>   Palliser Rd, W14, ☎ 0171-3385-2366.

Squash Rackets Assoc.
>   The Salons, Warple Way, W3, ☎ 0181-746-1616.

The Carlton Tennis Club
>   Alfred Rd, Westbourne Green, W2, ☎ 0171-286-1985.

Holland Park
>   Kensington High St., W8, ☎ 0171-602-2226.

Golf Courses

Airlinks
>   Southall Lane, Hounslow, ☎ 0181-561-1418.

Highgate
>   Denewood Rd, N6, ☎ 0181-340-1906.

Trent Park Golf Club
>   Bramley Rd, Southgate, N14, ☎ 0181-366-7432.

Bicycling

Go By Cycle
>   9 Templeton Pl, SW6, ☎ 0171-373-3657.

On Your Bike
>   52-54 Tooley St., SE1, ☎ 0171-357-6958.

Portobello Cycles
>   609 Goldborne Rd, W1-, ☎ 0181-960-0444.

Yellow Jersey Cycles
>   44 Chalk Farm Rd, NW1, ☎ 0171-485-8090.

Horseback Riding

London Equestrian Centre
>   Fith Manor Farm, N12, ☎ 0181-349-1345.

Ross Nye
>   8 Bathhurst St., Mews W2, ☎ 0171-262-3791.

SPORTS LINE

(info on all sports facilities)
☎ *0171-222-8000*
Mon.–Fri., 10:00 a.m.–6:00 p.m.

EXCURSIONS

*The water at the Baths has been the same temperature (116°F) since
the Romans first soaked their toes.*

Exciting and gloriously diverse as London is, we, who never
have enough time to spend on its great wealth of treasures, are
telling you that you should really leave it. But in the best possible
way, for a few immensely rewarding day trips. Travelling just a
short distance from London can put you in touch with historic
castles, medieval spas, and seaside resorts. We've suggested the
trips we feel would most enrich a visit to London without going
too far afield. This is probably the only time during your trip to
London that a car might come in handy, if you can overcome
left-hand-side-of-the-road-itis. Check at the hotel desk for rental
agencies.

Bath

Of all the day trips that are available from London, Bath is hands-down,
the most romantic. Not only is it a "living museum" and one of the best examples of a perfect Georgian city, but it is totally available to you by letting
yourself get lost in its winding streets and its ancient history.

The Romans were the ones who decided that the hot springs of Bath were indeed "hot stuff" in A.D. 43. It was no end of comfort to know that after a good orgy and a bit too much of the grape, they could drop into Bath for a major rehab. In gratitude, they built a temple to the Goddess Minerva with more sophisticated chambers to make use of the spa waters. A visit to the Roman Baths Museum is an eerie look at the past. The "pool room" itself has a pale green glow. The steam that rises from the water makes the whole place look like a moist mirage. The water has been at the same temperature (116 F) since the Romans first stuck their toes in.

In the 18th century, the Victorians rediscovered the spa led by the queen and Lord Nelson. Charles Dickens thought the water "tastes like warm flat-irons." But since it had become the spa of the moment, John Wood, one of the 18th century's most distinguished architects, laid out the terraces and squares of Bath in regal splendor.

Aside from the Roman ruins, Bath is a town for exploring. There are elegant shops, sweet little tea rooms, antiques and town houses that make it irresistible for the "unstructured stroll."

Another element of romance that can be part of a trip to Bath is the **Orient Express** which runs a day trip to Bath from Victoria Station. Talk about recapturing the past! Unlike its other exotic destinations that require sleeping aboard, this one leaves Victoria at 9:45 and returns in the early evening. You will travel in those meticulously restored coaches of the 20s and 30s, sipping a glass of champagne and feeling very much that Agatha Christie is sitting right opposite. Brunch and dinner are elegantly served at your seat. Once you arrive in Bath, you can tour with the other passengers (everything is included in the price of the tour) or you can break away and meet everybody at departure time for even more champagne and a "chi-chi" little supper on the way back to London. The Orient Express makes bath even more magical— if that's possible.

There are good cafes all over the town and there's the tiny bakery where "Sally Lunns" were first made. They are sweet buns, with a history.

If you decide to go to Bath by British Rail, you leave from Paddington Station and the 116 miles is covered in about an hour. Buses depart from Victoria and take about three hours. Of, of course, you can opt for a regular, set tour.

Brighton's Royal Pavilion is breathtaking inside and out.

Brighton

This seaside resort that came into prominence about 1750, was discovered by those who were looking for relief from tummy troubles. They thought that swimming in the water, rather than drinking it, would effect a cure. And so a resort was born. It was considered so trendy that the Prince of Wales decided to check it out. He loved it so much he built the "be all, end all" kitsch confection called the **Royal Pavilion**. The Pavilion is half-Arabian nights, half-Regency extravaganza. John Nash designed it for the Prince with a huge onion-shaped dome and roofs that look like the tops of Bedouin tents. It is breathtaking both inside and out. It's open for viewing from 10 a.m. to 5 p.m. (☎ *0273-603.005*).

Brighton's so-called beach is rocky and inhospitable for swimming, although it's always crowded with Brits who are testing the waters. The piers that jut out over the ocean are great fun in a faded, 30s amusement park sort of way, and the smell of the sea is bracing. What is totally unique about Brighton is that it is a perfectly preserved Regency setting right on the ocean. **The Promenade**, with it's cast-iron colonnade runs alongside the beach and past the beautiful crescents and squares that give Brighton its period look. Aside from the Pavilion and the **Brighton Museum**, which has an award winning art nouveau and art deco collection, **The Lanes** are the swinging part of Brighton. For those afflicted with terminal Victoriana, exploring the tiny cobblestone streets that are filled with antiques and collectibles, is the closest they'll come to (we hope) an orgiastic experience in Britain. By the time you find your way out of the winding maze of streets, all credit cards will be at half-mast.

Since Brighton has a year-round community, the restaurants are not only up to the level of the best of London, but in some cases, surpass it. Try **English's Oyster Bar or Manley's**. They're right in town. You can reach Brighton from Victoria Station by British Rail.

Greenwich

Royal Observatory, Greenwich is where Greenwich Mean Time originated.

Anyone who has ever herd of the Greenwich Meridian, which divides the world in two, or Greenwich Mean time, which is how the world sets its clocks, has to be fascinated by this prestigious town. You can actually stand with one foot on each side of the Meridian and know that you are standing in two hemispheres at the same time. This may even be better than "sitting on top of the world." Aside from these two very unique distinctions, this sleepy little village 10 minutes by train out of London, was also the birthplace of Henry VIII, the location of the **National Maritime Museum**, the **Royal Observatory**, and the berthing place of the *Cutty Sark*, the last of the 19th century tea clippers that sailed the world.

Aside from its rather earth-shaking significance, Greenwich also has a couple of antique, crafts and flea markets that are held on the weekend. It's true you can get to Greenwich in 10 or 15 minutes from **Charing Cross Station**, but it's a lot more fun to take a boat from **Charing Cross Pier**. It will bring you right along side the *Cutty Sark* and into beautiful downtown Greenwich, or you can take a boat from **Westminster Pier** (they run frequently) and get a blockbuster view of the **Tower of London** on the way. Greenwich is an absolute delight and as easy to visit as **Knightsbridge** or **Chelsea**. Kids especially, are really blown away by doing the Meridian "Cake Walk."

Stratford-upon-Avon

Shakespeare Center pays tribute to favorite son, William.

Wall-to-wall 16th-century England is hard to resist. Even if there was no W. S., no theatre, no edge-of-your-chair dramas, Stratford would still be England's Elizabethan *heartland*. But of course, everything goes back to the celebration of Stratford's favorite son William S. He was not "born in a trunk" as some would like to believe, but on Henley Street, which still has some of the original timbers of his home left. Today, that's the location of the **Shakespeare Centre**. His wife, Anne Hathaway, lived in **Shottery**, just outside of town, and her thatched cottage draws thousands of people, as does the **Holy Trinity Church**, where the Shakespeare family is buried. **Hall's Croft** is the preserved Tudor home of Shakespeare's daughter, Susanna (who, thank God, married a doctor). The other most visited exhibition is the **World of Shakespeare**, which is a multimedia extravaganza!

The Royal Shakespeare Theatre, which is located on the banks of the **Avon River**, is where **The Royal Shakespeare Company** performs between March and January. There is nothing better, if you love the plays, than to see them in the very place where Will dreamed them to begin with.

If you're planning just a day trip, you can leave from **Paddington Station** with a change at **Leamington Spa**. It takes about two hours, or go by bus from Victoria. Should you decide to see a performance and stay the night, there are endless B & Bs around. Try to book everything from London if possible so you don't lose time in last minute arrangements.

Windsor

Windsor Castle is the royal family's summer home.

The town of **Windsor** is not only the home of **Eton College**, but it also has the largest castle in the world that still has royalty in residence. **William the Conqueror** built it in 1078 and Queen Elizabeth had to endure its partial destruction by fire in her annus horribilis, 1993.

Once upon a time there were the *Merry Wives of Windsor*, including **Queen Victoria** who later, unfortunately, was called "the widder of Windsor." Today, very few of the Windsor wives have too much to be happy about, but the royal family (the ones that are left) still uses this magnificent castle as it's summer residence. Every king who lived at Windsor enlarged it. Edward IV began the chapel, Henry VIII built the vault in back of the choir, Elizabeth I added on the north terrace and Charles II redid the state apartments. Everybody put in their two farthings-worth until George V decided to use it as the family's weekend house. The Great Park that belongs to the castle is over 4000 acres and has deer, birds and the queen's corgis running through it. Now that Windsor is well on it's way to a complete recovery, it can be visited again except for several rooms that are still closed. The highlights are the State Apartments and Queen Mary's Dolls' House. To call it a mere dolls' house would be like calling the castle a fixer-upper. It has a full electrical system, and 200 teeny, tiny books in it's teeny, tiny library.

If you have time you can walk through the town for a bit; it's really lovely.

Windsor is reached by train from Waterloo. It takes about one hour. Greenline buses leave from Hyde Park Corner.

MUSEUMS

British Museum contains more than six million artifacts.

Even if you break out in a nasty rash at the thought of spending endless, backbreaking hours trudging through corridors and great halls, staring at pictures until your vision blurs, take a deep breath. This is, after all, London we're talking about. It is a city of museums. All kinds of museums from the sublime to the ridiculous. What other city has an institution like the **British Museum**, and just a few scant blisters away, the **Museum of Garden History**? London's museums are as much a part of the fabric of the city as **Big Ben**, **The Thames** and the **palace** itself.

The British Museum

Great Russell Street, WC1, ☎ *0171-636-1555.*
Mon.–Sat., 10 a.m.–5 p.m.; Sun., 2:30 p.m.–6 p.m. Admission is free.
Some say the greatest, most important museum in the world. (See "Top Sights," page 8)

Bank of England Museum

Threadneedle Street, EC2, ☎ *0171-601-5545.*
Mon.–Fri., 10 a.m.–5 p.m. Admission free.
They have exhibits to show the history of the bank, including a video display. High tech for high finances. Definitely no free samples.

Bethnal Green Museum of Childhood

Cambridge Health Road, E2, 0181-980-2415.
Mon.–Sat., 10 a.m.–5:30 p.m.; Sun., 2:30 p.m.–5:30 p.m. Admission free.
The perfect museum for children; wonderful collections of dolls, doll houses, costumes and toys.

Bramah Tea and Coffee Museum

The Clove Building, Butler's Wharf, SE1, ☎ 0171-378-0222.
10 a.m.–6 p.m. Admission £3, children £1.50.
A caffeine addict's dream come true.

Dickens House Museum

48 Doughty Street, WC1, ☎ 0171-405-2127.
Mon.-Sat., 10 a.m.–5 p.m. Admission £3, children £1.
This is the very house where C.D. wrote at least four of his novels. His study has been reproduced and the house itself could belong to Martin Chuzzelwit.

Design Museum

Shad Thames, Butler's Wharf, SE1, ☎ 0171-403-6933.
Mon.–Fri, 11:30 a.m.–6 p.m.; Sat.–Sun., 12-6 p.m. Adults £4.50, children £3.50
The museum's prime intent is to explain how everyday objects work, and the reason for their design.

Freud Museum

20 Haresfield Gardens, NW3, ☎ 0171-435-2002.
Wed.–Sun., 12-5 p.m. Admission £2.50.
If you really love your mother, you'd better drop by. This was Freud's last home. All his personal effects (of course, his couch) are on display.

Guard's Museum

Wellington Barracks, Birdcage Walk, SW1, ☎ 0171-414-3428.
Mon.–Sun., 10 a.m.–4 p.m. Admission £2, children £1.
Five regiments' (Grenadiers, Coldstream, Scots, Irish and Welsh) history for over 300 years. Uniforms, weapons and memorabilia on display.

Imperial War Museum

Lambeth Road, SE1, ☎ 0171-416-5000.
Daily 10 a.m.–6 p.m. Admission £3.70, children £1.85.
Four floors of exhibitions on W.W. I and W.W. II. Everything from ration books to a Blitz experience. It really captures the history and emotions of "Britain's finest hour."

Jewish Museum

Woburn House, Tavistock Square, WC1, ☎ 0171-388-4525.
Tues., Fri., Sun., 10 a.m.–4 p.m., April-Sept. Sun. and Fri., 10 a.m.–1 p.m., Oct-Mar. Admission £1.
Small, but very comprehensive history of the Jewish religion. Its most prized possession is a Venetian synagogue Arc.

London Transport Museum

Covent Garden, WC2, ☎ 0171-379-6344.
Daily, 10 a.m.–6 p.m. (last admission, 5:15). Admission £95, children £2.50.
Kids of all ages love this place. It has old trollies, buses and even a tube train. It also has "hands on" exhibits. You can actually put yourself in the drivers seat of a bus. Great fun and great souvenirs for sale.

Museum of Garden History

St. Mary-at-Lambeth, Lambeth Place, SE1, ☎ 0171-261-1891.

May 6-Dec. 11, Mon.–Fri., 11 a.m.–3 p.m.; Sun., 10:30 a.m.–5 p.m. Admission free.

Mary, Mary, quite contrary must have founded this place. Actually, the 14th-century church of St. Mary-at-Lambeth was restored and the 17th-century garden was re-created in the churchyard. The British are the most avid gardeners in the world, so there are permanent collections of tools, and an "Aspects of Garden History" exhibit.

Museum of London

150 London Wall, EC2, ☎ 0171-600-3699.
Tues.-Sat., 10 a.m.–6 p.m.; Sun., 12-6 p.m. Admission £3, children £1.50.
The history of London spread out in galleries arranged from the Roman period to present day. For a touch of glamour, the Lord Mayor's state coach is kept on display, except when it's used for ceremonial functions. The most fascinating exhibit of all is the Fire of London with special effects and lighting that makes it come alive in a chilling, realistic display. One of the newest exhibits is called Calico Crazy. It tells the history of the Calico printing industry with 18th century costumes and textiles.

Museum of Mankind

6 Burlington Gardens, W1, ☎ 0171-437-2224.
Mon.–Sat., 10 a.m.–5 p.m.; Sun., 2:30 p.m.–6 p.m. Admission free.
Actually, this is an arm of the British Museum, which deals with cultures of people who are not from western civilizations. It's the museum's Ethnographic Department that has been relocated to Burlington House. Eskimos, Amazon tribes, West Africans, Pacific Rim Asians, are all explored here through their artifacts, clothing and weapons.

Museum of the Moving Image

South Bank, SE1, ☎ 0171-401-2636.
Daily, 10 a.m.–6 p.m. (last admission 5 p.m.). Admission £5.50, children £4.
From Chinese shadow plays that were done in 2000 B.C., right up the age of television. MOMI is now considered the world's largest museum devoted to Cinema and Television arts. There are fabulous interactive exhibits that let you read the news on TV, animate your own cartoon or audition for a role in a Hollywood movie.

National Maritime Museum

Romney Road, Greenwich, SE10, 0181-858-4422.
Located in Greenwich, this museum of ships is any captain's paradise. They have a huge collection of model ships, navigational instruments, charts, uniforms and even fine paintings of naval scenes. Perhaps the most tragic of all shipwrecks is chronicled here in an exhibit of The Wreck of the Titanic. They do the sad story of the disaster from beginning to end.

Natural History Museum

Cronwell Road, SW7, ☎ 0171-938-9123.
Mon.–Sat., 10 a.m.–5:50 p.m.; Sun., 11 a.m.–5:50 p.m. Admission £5, children £2.50.
Dinosaur-heaven for kids; we love them too. There are over 65 million species (and that's only as we go to press) of plants, fossils, animals, minerals, that grew out of a collection of Sir Hans Sloane, who also was one of the founders of the British Museum. The exhibits tell

the story of the earth (where is Cecil B. DeMille when you need him). The gemstone collection is almost as much fun as the jewels in the Tower. One of the all time favorites here is the Creepy Crawlies Gallery, which, true to its name, leaves you with the ongoing desire to scratch yourself for hours. Super-enlargement of species with many arms and legs are made semi-adorable by clever film techniques. Our advice is, have lunch before you visit this one.

National Museum of Cartoon Art

Carriage Row, 163-205 Eversholt Ct, NW1, ☎ *0171-388-4326.*
Mon., Tues., Wed. & Fri., 12-6 p.m.; Sat.–Sun., 2 p.m.–6 p.m.; Thurs., 12-7 p.m.

A very new museum that chronicles 250 years of cartooning in Britain, from political to animation. We hope it will last, but call ahead just to make sure.

Fan Museum

12 Crooms Hill, Greenwich, SE10, 0181-858-7879.
Tues.–Sat., 11 a.m.–4:30 p.m.; Sun., Noon–4:30 p.m. Admission £2.50, children £1.50.

If you're feeling hot under the collar from the other museums you've visited, there is always a cool breeze blowing at the Fan Museum. They have 2000 fans on display from the 17th century to the present. The surprise here is the artistry that has been a part of Fan making through the ages. There is also a craft workshop so you can sometimes watch these delicate remnants of the past being restored.

Sherlock Holmes Museum

221B Baker Street, NW1, ☎ *0171-935-8866.*
Daily, 10 a.m.–6 p.m. Admission £5, children £3.

It doesn't take a brilliant sleuth to realize that if you adore Holmes, you'd want to see his very own "digs." If you want to make the "scene of the crime," look for the Victorian Bobbie stationed outside in front. Don't look for La Strade; he never thought Holmes was a "real" detective either.

Victoria and Albert Museum

Cromwell Road, SW7, ☎ *0171-938-8500.*
Tues.-Sun., 10 a.m.–5:50 p.m.; Mon., 12-5:50 p.m. Admission free.
(See Top sights, page 216).

The Museum of Torture/The Clink Exhibition

1 Clink Street, SE1, ☎ *0171-403-6515,* ☎ *0171-378-1558.*
Daily, 10 a.m.–6 p.m. Admission £2.

This one is really "pushing the envelope," unless you're devoted to SM. We don't know whether to call this place trendy or sick. Your choice! The exhibits include restraining and torture devices, as well as suits of armor and other things you wouldn't want Aunt Ruthie to see. It will either make you smile, or shudder, depending.

AGENDA INTELLIGENCE

If you've ever wondered where "the clink" came from in terms of prison jargon, wonder no more. There was an infamous jail-house in London, in the 1500s, run by an even more infamous warden named Clink. The most horrifying threat one could make was imprisonment in Clinks'. Later it just became, "the clink."

Shakespeare's Globe Museum

1 Bear Gardens, SE1, ☎ *0171-928-6342.*
Mon.–Sat., 10 a.m.–5 p.m.; Sun., 2 p.m.–5:30 p.m. Donation.
(See "The City," page 90)

GALLERIES

A collection of important people from Britain's past and present are immortalized at the National Gallery.

Barbican Art Gallery

Barbican Centre, EC2, ☎ *0171-638-4141.*
Mon., Wed., Sat., 10 a.m.–6:45 p.m.; Tues, 10 a.m.–5:45 p.m.; Sun., 12–6:45 p.m. Admission £4.50, children £2.50.
Varied art gallery in the Barbican Centre, changing collections.

Courtauld Institute Galleries

Somerset House, Strand W2, ☎ *0171-873-2526.*
Mon.–Sat., 10 a.m.–6 p.m.; Sun., 2 p.m.–6 p.m. Admission £3, children £1.50.
Old masters, Impressionists and Post-Impressionists.

Crafts Council Gallery

44A Pentonville Road, Islington, N1, ☎ *0171-278-7700*
Contemporary and historical crafts.

Dulwich Picture Gallery

College Road, 0181-693-5254.
Tues.–Fri., 10 a.m.–5 p.m.; Sat., 11 a.m.–5 p.m.; Sun., 2 p.m.–5 p.m. Admission £1.50, children £1.
The oldest public art gallery in England. It dates from 1815. Contains 320 paintings, 17th-and 18th-century works.

Hayward Gallery

South Bank Centre, SE1, ☎ *0171-928-3144.*
Mon., Thurs., Fri., Sat., Sun., 10 a.m.–6 p.m.; Tues.–Wed., 10 a.m.–8 p.m. Admission £5, children £3.50.
Revolving exhibitions of British and worldwide artists.

Chalk Farm Gallery

20 Chalk Farm Road, NW1, ☎ *0171-267-3300.*
Daily, 10 a.m.–6 p.m. No admission fee.
Paintings, ceramics, glass and sculptures.

20th Century Gallery

821 Fulham Road, SW6, ☎ *0171-731-5888.*
Mon.–Fri., 10 a.m.–6 p.m.; Sat., 10 a.m.–1 p.m. No admission fee.
Post-Impressionist and modern British.

Mathaf Gallery

24 Motcomb Street, SW1, ☎ *0171-235-0010.*
Mon.–Fri., 9:30 a.m.–5:30 p.m. No admission fee.
19th-century Oriental paintings.

National Gallery

Trafalgar Square, WC2, ☎ *0171-389-1785.*
Mon.–Sat., 10 a.m.–6 p.m.; Sun, 2 p.m.–6 p.m. Admission free. Charge for special exhibitions.
Over 2000 paintings in an unrivaled collection of Western civilization's art from the 13th to 20th centuries. It was founded in 1824 when George IV persuaded the pence-pinching government to buy 38 old-masters' paintings. The rest, as they say, is history. The very controversial Sainsbury Wing, which Prince Charles detests, was opened in 1991, to house the early Renaissance collection.

National Portrait Gallery

St. Martin's Place, Trafalgar Square, NC2, ☎ *0171-306-0055.*
Mon.–Sat., 10 a.m.–6 p.m.; Sun. 12-6 p.m. Admission free.
Right around the corner from the National Gallery, this is a collection of historically important people from Britain's past and present, starting with the Tudors. It's not half as uplifting as the National Gallery, since it's mostly a collection of staring faces, even if most of them are royal, and no matter how famous they may be to a resident, to a visitor it's like looking at someone else's wedding photos. Still, some of the artists are old masters, so it might just be worth a quick stroll-around.

Queen's Gallery

Buckingham Palace, Buckingham Palace Road, SW1, ☎ *0171-799-2331.*
Tues.–Sat., 10 a.m.–5 p.m.; Sun., 2 p.m.–5 p.m. Admission £3, children £1.50.
The riches of the royal collection spread out in front of you. The queen has always been a topnotch collector of paintings and furniture and has the single most important Faberge collection outside the Kremlin. When she displays her knickknacks, it's well worth a look.

Royal Academy of Arts

Burlington House, Piccadilly, W1, ☎ *0171-439-7438.*
Mon.–Fri., 10 a.m.–6 p.m.; Sat.–Sun., 11 a.m.–7 p.m. Admission £5, children £2.25
(See "Piccadilly," page 66).

Saatchi Gallery

98A Boundary Road, NW8, ☎ *0171-624-8299.*

Tues.–Sun., 12-6 p.m. Admission £2.50, children £1.50.
An amazingly designed space that was once a paint factory, it's a work of art by itself. It houses the Saatchi collection of international contemporary art. Ongoing guest exhibitions during the year.

Tate Gallery

Millbank, SW1, ☎ 0171-887-8000.
Mon.–Sat., 10 a.m.–5:50 p.m.; Sun, 2 p.m.–5:50 p.m. Admission free.
The Tate has two major collections with which they continue to dazzle art lovers. One is British art from the 16th century to the 20th; the other is international modern art including the Impressionists up to the present. All the greats from Rodin (*The Kiss* is at the Tate), to Warhol, to Picasso, are displayed, although the Tate's holdings are so numerous that only a part of them can be exhibited at any one time. The British collection dates from 1545 up to today, and highlights Gainsborough, Reynolds and Hogarth, among others. The Tate is world-famous.Don't miss it.

Whitechapel Art Gallery

80 Whitechapel High Street, E1, ☎ 0171-522-7878.
Tues.–Sat., 11 a.m.–5 p.m.; Wed, 11 a.m.–8 p.m. Admission £3.50, children £2.
Experimental and modern artists in a very high profile gallery with two levels for decorative displays. There are a number of permanent artists who give lectures and run workshops as well.

AGENDA TOURS
OF LONDON

London's sights can be enjoyed on walking, bus and river tours.

London is a walking city and the joy of exploring it can best be realized on foot; however we've always, upon arriving in a new city, booked a half-day tour to get our bearings and a less confusing lay of the land. Once that's done, you'll be able to make up your agenda for walking the city with a good idea of the areas you want to focus on.

Guided Bus Tours

Original London Transport Sightseeing Tour

Tickets are, at press time, £9, for children £5. ☎ *0171-828-6449.*
Visits all major sights in Central London. It's operated by London Coaches. They leave very frequently from Victoria, Piccadilly Circus, Marble Arch and Baker St.

London Transport's London Plus

Tickets are at press time, £12, for children £6. ☎ *0171-828-6449.*
Double-decker buses, open top in the summer months, have guided tours with 30 stops at points of interest. You can get on and off, just catch the next tour bus to come along.

London Transport Royal Westminster Tour

Tickets are £11.50, for children £5, under 4. ☎ *0171-828-6449.*
This includes a view of the Changing of the Guards at the palace and takes three hours.

London Transport City Tour (three hours)

Tickets are £16.50, for children £15.50. ☎ *0171-828-6449.*
This includes the Tower of London and St. Paul's Cathedral.

London Transport Full Day Tour

Tickets are £27, for children £25, lunch included. ☎ *0171-828-6449.*
A combination of the Royal Westminster tour and the three-hour city tour, which takes the day and includes lunch.

Harrods Sightseeing Bus

Tickets are £15, for children £7. ☎ *0171-581-3603.*
Double-deckers in the famous green and gold colors of the store leave from entrance No. 8 (ask doorman) on Brompton Rd, at 10:30, 1:30 and 4p.m. The bus, or Harrods on wheels, tours all the major sights and serves coffee, tea, orange juice and cookies.

Evans Evans

☎ *0171-930-2377.*
Full day bus trip (various buses).

Frances Richards

☎ *0171-837-3111*
Full day bus trips (various prices).

The Big Bus Company

☎ *0181-944-7810.*
Different durations and prices, but they pick up visitors at their hotels at frequent intervals.

River Cruises

There are all manner of river tours of different durations, some with lunch, dinner and even tea. Call ahead to find out the options available at the time of your visit.

Westminster Pier, ☎ *0171-930-4097*
Charing Cross Pier, ☎ *0171-839-3312*
Tour Pier, ☎ *0171-488-0344*
Catamora Cruisers, ☎ *0171-839-3572*

Private Car and Driver Guide

Take-a-Guide Ltd

43 Finstock Road, W-10, ☎ *0181-960-0459.*

Good Company

48 Prince of Wales Road, NW5, ☎ *0171-267-5340.*

Walking Tours

Original London Walks, ☎ *0171-624-3978*
City Walks, ☎ *0171-700-6931*
Streets of London, ☎ *0181-346-9255*
Citilights, ☎ *0181-806-4325*

LONDON DAY AGENDAS

A terrace brings visitors closer to Tower Bridge.

One-Day Agenda for London

The following is elemental London, a quick look at the city to include at least our top three sights and just a whiff of the heady scent of "royalty." If you have only one day here, this is the best way to spend it.

Since it is an impossible task to get more than a taste of London in as brief a time as one day, the least frustrating route to take is to spend just a short while at each of your stops, no matter how hard it is to tear yourself away, because, in truth, you could easily devote days of fascinating exploration to each of them. Remember, this is just a taste, your next visit will be a banquet.

Morning

Start off with a "proper" British breakfast. If your hotel isn't the kind of place that offers a thrilling experience, then don't even reach for that limp toast; head for the **Connaught Hotel** (see "Hotels," page 29). We know it will cost a queen's ransom, but can one put a price on crisp sausages, perfect eggs, richly marbled, meaty bacon and the crispiest toast slathered with the best marmalade in town? And the setting is one that will start your first day with as much "pomp and circumstance" as you can get in the early morning.

Now you're ready to play the palace. It's essential that you get there by 11a.m. so that you have the best possible vantage point from which to see the **Changing of the Guards**. The ceremony takes place from 11:20-12:05. In the summer months it is performed daily. From the end of August to March, it's scheduled for every other day. Check with your hotel to make sure *your* day is the same as *their* day. Even if you miss the ceremony, you can still gaze at the Windsor Wonderland from outside, or if the queen is out of town (her flag will not be flying), you can always take the **Palace Tour** (see "Top Sights," page 4). Again, if you only have one day, this is a quick "close encounter of a royal kind."

Next, it's time to hop on one of those **big red doubledecker darlings** for a two-hour guided spin around London just to get your bearings. You can walk over to Victoria from the palace and catch one there. It's worth every pence to ensure your first real glimpse of the city is relaxed and hassle-free.

Afternoon

You've just spent half the day having a "blitz" look at London, so you should be ready for some major sustenance. What could be better than combining a **cruise on the Thames** with both lunch and the **Tower of London**? Arriving at the Tower by boat is the very same way some of it's most notorious alumni made their entrances (not many of them lived to make their exits). You can get a boat from **Charing Cross Pier** (Victoria Embankment, ☎ *0171-839-3312*) that serves a lunch included in the tour, and cruise down to the Tower with some of the best views of London as a bonus. If you prefer not to take to the water, this might be the perfect opportunity to have your first below-ground experience in **THE TUBE**. Since getting around in London by tube is ridiculously simple and great fun as well, just flash your travel card (see "Priorities," page 3) and take the Circle or District Line to Tower Hill. Then just follow the crowd.

Now that you've seen the jewels, the ravens, the beefeater and a few assorted dungeons, you're ready for an express viewing of **Westminster Abbey**. If you're taking the boat back to the Embankment (Charing Cross Pier), you can catch the Tube (Circle or District lines to Westminster, or take the tube (same lines), from Tower Hill to Westminster. In most cases the tube will be the fastest way to get around, since the traffic in London is so appalling!

Having just a quick look at Westminster Abbey seems as easy to accomplish as spending your coffee break touring the Pentagon, but be of good cheer; every gigantic national monument has its highlights. On your mark, get set, sightsee! Here are the bases you should touch before leaving: **Poets Corner, Henry VII Chapel, Royal Airforce Chapel, Tomb of Elizabeth I, Tomb of the Unknown Warrior, Tomb of Mary, Queen of Scotts**. Always look down as you walk through the church to see what famous person is buried underfoot, and if at all possible stop for 10 or 15 minutes to do a brass rubbing at the Rubbing Center, on the way out.

Even if you had winged feet, and fairly flew from place to place, it must be time for tea by now, so you're going to head back to the Strand (Embankment tube stop), for **tea at the Savoy**. We couldn't risk you're missing the Savoy or it's history and besides, after a delicious selection of their goodies, you can cross the Strand to **Covent Garden** for a whirlwind tour of the shops and the Piazza before heading back to your hotel. After a pit stop and a chance to pick up the tickets your concierge got for one of the hits at the **National Theatre**, your ready for a night on the town.

Evening

If tea at the Savoy was as decadent and extravagant as we remember, you probably won't want dinner before the theatre, so try to get to the National well before curtain time. You can have a drink and nibbles at one of the outdoor cafes or at one of their indoor bars. The area is wonderful for walks along the river or exploring the theatre complex itself. By the time the curtain comes down you're ready for some serious dinner. We think if you have only one night in London, dinner should be an occasion. Head for one of the hot spots such as **Bibendum** or **Quaglino's**. If you're too tired to cope with mega-glitz, there's always **Chinatown**, where you can keep a low profile and eat with your fingers. Before you're off to your dinner choice, try to walk back from the theatre over **Waterloo Bridge**. If you have to leave London in the morning, the view of **Parliament**, **Big Ben** and the **Thames** in the moonlight is the one you'll want to remember.

Agenda for the 2nd Day of a 2-Day Trip

Now that you've gotten the "superstar" sights out of the way, it's time to break out and see more of what makes London swing.

Morning

You're off to Parliament so get another early start with a pub breakfast at the **Silver Cross**, *33 Whitehall*, a pub that's been there since 1647. It's a hangout for newspaper people who cover Parliament, so not only will you have a great "trenchman's" breakfast, but you'll get to rub elbows with the "fourth estate." Now on to **Parliament Square** and the Houses themselves (see "Sights," page 11). You may be able to get into the Visitor's Galleries in the House of Commons, but with a few exceptions, most areas of Parliament are off-limits. But the views of the Houses and Big Ben are picture-postcard perfect. You're not far from **Downing Street** (you know who lives there), and also the **Cabinet War Rooms**, (Clive Steps, King Charles Street). They're a compelling reminder of Churchill and World War II.

If you walk down Whitehall, you can get to the **Strand** and **Trafalgar Square**. Spend some time with the lions who have the most benign demeanor and are willing patsies for the pigeons who lounge on them.

Lunch might be in **The Cafe**, in the Crypt, a ghostly "haunt" for people who love atmosphere with their bread pudding. The Crypt is under the Church of St. Martin-in-the-Fields, located alongside Trafalgar Square. The food is terrific, served cafeteria-style and inexpensive. It's a top choice for an informal lunch and tombstone rubbing.

Afternoon

The National Gallery is close by so you can pay a visit and still have time to walk on to **Piccadilly Circus** and be overwhelmed by the sound and fury. Don't stop now, **Fornum and Mason** is just down Piccadilly. It will only take a minute to take a turn around the Food Hall before taking the tube at Green Park (Piccadilly line) for the short ride to Knightsbridge, and your very first exposure to **HARRODS**!!! Even though you could spend hours, and all your money in the Food Halls alone, if you're not staying in town another day or two, the **Victoria and Albert** and the **Natural History Museums** are just down the road.

Don't have tea at Harrods; instead, go across Brompton Road to the very fashionable **Hyde Park Hotel**. It's a stunner and the Queen Mother always took the little princesses there for tea. Need we say more? If you've gotten to the V and A or the Natural History before tea, you can spend the late afternoon exercising your charge cards while exploring **Beauchamp Place**, the street of snazzy boutiques.

Evening

It's back to the hotel for a bit of R & R because tonight is the night to pull out all the traditional stops and visit the **Royal Opera House**. In New York, you had the foresight to reserve seats for a performance of either the opera or ballet, and now all you have to do is pick the perfect place for a drink (**The American Bar at the Savoy**) on the way to **Covent Garden**, and then, dressed to the nines, you can spend the evening in the most chic of all London entertainment choices. And don't forget to have a glass of champagne during the "interval"; you've earned it.

After the opera, there you are, all dressed up and you certainly do have someplace to go.

If you ask anyone near the opera house, they'll direct you to a tiny alley that opens onto **35 Maiden Lane**, which is where the 200-year-old Rules is. It is *the* place for after the opera and it will take you back in time. Some of the men seated around the rooms will be wearing formal dress and medals (see "Restaurants," page 171). If you want something a little less Dickensian, try the **Ivy** for its very "in" clubby atmosphere (see "Restaurants," page 164).

If you still have some energy left, there are clubs where you can dance the rest of the night away, just like Eliza, but remember, we're going to get you up early for your third, and possible last Agenda day.

Agenda for the 3rd Day
of a 3-Day Trip

The Changing of the Guard remains a popular London spectacle.

Your third day may be your last (in London, that is). That seems to be the most popular length of stay for most visitors. So this is do-or-die until you return to see all the hot spots you weren't able to squeeze in on this trip. What better reason for another triumphant tour as soon as possible?

Since you've covered most of "important" London briefly over the past two days, this would be the perfect time to see where London began, so today the agenda is focused on **The City**. It may be confusing to understand (see "The City," page 90), but it is truly the most mesmerizing part of London because it is a trip back in time to the haunts of Shakespeare, Chaucer, Johnson and of course, Dickens.

Morning

There's so much to see in the city, breakfast should be a quick pick-me-up and part of the downtown scene, and since you're going to start at the **Museum of London** (See "Museums," page 215) to learn all about London's beginnings, the cafe at the museum is the perfect spot for a fast cuppa and a great ham sandwich. They open at 10 a.m. After the inside story of London's first 2000 years, you're ready to hit the streets for some firsthand knowledge. As you walk through the narrow lanes you can almost feel Oliver and Little Nell walking behind you. The highlights that are absolutely not to be missed, in any order you choose to do them, are: **The International Shakespeare Globe** center and museum (where they have almost finished recreating the Old Globe); **The Monument** (to commemorate the Great Fire), which stands almost on the very spot in Pudding Lane; where the biggest "Hot Foot" in history started; **St. Paul's Cathedral** (Wren's masterpiece, see p...); **The Bank of England** (Princess Di hopes it will be part of the divorce settlement). If you didn't cover the **Tower of London** on the first day's agenda, you can certainly make it part of your City walkabout.

Lunch down here should be as steeped in history as the sights, so stop into the **George and Vulture**. It was the pub Dickens set *Pickwick Papers* in. Today, it is a fine restaurant with all the old favorites, done a far, far better way than in most places in the area. The other terrific lunch choice is **Balls Brothers** at the back of St. Paul's, where they serve meat-stuffed sandwiches of gigantic proportions. You can have one of their best, a beer, and be on your way.

Afternoon

After a whole morning in The City, it's time to flex those charge cards again. Take **the Tube** (Central line at Common St, or St. Paul's, and get off at Oxford Circus) and get to know Oxford and Regent Streets. Most importantly, a visit to **Liberty** (see "Department Stores," page 148) is not only a chance to snap-up some of those famous prints, but also the "**Tudor**" building itself is worth the trip. The shop-till-you-drop atmosphere of **Oxford St.**, with the mammoth **Selfridges**, makes tea in a nifty spot today a vital necessity. **Browns** fills the bill, as well as the cup, in every way. It's our very favorite place for a delicious, relaxed tea in all of London. They're at **30-34 Albemarle St.**, right off Piccadilly. Browns is the epitome of grace, charm and comfort; the clotted cream is great too. After, perhaps a walk in the park, **Green Park** in fact, which is lusciously green and blissfully peaceful. An alternative for the afternoon might be the **British Museum**. In that case, set aside the whole afternoon—it's formidable.

Evening

If this is to be your last night in London, it seems to us imperative that Shakespeare should be one of the last voices you hear before you go. But first things first, in this case, a very classy cocktail at the **Dorchester**, the perfect place to see and be "scene" before the theatre. If there's no Shakespeare in the big houses in "Theater Land" then you can always try **The Old Vic**, or the **Barbican Center**—there is usually a production of the bard somewhere in London. If you've had a tea complete with scones, sandwiches, and pastries, and you've downed a few hundred hor d'oeuvres, you'll probably have dinner after the theatre. Since this is your last night, you should be able to remember London with its lights twinkling and the Thames a-shimmer in the moonlight. **La Pont de la Tour** is the perfect place (see "Restaurants," page 167) for both a fish and a fitting last look at the City at its most romantic. In summer there is a terrace right on the water to bring you even closer to the lights of **Tower Bridge**.

We haven't listed any of those great markets (see page 149) we love in the previous day agendas because they all take place on different days of the week or weekends. If your schedule permits, you can always make time for one or two when you know which days of the week you'll be in town.

Children's Agenda

Even though London appears to be a place where children traditionally are seen but not heard, that was back in the days of Oliver, Pip and Estella. Today London has all sorts of exciting things for kids to do and sights that will delight them, starting with a ride on the top of a double-decker. Even the Tube is astonishing because of its nontraditional subway look. A little common sense and realizing that the mainstream of society here refrains from a great deal of boisterous activity, will make smooth sailing for most of the usual sight-seeing expeditions. Remember this is a city that loves Christopher Robin and Peter Pan.

The following is an agenda in no particular order (since kids have unpredictable needs) which can be used to make up an exciting day for the biggest small fry:

Natural History Museum
(see page 215)

London Transport Museum
(see page 214)

London Toy and Model Museum

Bethnal Green Museum of Childhood
(see page 230)

Museum of London
(see page 215)

Rock Circus London Pavilion
Piccadilly Circus, ☎ *0171-234-8025*

London ZOO, Regent's Park
(see page 129)

Tower of London
(see page 6)

Madame Tussaud's
(see page 13)

St. Paul's Cathedral
>   *Whispering Gallery (see page 15)*

Brass Rubbing Center
>   *Westminster Center, Piccadilly,* ☎ *0171-439-1791 (see page 226)*

Guiness World of Records
>   *Trocadero Centre, Piccadilly,* ☎ *0171-439-1791*

Hard Rock Cafe
>   *150 Old Park Lane,* ☎ *0171-629-03382*

Chinatown

The Little Angel Marionette Theatre
>   *14 Dagmar Passage, Cross St.*

Hamley's
>   *188-96 Regent St, W1,* ☎ *0171-734-3161*

Smollensky's Balloon
>   *1 Dover St, W1,* ☎ *0171-491-1199*

Puppet Theatre Barge
>   *Little Venice, Bloomfield Rd., W9,* ☎ *0171-249-6876*

Changing of the Guards
>   *(see Top Sights, page 4)*

Unicorn Theatre for Children
>   *Great Newport St, W2,* ☎ *0171-379-3280*

The Sea Shell Restaurant
>   *(Fish & Chips), 49-51 Lisson Grove,* ☎ *0171-723-8703*

Camdon Lock Market, Chalk Farm
>   *(see Markets, page 151)*

Greenwich
>   *(see page 209)*

Young Vic Theatre
>   *66 the Cut, SE1,* ☎ *0181-699-2339*

Horniman Museum
>   *100 London Rd., SE23,* ☎ *0181-699-2339*

Christmas Agenda

The Christmas season in London is a Dickens dream come true. Maybe you won't hear anyone saying "bah, humbug" but you do hear lots of "Christmas is coming, the goose is getting fat" all over the city. Perhaps if Scrooge awoke on Christmas morning in the 90s, he would have felt as happy as he did back in 1800 something. Most of the hotels have Christmas festivities and menus, the stores are packed and even though we can't promise snow, we certainly can predict that from the middle of November London is completely Christmas-driven.

Since London starts to fill up in November with people coming in from the countryside to shop, if you're planning to travel at that time or even worse, in December, you had better book as early as possible and that applies to restaurants and entertainment as well. As for getting around the City, forget buses and cabs; you will spend your day sitting in the middle of Piccadilly praying for an out-of-body experience. Tube from place to place if you want to retain your sanity.

We can't think of a more exciting place to do Christmas shopping than London, so if you really want to impress the folks you've left behind, start early for maximum coverage of all the Christmas wonderlands. Since most of the department stores have good restaurants, have breakfast on the go. Or if you want a festive, elegant, start to the day, drop into the **Capitol Hotel** down the block from Harrods for your own Christmas treat. Then on to **Harrods** for some guerilla shopping. How many people back home have presents with Harrods gift wrap? This is surely the way to make points with Aunt Sophie. Of course, you'll want to see the lights on **Regent Street** (the best light display in the city), and the giant tree in **Trafalgar Square**, and perhaps even join the caroling that takes place there everyday during the season. Aside from Regent Street, there are Christmas lights at all the shopping meccas; **Kensington High Street** even has lit-up Christmas trees attached to the lampposts so the whole avenue glows.

The department stores try to outdo each other with the extravagance of their windows and Christmas merchandise, but the museum shops (particularly the **V and A** and the **British Museum**) always have much more individual choices.

One of the most moving events of the season is a performance of Handel's *Messiah* in the magnificent **St. Paul's Cathedral**. All over town, in fact, great Christmas music is being performed. **The Choir of Westminster Abbey** is particularly angelic.

The British have a tradition of what they call Pantomimes (Pantos) that they put on for the holidays. If you have children with you, these productions are a delight. The **Barbican Center** often does *A Christmas Carol*; elsewhere around town there are special circuses, fairy tales and usually a performance of *The Nutcracker*. If you're in London for New Years eve, the custom is to see the New Year in along with the thousands of celebrants that jam **Trafalgar Square** to sing "Auld Lang Syne" at midnight. Big Ben tolls the year in. The next day, January 1, marching bands parade around town, so try not to have a headache.

You're sure to have a Merry Christmas in London, "God bless us, everyone…"

AGENDA FOR TRAVEL ARRANGEMENTS

Having a successful trip requires as much planning and imagination as a successful marriage. Because travel is an equally maddening combination of pleasures and pitfalls, what you do *before* you go is your best insurance.

The first travel arrangement you make is in your head. Take a little time to decide what you want to do, and see, in London. Make your own agenda for the most important things, not just "shopping" or "theatre" but which shops and what shows. Same thing with restaurants. *Do not* leave all of these choices to be made once you arrive. Why spend precious London minutes planning instead of experiencing? You can access all the information needed to make a decision before you go.

Once your travel reservations are confirmed, get a copy of the London *Times, What's On in London* and *Time Out* at an international newsstand. Every city has them. Go to the library and fine out what articles have appeared recently on London. Contact The British Tourist Authority, *551 Fifth Avenue, New York, NY 10176,* ☎ *(800) 462-2748.* In London, call the London Tourist Board, ☎ *0171-971-0026,* for brochures. We promise that your advance planning efforts will pay off by allowing you to arrive in town with reservations at Bibendum and tickets to *Sunset Boulevard.*

London Weather

It may start out to be bright and sunny and then an hour later, there will be a steady downpour for the rest of the day. It may start off with fog and drizzle and then an hour later there will be a steady downpour lasting the rest of the day. Or the day may start out with a steady downpour and later in the afternoon it's turned into a full blown storm. There is a lot of heavy mist (RAIN) in London, but no one will mind except you. The universal picture of the Englishman, never without his umbrella, is not an overstatement. But the good news is that the temperature year round is mild. Spring in London is usually sunny and the grass turns a bright emerald green. If London's weather could be summed up in a word, that word would be **UN-PREDICTABLE**.

	Jan.	Feb.	Mar.	Apr.	May	Jun.	Jul.	Aug.	Sep.	Oct.	Nov.	Dec.
AVERAGE TEMPERATURE & PRECIPITATION												
Avg. High (°F)	43	44	50	56	62	69	71	71	65	58	50	45
Avg. Low (°F)	36	36	38	42	47	53	56	56	52	46	42	38
Avg. Days w/rain	15	13	11	12	12	11	12	11	13	13	15	15

Probably the best times to be in London, if the choice is yours, would be spring and fall. The next best time, despite the incredible crowds, is between Thanksgiving and New Year's. London dresses up for Christmas and the very British approach to the holidays make the whole city even more exciting. If you must come during the summer months, London has an extremely mild climate and the temperature rarely moves above 85. The British would never stand for it being much hotter.

Dress Code

Most Londoners like to dress up. It's part of their social identity. As a visitor you may not feel at ease being quite as informal as you might be at home, particularly in the evenings. If you're off to tea at some fashionable hotel, you'd probably feel more comfortable in a jacket (this may not be required, but ask) or a smart outfit. Perhaps the most appropriate phrase is "designer casual" (even if you're not from L.A.). For sightseeing around town, jeans or slacks are fine, but shorts in churches or theatres in our opinion is "major tacky." You'll need a jacket or sweater from September through May because it cools down considerably in the evening. Your two most important travel aids: an umbrella, and a comfortable pair of shoes.

Travel Documents

All U.S. citizens, even babies, need a valid passport to enter Great Britain for a stay of up to six months. No visa is required.

Customs

British customs allows you to enter the country with 200 cigarettes, or 50 cigars, 2 liters of wine and 1 liter of hard liquor, or 2 liters of wine, 50 grams of perfume, 9 oz. of cologne and gifts that you wish to bring into the country, with a value of no more than about $50.00 (at press time).

Upon your return, you are allowed, duty-free, up to $400 per U.S. citizen. If you are out of the country for a shorter time than 48 hours, you are only allowed $25. There is a 10 percent customs duty on the next $1000 over your permitted $400. Your $400 allowance may include one carton of cigarettes (200), 100 cigars, and one liter of wine *or* liquor.

Money Madness

The British currency is based on the pound sterling (which is made up of 100 pence. The paper notes are in the denominations of £5, £10, £20, £50.

The coins are, 1p, 2p, 5p, 10p, 20p, 50p, £1. Sometimes the £1 coin is referred to as a "quid." As we went to press, the U.S. dollar against the £ was $1.50-$1.60. Unfortunately, the dollar, of late, has been weaker than Roseanne's diet resolve, so we can only hope it will rise beyond $1.50 per £ before you arrive. And even though London is outrageously expensive at the moment, we prefer to regard the money we spend there as an investment of the kind we would make in a fine antique, rather than our vacation budget (talk about rationalizations).

In London, most U.S. credit cards or traveler's checks are accepted everywhere; however always check with restaurants and clubs, just to make sure, since policies change. If you can, charge your purchases and meals to your credit cards. The rate of exchange is usually better, and it will help to have a record of what you have spent. If you plan to attend an antiques market try to take cash. The dealers will be more apt to strike a good bargain.

It would be wise to convert about $100 into £s before you leave for London so that when you arrive, you won't need to bother with money matters till you've reached your hotel and had some rest. Usually, we tell our readers to always try to change money at the bank rather than at the hotel since the rate will be better. Well, times are changing as well as money; we noted in several instances that hotels were giving as good a rate because they usually don't add a service charge. Be most careful at all those "Bureaux de Change" booths around London. They usually impose an even steeper service charge while quoting seemingly low rates.

These days, the most important thing about money, no matter where you are, is being careful to protect it from the random crime that seems to crop up everywhere. Carry just the money you will need for the day in your inside jacket pocket, or purse. The rest should be in one of those nylon carriers that go around your waist or around your neck, under your clothes. You can keep your credit cards, traveler's checks, and passport safe.

To Tip or Not to Tip

Many restaurants around town add a service charge to the bill. In that case you may want to leave five or ten percent extra, if they've been sweethearts. Otherwise, if service is not included, tip 15 to 20 percent, which is the norm.

Cab drivers expect about 15 percent and £1.50 for each suitcase.

Doorman - £1 for hailing a cab.

Bellhop - £1 per bag. £1 for room service.

Telephone Facts

There are two area codes in London: *0171* for most of the city, *0181* for places farther from the center.

To call the U.S., dial 010 (international access) + U.S. country code + area code + local number.

If at all possible, try to make your calls to home from the hotel lobby phone, or from street phones. If you call long distance from your room, the hotel imposes a horrific service charge that is out-and-out thievery. Sometimes it's as high as $5 or $6.

London Holidays

New Year's Day (January 1)

Good Friday

Easter Monday

Mother's Day (May)

Spring Bank Holiday (May 30)

INDEX

Favorite People, Places & Experiences

ADDRESS:	NOTES:

Name

Address

Telephone

Name

Address

Telephone

Name

Address

Telephone

Name

Address

Telephone

Name

Address

Telephone

Name

Address

Telephone

Name

Address

Telephone

Favorite People, Places & Experiences

ADDRESS:	NOTES:

Name

Address

Telephone

Name

Address

Telephone

Name

Address

Telephone

Name

Address

Telephone

Name

Address

Telephone

Name

Address

Telephone

Name

Address

Telephone

Favorite People, Places & Experiences

ADDRESS:	NOTES:

Name

Address

Telephone

Name

Address

Telephone

Name

Address

Telephone

Name

Address

Telephone

Name

Address

Telephone

Name

Address

Telephone

Name

Address

Telephone

Favorite People, Places
& Experiences

ADDRESS:	NOTES:

Name

Address

Telephone

Name

Address

Telephone

Name

Address

Telephone

Name

Address

Telephone

Name

Address

Telephone

Name

Address

Telephone

Name

Address

Telephone

Favorite People, Places
& Experiences

ADDRESS: NOTES:

Name

Address

Telephone

Name

Address

Telephone

Name

Address

Telephone

Name

Address

Telephone

Name

Address

Telephone

Name

Address

Telephone

Name

Address

Telephone

Favorite People, Places & Experiences

ADDRESS:	NOTES:

Name

Address

Telephone

Name

Address

Telephone

Name

Address

Telephone

Name

Address

Telephone

Name

Address

Telephone

Name

Address

Telephone

Name

Address

Telephone

Favorite People, Places & Experiences

ADDRESS:	NOTES:

Name

Address

Telephone

Name

Address

Telephone

Name

Address

Telephone

Name

Address

Telephone

Name

Address

Telephone

Name

Address

Telephone

Name

Address

Telephone

Favorite People, Places & Experiences

ADDRESS:	NOTES:

Name

Address

Telephone

Name

Address

Telephone

Name

Address

Telephone

Name

Address

Telephone

Name

Address

Telephone

Name

Address

Telephone

Name

Address

Telephone

Favorite People, Places
& Experiences

ADDRESS:	NOTES:

Name

Address

Telephone

Name

Address

Telephone

Name

Address

Telephone

Name

Address

Telephone

Name

Address

Telephone

Name

Address

Telephone

Name

Address

Telephone

Favorite People, Places & Experiences

ADDRESS: NOTES:

Name

Address

Telephone
_____

Name

Address

Telephone
_____

Name

Address

Telephone
_____

Name

Address

Telephone
_____

Name

Address

Telephone
_____

Name

Address

Telephone
_____

Name

Address

Telephone

Favorite People, Places & Experiences

ADDRESS:	NOTES:

Name

Address

Telephone

Name

Address

Telephone

Name

Address

Telephone

Name

Address

Telephone

Name

Address

Telephone

Name

Address

Telephone

Name

Address

Telephone

Favorite People, Places
& Experiences

ADDRESS:	NOTES:

Name

Address

Telephone

Name

Address

Telephone

Name

Address

Telephone

Name

Address

Telephone

Name

Address

Telephone

Name

Address

Telephone

Name

Address

Telephone

Favorite People, Places
& Experiences

ADDRESS:	NOTES:

Name

Address

Telephone

Name

Address

Telephone

Name

Address

Telephone

Name

Address

Telephone

Name

Address

Telephone

Name

Address

Telephone

Name

Address

Telephone

Favorite People, Places & Experiences

ADDRESS:	NOTES:

Name

Address

Telephone

Name

Address

Telephone

Name

Address

Telephone

Name

Address

Telephone

Name

Address

Telephone

Name

Address

Telephone

Name

Address

Telephone